40p.

Th
be
boo
re

MARGERY FRY

In 1948

MARGERY FRY

The Essential Amateur

by

ENID HUWS JONES

LONDON
OXFORD UNIVERSITY PRESS
NEW YORK   TORONTO
1966

Oxford University Press, Ely House, London W.1

GLASGOW NEW YORK TORONTO MELBOURNE WELLINGTON
CAPE TOWN SALISBURY IBADAN NAIROBI LUSAKA ADDIS ABABA
BOMBAY CALCUTTA MADRAS KARACHI LAHORE DACCA
KUALA LUMPUR HONG KONG

Printed in Great Britain
by W. & J. Mackay & Co Ltd, Chatham, Kent

To R. H. J.

CONTENTS

ILLUSTRATIONS

ACKNOWLEDGEMENTS

THE letters and documents on which this book is based were lent by Mrs Pamela Diamand, whom I thank not only for this but for her constant friendship and encouragement. I have called almost as often, and as successfully, on the Secretary and staff of the Howard League for Penal Reform. I should like to thank the Home Office for permission to use some passages of unpublished evidence, the British Broadcasting Corporation for the use of scripts, Mr Leonard Woolf for leave to quote from *To the Lighthouse* by Virginia Woolf.

It would be impossible to count those who have given me generous help: the librarians who have produced material I should have missed, the people who have searched out memories, letters, and newspaper cuttings. A few knew Margery Fry in her childhood, many for more than fifty years, some (whose contribution is also significant) met her only once. Some of their names would be known to anyone who reads this book, others are unknown even to one another. I have been fortunate to live for a few years among Margery Fry's friends.

E.H.J.

I

A Place in History

A CHINESE lacquer cabinet, handed down from one eldest daughter to another for many generations, came to Margery Fry's mother at three years old and remained with her for ninety-four years. Nine of its drawers held in time the treasures of her children. Ceremoniously, not too frequently, Mariabella would gather her children round the cabinet and unlock its doors. As the gold-dusted drawers slid open the children breathed in the special fragrance which Margery later recognized in the Temple of the Ancestors in Peking.

The plaited straw pig, which Margery remembered as the first of her Chinese adopted children, has gone from her golden drawer, but her parchment drum-rattle is still there, Victorian brown boot-buttons replacing the worn-out Chinese knots. There is a paper puppet—probably the 'painted man' which she carried home from a tea-party in the 'seventies—some objects brought from much-loved places in a long life of travel, a scrap of richly coloured tapestry worked in old age. Among Margery's eight brothers and sisters only one drawer closed on a short life—that of an older sister who died of scarlet fever before she had finished, in her firm four-year-old hand, a row of mock capital letters in her notebook. The others grew up to paint Christmas cards, to copy texts, finally to write an account of themselves to their mother whenever they were separated for a few days.

All these records Mariabella Fry kept. She also had her children photographed, the boys separately, the girls in pairs, Mab and Joan, Isabel and Agnes (the twins), Margery and Ruth. Each pair was dressed alike in every detail, but in each pair a contrast of personality survives with extraordinary vigour the tedium of sitting and the disguise of Sunday clothes. Their letters were tied up in bundles with pink tape.

Inevitably, the lives which moved farthest from their parents were the most fully recorded. The daily devotion of those who stayed at home is hidden. The conversations round the library fire, decisive in the lives of returning travellers, can only be conjectured. Mariabella Fry could lock away her children's lives in letters hardly more comprehensively than in the Chinese cabinet. But although letters home became in time circumspect they continued to arrive faithfully. To the end of her long life Lady Fry continued to sort and preserve them, even though grandchildren showed diminishing enthusiasm for tying up old letters as a holiday occupation. As for Margery Fry, it had long before seemed to her, as she stood clutching the door-knob in her hot hand, waiting for her mother to turn from her desk and listen to news of nests in the orchard, that the past had no business to steal the present moment.

To a Chinese audience Margery Fry once said, in apology for some anecdote of her childhood, 'To learn the unimportance of one's own first footsteps in the world is an elementary exercise in good manners.' Yet all her experience and study deepened her interest in the development of personality. More than once she urged the importance of recording the early memories of prisoners, and indeed of all kinds of people whose lives had taken an unusual turn.

In such recording, though she had no conscious social motive, Lady Fry had been a natural expert. With the scruples of a scientific investigator she discriminated between what was remembered and what was told. We can read, in a few pages she wrote for her eldest daughter, what it felt like to be Mariabella Hodgkin, aged two, on the beach at Broadstairs in 1835:

(I remember nothing about the sea, but I am told that I was there) and standing in a pit dug in the sand (probably by my two brothers and the nurses) while an old woman stood near, who sold buns. All that I see in the picture, is myself, the pit, a woman, a bun, and vague figures around; the details are filled in by other witnesses, but the one bit of internal evidence of truthfulness is, that I am more than waist-deep in the pit, which I don't think any but a little two-year-old would have been, in such an excavation.

From this sharpness of memory, this knowledge of what it felt like to be a little child, sprang perhaps that 'great and expressive tenderness towards the very young' which gave Mariabella's children, according to Margery, 'a confident expectation of loving-kindness—none of her children grew up with any shrinking from human contacts. Even where shyness intervened we have *wanted* people.'[1] Whatever conflicts and misunderstandings came later, this was where the children of Mariabella and Edward Fry started.

Agnes Fry's edition of the memoirs of her father, Sir Edward Fry, published in 1921, is still to be found uncut on the shelves of Friends' Meeting Houses: to the loss of their congregations, for there is splendid stuff in it. Out of her love and reverence Agnes Fry presented a great man, his dignity unscathed by her honest recording of such limitations as she was able to see. Sir Edward Fry died knowing he need not fear his biographer.

Gossip [he had written] threatens to add a new terror to death. Men of letters think it fitting, in volume after volume, to give us the details of the state of the digestive organs, or the family discords of their deceased brethren. I am no advocate for the false and stately panegyrical style of biography, but it is possible to write perfect truth with something of dignity, with a certain sense of proportion, with a certain power of repression and condensation.[2]

Sir Edward Fry had commended in Eleanor Rathbone's life of her father, William Rathbone, the impersonality which somewhat shocked her contemporaries: the life of a public figure, he believed, could well be limited to his public works. Yet when soon afterwards one of his own few intimate friends, Lord Hobhouse, was commemorated in this way, Sir Edward admitted that the picture was not only incomplete but false: his friend was barely to be recognized without 'the small pleasures and graces of life . . . the little acts of kindness and thoughtfulness'.

Margery Fry saw greatness in two men of her immediate family, her father and her brother.

If one is honest [she wrote], how hard it is to recognize with any certainty, not only in the arts, but in thought, in action, in people, this spark of the authentic spirit. Slowly, as generations pass, the works of art, the lives of men warmed by it, glow more and more brightly, and perhaps this power of survival, of burning again in the hearts of later generations, is the one sure test of greatness.[3]

She lived to see the teaching of her brother, Roger Fry, burning in the hearts of two generations, and as far away as Peking. She was

---

[1] *What Life Has Taught Me* (ed. Sir J. Marchant, Odhams Press, 1948), p. 52.
[2] Agnes Fry, *Memoir of Sir Edward Fry* (Oxford University Press, 1921), p. 246.
[3] *What Life Has Taught Me*, p. 62.

able to hand his papers to the biographer whom he as well as she had chosen. Virginia Woolf's *Roger Fry*, the last of her books published in her lifetime, appeared in 1935.

Twenty-four years later the life of Joan Mary Fry was printed in one of those modest pamphlets by which the Society of Friends nowadays acknowledges its saints. A few days before her own death, Margery Fry gave her blessing to the writing of the life of Isabel Fry, in the *Portrait of a Great Teacher* set down by a former pupil still warmed by her 'obsessive image'.[4]

'And Margery, what is Margery going to do with her life?' one of the old men at Oxford had asked her friends in 1897, when three-quarters of her life still lay ahead. She neither preserved nor destroyed the records. She perpetually wove threads of personal memory into her writing and talking. She kept old pocketbooks, official letters, which might serve the historians of the causes she valued. She kept letters: one day there might be time to relive old journeys, to retrace the beginnings of friendships. There never was time. The present always held something more urgent than the tidying-up of the past. Notebooks, letters, diaries, the enduring with the ephemeral, plans for an international campaign for penal reform along with details of an acquaintance's new baby, congratulations from the eminent, demands from the humble, together with the warm, wearying, sustaining interplay of family relationships, were thrown into boxes, moved from one house to another, for more than seventy years.

Much of her life, she remarked towards the end of it, had gone into the wastepaper basket. A memory so prodigious is particularly aware that life is complex, that among a diversity of gifts there is great waste. In the last weeks she felt she would rather her life slipped altogether into the wastepaper basket than that it should become a ponderous tome, an infliction on her friends. She had fought battles, but without extremes of heroism: all the way there had been the loving support of her close family, material comfort, and easement. Behind her achievements there was the silent labour of countless people. She knew also that what were commonly called actions and achievements, things shaped so abundantly by her abilities, were only a part, perhaps even the less significant part, of living.

This liveliness of being, fertile in action but undiminished when

---

[4] Beatrice Curtis Brown, *Isabel Fry* (Arthur Barker, 1960), p. 1.

at rest, had been open to everyone who met her. 'We did not even know she was a penal reformer,' said one who as a schoolgirl often visited her at Holland Park, 'but she seemed to know how to live.' Such knowledge, like the development of the delinquent personality, has a lifelong history, and it may be as valuable to preserve the records of the one as of the other.

Margery Fry saw herself always as one of many, though in her later years as one of a group fast disappearing—the single woman of independent means. In this sense, although to others she seemed timeless, she was perfectly clear about her place as an historical figure. She was much else besides, but she was undoubtedly a Victorian spinster, a maiden aunt. She brought to public life an educated judgement, but she also brought the undemanding loving-kindness learnt as a daughter and a sister. On the 'surplus women' of her generation and the next, civilization leaned heavily during half a century of violence. Her life was more varied and colourful than most, but the pattern was the same. A few women, like her, became eminent. Few are remembered beyond the annals of one school, one hospital, or one voluntary society. Margery Fry once said that her main work had been to make known the ideas worked out by other people. The work of many spoke through her voice, a voice of great beauty and power. The lives of many may also speak through her life.

II
Highgate: 1874-1887

MARGERY FRY was born on 11 March 1874, the eighth child and sixth daughter of Edward and Mariabella Fry. On both sides her ancestry went back to the seeking and enduring Quakers of the seventeenth century. For the established Quaker families of the nineteenth century that pedigree was long enough, though they could easily have gone farther if they had cared to look. Such families as the Frys and Hodgkins had then, by intermarriage and 'steady money-making in quiet businesses'[1] (Oxford and Cambridge, and hence the professions, being closed to them), formed an aristocracy in the Society of Friends: fifty years ago when a young Friend travelling in Australia met a branch of the Hodgkin family he saw them as 'princes in the House of Israel',[2] until he experienced their unassuming friendship.

Even when the universities were opened to them the Quakers were set apart by a certain lack of worldly ambition. It was not until the present century that they merged completely with the families of that intellectual aristocracy which, according to Noel Annan, had fifty years earlier begun 'to share the spoils of the professional and academic worlds between their children'.[3] Because the faith of the Quakers was experimental, science lay open to them. Held back by moral scruples, they lived in a state of tension on the edge of those worlds of politics and art which they had the gifts and the leisure to enter. There was tension also in their material lives, their contact with their neighbours: they had their comfortable houses, their acres of garden, their servants and carriages like other well-to-do people: but in general they dressed plainly, did not dance or go to the theatre, rarely listened to music. None of these restrictions was imposed by written law, except by general advice embodying the

[1] *Memoir of Sir Edward Fry*, p. 14.
[2] *Memoir of Lucy Violet Holdsworth* (privately printed, 1956).
[3] Noel Gilroy Annan, *Leslie Stephen* (MacGibbon and Kee, 1951), p. 1.

'sense of the Meeting' and intended to be interpreted by the individual conscience. Each family, each household practised Quaker plainness in its own way. Thus from childhood each family circle was aware of its own integrity.

Edward Fry, born in Bristol in 1827, and Mariabella Hodgkin, born in Tottenham in 1833, had been reared in a Quaker community around a Meeting House. This was not so in Highgate, where all their children grew up. Before the church bells rang for matins in Highgate the Fry carriage was ready to take the family to Meeting in St Martin's Lane, Westminster. The faces the Fry children saw on Sunday were different from those they met in their daily walks.

Edward Fry had travelled in half a lifetime from an unpretentious house in Bristol, where the cocoa business, still precarious, was carried on in a shed at the end of the backyard, to a position of eminence at the Bar. His self-education in natural science is as fascinating a story as any in his family. Until his marriage in 1859 to the sister of his friend, Thomas Hodgkin, much of the journey had been lonely and austere. Yet it need not be supposed that none of Margery Fry's gaiety came from his side. There are familiar traits in the portrait of his mother, Mary Ann Fry, always talking, witty without malice: 'though her opinions were decided, she never wrangled. You might feel she was unconvinced but never that she was annoyed or vexed by opposition. She was exceedingly hopeful, so that she led others to take the same bright and trustful views which she held; and this made her a delightful companion in daily life.'[4]

Though Edward Fry had given up, and even written against, the Quaker peculiarities of dress and address, he was perhaps more deeply affected than his wife by his minority upbringing. Her childhood was bound by similar restrictions, yet there is something almost romantic in her early photographs. Her mother, daughter of Luke Howard, whose treatise on the clouds had inspired a poem by Goethe, had died before she was three: but not before casting her shining mantle on Betsy, the nurse, whom Margery Fry's elder sisters loved to visit in her old age. Mariabella grew up among good, simple people. In her grandmother Howard, Margery Fry's great-grandmother, the Fry sisters are already visible. In the eighteen-thirties she allowed her grandchildren to have their own gardens ('shared indeed with other cousins' grandchildren, but each family in turn, as it paid its visit, tormented the soil as it pleased'),[5] to

---

[4] *Memoir of Sir Edward Fry*, p. 16.   [5] MS. Recollections of Mariabella Fry.
MF—B

camp in the toolhouse, light fires, and even as a special treat to wash up their tea-things.

Mariabella Fry was at ease with all babies and very young children, but she had from the beginning a special relationship with her eighth child. Though she was nearly forty when Sara Margery was born, it is said that this was the only infant she suckled for several months. Perhaps this was because of all her children Margery most closely resembled the little dead Alice, a child of great vigour and promise. Yet if jealousy arose among the group where there were so many to compete for favours, it was quickly acknowledged and thrown off. All, except perhaps the youngest, born when her mother was forty-four, had learnt their earliest relationships in the radiance of her mothering. Joan Fry could not forget in old age the face of her five-year-old sister Isabel when she first saw the new baby who was to push her from her mother's lap: yet in two or three years Isabel was lifting Margery on to the garden wall to look at the sunset, her first conscious contemplation of beauty.

The Fry children all inherited clever hands from their mother. She showed them how to use them, though it was unthinkable in her time and circumstances that she should perform any menial tasks. It is tempting to imagine that this intelligent but not intellectual woman, busy in her lively nursery with scissors and paste, would have been an even more excellent mother of a later generation: cheerfully fragmenting her life for husband and children, finding relief rather than regret as they grew to independence. But such fancies are inappropriate to this biography, as in such conditions her childbearing would have been unlikely to extend beyond fifteen years or five or six babies.

There she was in the spring of 1874 writing to her sister, Lady Waterhouse. Her eighth baby was in the cradle, still too new to have acquired a nickname—'Mabby and Kizzy [Joan] and the twins and Sara Margery are helping Mother to make a screen for baby Sara Margery's nursery. They cut out pictures, paste them, then hand them and Mother sticks them on.' They were in the nursery at 5 The Grove, Highgate—a beautiful red-brick Georgian house, the third and largest which the family had rented at Highgate. Margery Fry believed that her first conscious memory, like her mother's, was not of home but of the seaside—'a creature of two and a half staggering down to the beach through a little gate, with my father behind me, going to discover the truth about an incredible statement made by "The Others" (that tribe of friendly brothers and sisters) that the sea was salt. That is how life opens for me—with a question.'[6] There, as in the earliest memory of most children, is the jerk of strangeness: but the durable texture of her childhood was woven at Highgate.

Beyond the garden wall where the children watched the sunset lay the domain of the Baroness Burdett-Coutts. Farther still was the vast untrodden park and woodland of Ken Wood, the property of the almost mythical Lord Mansfield. Roger Fry remembered skating there with his father and Margery was taken there at least once by their neighbour, Mr Tomlinson, before whom the great gates were mysteriously opened. Charles Tomlinson was not, as was believed in the village, a professor, but he was a Fellow of the Royal Society. With him the children visited factories and the National Gallery. They were invited to his dusty study, where he played 'Rule Britannia' on glasses or made sand dance to his violin. Margery was the youngest, hanging on, but raised to a sense of occasion by the enthusiasm of Roger and the twins. To the end of her life scientific toys were more than interesting; they moved the heart like magic.

In Highgate she became aware of people outside the family: of the 'cheerful mob of brats' roaring up and down the green (for Highgate was still socially balanced, almost an ordinary village)— 'almost more remote from us than the Zanzibar boys for whose conversion we saved rather unwilling pennies and sewed marble bags':[7] of eccentrics like the Indian man who sold tea and seemed to think that India was at least as good a country as England. In Highgate she knew the vast terrors of childhood, unavoidable even in the most civilized environment. When the Volunteers beat their drum in The Grove her bedroom door was left open and a grown-up person stayed within screaming distance, but to other terrors even her tender and apprehensive mother abandoned Margery: the dark passage by the backstairs, the sordid and violent tales whispered by the visiting sewing-woman to the nurse as Margery crept under the table, close to the cat, which seemed 'not only older but wiser and more important than I was, gravely kind and condescending'.[8] Remembering these things, she was later infuriated by the commercial exploitation of children's terrified curiosity.

[6] *What Life Has Taught Me*, p. 51.   [7] Ibid., p. 52.
[8] 'Some Horrors of Childhood', broadcast in the B.B.C. Home Service, 9 August 1956.

In Highgate she learned the ways of her father, who disappeared every morning, walking powerfully in the middle of the road (accompanied to the end of The Grove, on sunny mornings, by two or three little girls in house-shoes), and turned his key in the lock every evening at six. He spent all his leisure at home: if he travelled, his wife and later one of his daughters went with him; if work prevented him from going for a distant holiday, a house must be taken for the family within reach of London. Though Sir Edward Fry held no higher opinion of babies than that 'they would improve with keeping', when they began to talk he enjoyed their company within the merciful limits granted to professional men in his time. He would romp with them, but, says Agnes, 'there were bounds not to be overpassed'. He would take one or two children on some special expedition. Law as well as order prevailed. At the twins' request he drew up a charter of rights for the nursery: when Margery outgrew her dolls' furniture she leased it to Ruth.

Even Agnes admits that Edward Fry was not gifted as a teacher of children. It was to her alone that he was able to communicate his special scientific enjoyments. Yet Margery says:

The dominant influence in our education was undoubtedly the personality of my father. He was a somewhat austere man, his pleasures were almost entirely intellectual, his friendships few, his mind powerful and rather intimidating. I have never known anyone with a more sensitive feeling for honour, truth, and scrupulous justice—that 'most unpopular of the virtues' as he used to call it. He tried to give us his own high standards, he hated inaccuracy and sloppy thinking. He had come far, perhaps he himself hardly realized how far, from the orthodoxies of his youth (the generation for whom Darwin was the great revealer of new thought) but he held, as the one vital element of faith, to a profound belief in the spiritual meaning of the universe.[9]

Such benign influences from both parents, as they played their Miltonic parts in their children's early lives, Margery was able to set against the almost inevitable asperities of the nursery in their age and social class, even the fearful moral indictments descending to all appearance arbitrarily, because never focused to a child's judgement.

The records of these honest and articulate people show that no two children have the same background. At four years old Joan Mary Fry lost an eye in a nursery accident: two years later her little sister died. Margery grew up without tragedy except for the slow

[9] *What Life Has Taught Me*, p. 53.

deterioration in health of Portsmouth, her eldest brother. Even the vagaries of nurses and governesses, which probably made the Victorian nursery a less stable place than it seems to us from outside, seemed to touch her more lightly than her brothers and sisters. She escaped the threats of hell-fire which tormented Roger, though, unlike Roger, she had to eat up the crusts which the baby rejected. But her greatest luck was in the gift of happiness, obvious in her physical presence, as in her paternal grandmother's. Her face, said a governess (quoting Browning, in the way of governesses) was—

> Like a Catharine-pear,
> The side that's next the sun.

Margery was no doubt among those who trooped downstairs in 1877 to hear their mother's solemn announcement that their father was to be a judge: an occasion which impressed ten-year-old Roger as a call to humility (since their father would be knighted) and to the acceptance of economy (since, as Roger later calculated, his father's income would be halved to 'a miserable £5,000 a year').[10] To Margery other family landmarks would be more important: the birth of Anna Ruth, the last baby, when she was five, and, a few years earlier, the purchase of Failand, a country house in Somerset, near the Bristol Channel. There her cousin Nelly Hodgkin (Mrs R. C. Bosanquet) remembered Margery at six years old, playing with her younger cousin under a great ilex tree, then, 'a little woman of the world . . . dashing through that formidable door and reappearing with a piece of bread and cheese for each of us'.

'It is worth-while', said Margery Fry in 1940, 'to remind ourselves with what anxious care the wealthiest classes procure for their children in their holidays just the sort of wild-life conditions so completely forbidden to poorer boys and girls.'[11] Wild-life was circumscribed, even in Somerset. It had to be caught in snatches, between the fences set up by a punctual household. At regular intervals the children had to be at table, scrubbed and docile, not 'rompy'. Visits must be paid to relatives, for this was Fry country. 'Bay [Baby] was very good, and not shy,' it was reported, but Margery's dictated letter, after a tea-party in the ornate gardens of an uncle's house, shows that her social sense already veiled a critical spirit: 'I did not like some marmalade and there was not any fruit and we

[10] Virginia Woolf, *Roger Fry* (Hogarth Press, 1940), p. 28.
[11] *The Ancestral Child* (Clarke Hall Lecture, 1940), p. 39.

had no table. I do not like the grotto, I did not much care about the
lions and I did not go through the tunnel.' Croquet and tennis were
arranged at Failand for visiting children, cousins or well-established
friends from Bristol. When the children were left with nurses at
Failand permission had to be asked from London for any unusual
activity: 'Ruth and I want to have a seed-sale. May we take some of
the common seeds from the garden?' The seed sale went at least as
far as the issue of a prospectus, headed, 'Messrs Friancisteurs: the
profits of this sale will be given to the Children's Bible Society except
that realized by S.M.F. who will sell some of the Honesty Seeds the
products of her garden.'

There were, however, besides the painting of texts and Bible
clocks, the readings from Stanley's *Jewish Church* on Sundays and
from *Enoch Arden* on week-days, the sights and smells of the
country, bird-songs to be identified, a jackdaw to be tamed and even
taken back to London. Below the wooded slope called Durbins
Batch (from which Roger Fry named his house at Guildford) they
made a water-wheel by the stream, built a den, and roofed it with
bracken. The sea—or at least the tidal Channel with the Welsh hills
beyond—was near, 'offering rather moderate attractions one would
fancy at low tide', wrote kind Aunt Sarah Fry, when she had seen off
a party with a picnic hamper. She was wrong. 'Right out over the
rocks and mud', writes Margery at twelve years old, 'I found lots of
sea-anemones, one was all over rosy red some were grey and red,
green and red-grey. I brought one dull little fellow on a loose stone
up to Ruth and left him in a pool by her where he opened out so
that she could watch him as Harry [the nurse] did not like her to go
far on the rocks, as they were very slippery.'

So she shared with her sister, still caught in the trammels of
babyhood at seven years old, this wonder of the 'dull little fellow'
transformed by the tide: an image which more than once recurred
to her, though, as she reflected many years later, the tides which
transformed human beings were less calculable than those governed
by the moon. As the years went by the gardens at Failand were
planted and flourished, relations with the village became established
though never familiar. Failand began to stand for permanence and
continuity. When Margery was thirteen they left No. 5 The Grove,
and though sometimes afterwards she walked past the house Margery
never saw the backstairs or the garden wall again.

III

Bayswater and School: 1887-1892

THE house in Bayswater to which the family moved in 1887 over-looked the Broad Walk and Kensington Gardens. A walk through Hyde Park to a point where he could hail a cab to the Law Courts had become a more accessible pleasure to Sir Edward Fry than the garden at Highgate. He was at the most arduous stage of his working life, not only on the Bench but also on the Senate of the University of London, to which he had been appointed two years earlier by the Crown. The Senate was engaged in the enormously complicated task of transforming the University of London from an examining body into a teaching university. With such labours in hand the reappearance of 'the dear Father' at six o'clock in the evening could no longer be counted on. Lady Fry also wanted more space for the household, which included eight grown-up or adolescent children all living at home, and the domestic staff necessary in a judge's house even to maintain plain living: 'plain living and high ceilings', jested Sir Edward Fry, nostalgic perhaps for the comely proportions of The Grove.

To Roger Fry the Bayswater house was repulsively ugly, typical of a growing stiffness in their family life. Yet some who visited it as children remember it as 'a dear old house' where fresh experiences were always to be found. Certain fears gave pungency to these visits: encounters with the Fry parents, who courteously but inevitably corrected inaccurate statements, not only by their children but by their children's guests; cruder alarms from Jack Daw, who would fly down from Margery's shoulder to peck the ankles of strange girls. But there was another, gentle little bird called Nicholinka which perched on Ruth's finger; there were musical games like the Toy Symphony which Isabel had arranged at Highgate ('Harmonicum: Miss S. M. Fry'); there were puzzles with string and paper.

There was Roger, no longer a nursery tyrant but the kindest of elder brothers. He would come in from the Hammersmith studio where he was working, bring a plate of sandwiches, and eat them by the schoolroom fire. Margery persuaded him to review the sketches sent in by cousins and one or two friends who joined her correspondence club for circulating essays, drawings, and book recommendations. 'At last', he wrote to Nelly Hodgkin, 'I believe you have been reading the remarks I trouble to write; for at last you have really looked at the thing you have tried to paint.' When he was away he dashed off letters to Margery, wasting no time over formalities, but plunging straight into a description of the Bayeux Tapestry or a cartoon by Michelangelo. She replied with a description of Burne-Jones's 'Briar-rose'—'very pretty but I couldn't help feeling a little sorry it was all so very browny-grey and all the girls looked so yellow and jaundicy! But some of them are very pretty and the armour and the drapery are lovely'—or of a more exhilarating visit with Mademoiselle ('awfully jolly and so mad') to the Niagara Panorama— 'The rummiest hole you ever saw—There are a few dead firs and chestnuts with artificial leaves and telegraph posts stuck into a lot of dead turf and you can't see where the real ends and the picture begins. It makes you feel rather cross for being so like and yet so unlike a real place.'

At fifteen Margery went away from her family for the first time. She was invited to stay in Norfolk with the daughter of one of her father's colleagues. Though she was absent only a fortnight, the tender solicitude of mother and sisters followed her in a handful of letters. Her replies show some anxiety lest, excited by a rowing-boat on a lake, a couple of swans, a nut-hatch, a moorhen, a kingfisher, Connie's big brother, and Connie's brother's friend, she may have given way to 'rompiness'. She was clearly in a more permissive family than her own and the very stars shone more brightly in Norfolk than in Somerset. The friendship was encouraged to continue. Roger took Connie and Margery to the New English Art Club and Connie came home to tea at Bayswater. Afterwards they tried to make toffee on the schoolroom gas-ring. The occasion was 'somehow rather flat', thought Margery.

In these years at Bayswater, dull as they seemed to the six sisters, Margery was practising all those minor skills which were to delight those around her for the rest of her life. Her mother had taught her to observe stars and birds from her babyhood. Though 'fancy-work' was a derisive word in her family, its members valued a home-made present: embroidery took in Margery's life a place perhaps similar to novel-reading in the lives of her friends. In particular she was as clever as any sailor in knotting. Isabel and Ruth could play the piano and sing: Margery's piano lessons ended in tears, but some time in her teens she discovered the flute, the successor to the mouth-organ she had played in the nursery. Theatre-going was forbidden, but dramatic talent flourished: the sisters only lacked an audience for their dressing-up and mimicry. Yet Bayswater, by comparison with Highgate, was unloved. Lady Fry had brought with her to Bayswater her bundles of letters, but the brothers and sisters had left their childhood behind at Highgate. Only Margery and Ruth were still in the schoolroom. The elder sisters were assumed to have settled into those corners where they could carry on their harmless or even beneficent occupations, sheltered from the immense, if vaguely conceived, perils of the world. Mab, the eldest, in whom an overruling interest in babies had developed early, was permitted to take a nurse's training: not indeed to become a hospital nurse, but to exercise her profession from home, especially in looking after relatives. Joan, the second sister, accompanied her mother in those good works which Lady Fry performed in no great spirit of enterprise, but nevertheless with courage, for she had regularly visited a cancer ward in the Highgate Workhouse Infirmary. Joan, like the others, had found the two-hour Quaker Meetings of her childhood a test of endurance, but endurance strengthened her mysticism. In her early twenties she was bidden to accompany her Uncle Tom Hodgkin to a special Meeting at St Martin's Lane. It was a thin, unpromising gathering in the cold light of a week-day morning.

The time had passed when the meeting generally closed, and the Elders intended to break it up. I suppose one was about to give his hand to Bevan Braithwaite when the latter said that he felt someone in the meeting had not expressed what was on their mind. To my great amazement this was myself, and in consequence I got up and quoted Isaiah XXX v. 15. 'In quietness and confidence shall be your strength.'[1]

Lady Fry was not particularly pleased by this display of enthusiasm, but Joan from that day devoted her great energies to the life and worship of the Society of Friends.

Whatever defects Roger had noticed in his education, he had been given at Clifton and King's College, Cambridge, the normal opportunities of a boy of his social class. The only sister who had

[1] Ruth Fawell, *Joan Mary Fry* (Friends' Home Service Committee, 1959), p. 15.

so far received any academic education outside home was Isabel. She had not been, like Margery, a child obviously attractive and lovable. She had been obstinate with nurses, tiresome with governesses, refusing to answer their questions, and raising awkward problems of her own. Her parents decided to send her away to school for a year. Then she returned to Bayswater to join her gentler twin, Agnes, who was already immured by the severe deafness which had come upon her at adolescence. Devotion to her father and to his scientific interests brought some fulfilment to Agnes: for Isabel there was the Bach Choir, a singing-class for working girls at Westminster Meeting House, and the long hours in the drawing-room, watching the impassive face of the clock.

Margery's elder sisters were presented at Court. It was a duty owing to their father's position, unaccompanied by gaieties. They were not out in the world looking for suitable husbands. Neither were they wholly in the smaller Quaker world in which their parents had met, with its quiet sociability, its private jokes, its comings and goings, where women as well as men took their part in the ministry or business of the Society of Friends. When their father rose in Meeting to read a passage of scripture and to comment on it in the light of recent scholarship, they knew his Quakerism was not of a piece with the cheerful evangelicalism of their cousins. He had little desire for company, either in the Society of Friends or out of it. As to Lady Fry, after the birth of her ninth child, she seems to have slipped into that mild valetudinarianism which carried so many of her generation through to a wonderful old age. She could not be expected to entertain, beyond the strictest demands of duty.

'I think we were hungry for other young people,' said Margery, looking back on these years. There were cousins, of course—over sixty in the first degree, according to Isabel; cousinhood introduced them to an astonishing variety of social scenes (all, however, of a high level of respectability and indeed of worldly success). But cousins suffered from a common ineligibility: they were not freely chosen as friends.

Early in 1891, Margery wrote to Roger: 'I really am going to school after Easter.' Bedford College, Queen's College in Harley Street, Miss Buss's school in North London had all been founded forty years earlier. Girls had been sitting for the Cambridge Local Examinations for nearly a quarter of a century. Before Margery had learned to read and write there were two women's halls in Cambridge, two in Oxford. Lady Fry had no interest in these institutions. She would have liked another boy to send to Cambridge, in fact Margery had given her mother, she told her later, 'a little shock of disappointment in not being a boy. . . . The little mistake was soon forgiven. . . . Indeed, now I think that daughters, who may bide at home and not have to fight all the battles of life while their parents watch them anxiously, are quite as much to be coveted as sons.' If these daughters at home showed intellectual tastes, they had their father's conversation and the books in his library.

Margery was just seventeen when she went to Miss Lawrence's school at Brighton, which later became Roedean. Ruth and the governess were left desolate. The governess, assuming cheerfulness, suggested a walk in Kensington Gardens, to watch the sheep-shearing. Ruth, like the sea-anemone, shut up her heart until Margery should return on the tide of the summer holidays.

Miss Lawrence and her sisters—there were five of them teaching or helping in the school, three others on the periphery—prepared pupils for the Junior and Senior Cambridge Locals, and sent some of them on to Newnham. They believed in short, concentrated hours of study and for the rest of the day drove their pupils into the open air, insisted on their playing team games. They encouraged them to make speeches, to write and produce plays. They allowed them to draw and read secular books on Sundays. Margery recalled her four terms at Brighton as 'complete bliss'.

She was to write home twice a week, but to keep the postage within bounds she must not use more than four sheets of the bulky paper then fashionable. The free, square handwriting might be taken for that of a schoolgirl today—at first, perhaps, a girl of fourteen rather than of seventeen. Though much labour was spent in allaying Lady Fry's anxieties, these were intimate letters, sharing her growing self-knowledge with her mother with a freedom surprising to those who ever entered that severe presence. To each of her sisters and to Roger she wrote separately. Each sister sent her own small news. 'How I envy you all this capital teaching!' sighed Agnes. But there was nothing destructive in her envy. In Margery the sisters offered up their own desires and aspirations with an integrity almost sacramental.

A letter survives even from Mab, the younger Mariabella, eldest and most docile of the sisters, whose life-story contrasts more completely with Margery's than any other in that generation. Her knowledge of nursing singled her out for exile with Portsmouth at Weston-super-Mare, where it was hoped that sea air might check his physical and mental decline. There, in her thirties, a country doctor fell in love with her, for she was gentle and beautiful. He went to Failand to see her father. The library door closed on him and she never saw him again. Portsmouth also found romance at Weston-super-Mare. The lady, the family agreed, was not 'their sort', but she married Portsmouth and was a kind companion for the long remainder of his life. Mab was set free to return to her parents' house. They bought her a donkey-cart and she went out caring for mothers and babies in the surrounding villages. She never had a baby or a home of her own. In her uniform she was a Fry, formidably competent. Out of it she was the contented daughter at home, happy in small things.

In the Bayswater drawing-room Isabel continued to gaze at the clock. Every detail of her life, at twenty-two, was under her mother's scrutiny. She had been at school one year. She had no qualifications for any kind of work and she felt that she lacked the social grace which could win influence in a world where qualified women were still extremely rare. She was determined that Margery should not have to tread the same path. Margery, like her, had intelligence and a powerful will. She had also the inestimable art of getting her way without open rebellion. Isabel pushed her towards perfection, scolding her fiercely at the first sign of emotional enslavement to a teacher, upholding for her sister the faith which so often forsook her in her own battles. At seventeen Margery was becoming by democratic choice the centre of her family, a position she was to hold even in the long and unrelaxing reign of her mother.

The Misses Lawrence were Unitarians, at a time when the scholarly Gothic chapels of Unitarianism, enriched with Burne-Jones windows and Morris tapestries, were filled with vigorous and influential people. The school offered alternative Bible lessons, with a visiting clergyman and with one of the young teachers. Lady Fry on the whole favoured the clergyman, but as there was no knowing whether he was 'High' by Fry standards, Margery was to try him out for a few lessons. Miss Lawrence would stand no nonsense. Taking one look at Margery (perhaps also, though the surmise may be quite unjust, at the clergyman), she realized that if Margery left his class all his other pupils would follow. Margery therefore attended Miss Crommelin's Bible classes and reported them 'very thoughtful and open-minded'. Pressed harder to show the benefits of her own upbringing among the girls, Margery replied: 'In ordinary matters one cannot do much but try hard to keep the rules and not do anything a bit mean or double', indicating also that girls from other homes were not without standards.

It was on Sunday that she missed home most. On Sunday 'the dear Father' had always been with his family. The day had been solemn, but richly textured. At school the Sunday chatter of the girls depressed her. The freedom of Sunday afternoon, she recognized, sprang not from indifference but from Miss Lawrence's principles. There was a sketch club, the girls could relax with a book. Margery had no taste for novel-reading, but she wrote home about the sketch club. There was no sharp demand or curt refusal: all was gentle suggestion and counter-suggestion. Margery was quite right in supposing her mother would not like her to join, '*yet*: you may find some quiet girl who would like you to join in some rather more Sundayish occupation'. Later Margery turned down a suggestion of Sunday play-rehearsal—being careful to report home this act of grace.

Attendance at the Friends' Meeting in Brighton proved impracticable. Meeting House Lane was a great distance from Miss Lawrence's. No escort was available unless she could press the Jews into service. Once or twice she persuaded these kind girls to hurry through their bed-making and walk with her, but as a regular practice she joined the crocodile to church. She gave to the sermons a lively, critical, and often responsive ear, but it was the music and liturgy which drew her. Soon she was attending church twice every Sunday. At church she was relaxed. Between the services she wrote home, and by this weekly process of self-justification learnt to know herself and her surroundings.

Girls in those days went to school late if they went at all, leaving homes where they had lived in almost total physical dependence on nurses and maids. The supervision given to these girls of seventeen would rarely be acceptable today to any girl above a junior form. 'We are kept in fearfully good order as to our rooms and drawers being tidy and our clothes mended. I believe they look at all our drawers daily.' The day was as simply planned as in a convent. From eight until ten in the morning the girls were on the playing-field. From ten till one (no longer) they had lessons. From dinner until tea they played hockey or cricket. From four to seven they studied.

At half past eight they went to bed. Occasionally they went to a shop
—once to buy fives-balls and once, rather daringly, to be photographed (a dozen for half a crown), to exchange with other girls.
They saw an occasional illustrated periodical, but no newspaper.
They knew nothing, until parents wrote, about a shipwreck on the
beach a few miles from Brighton. Astronomy was an examination
subject, but the teachers were at first taken aback by Margery's
suggestion of going into the garden to look at the stars.

Yet she found nothing irksome in the school routine. Though,
like her mother, she was perpetually chilly indoors, she did not mind
being driven into the cold air to play. 'She played to win,' said one
of her contemporaries, smiling seventy years later at the image of
Margery Fry dashing down the wing. She found all the lessons
(apart from the 'extras') exhilarating, only doubting her own intellectual adequacy. She never (except when she was kept away from
church for some minor or unknown reason) complained that the
discipline was arbitrary. She was, in fact, surprised by its generosity.
'We are a good deal trusted and not continually spied on by governesses. You see we never have anyone in the room with us in prep.
time or out of school.'

There was no school uniform, of course, and Margery's outfit
was not extensive.

I should be very glad if you would not find it too much trouble if when
you come you would bring my drab frock please for my flannel jersey is
too floppy to be very tidy, and the one Joan got me is not any good now
it has been washed I'm afraid, it has shrunk so much: then we can't have
print skirts washed and sad to say I have torn my pink print skirt so
seriously that I thought it would be better not to try to mend it, but leave
it to see what ought to be done.

She reported with relief that she had only been spoken to about her
hair once, when it refused to stay up after washing, but the girls
told her she wore it hideously. She thought vaguely of measures for
improvement, but did not worry overmuch: the Fry girls had never
since childhood been led to hope they could look pretty, or to suppose that to impress by a fine appearance was a worthy aim.

Nevertheless she looked around with confidence. To those
reared in a less bracing climate than that of the Fry schoolroom her
outspokenness, her flashing eyes, and her splendid voice could be
alarming. At least one octogenarian shuddered to remember Margery

Fry exclaiming, as she herself had scuttled past a group of older girls, 'I hate a fool!' She was never gentle to pretentious fools and she disliked people in the mass. In fact, she hardly ever saw people in the mass. One by one in her letters the girls detach themselves from the bundle of movement and chatter into which she came as a new girl: with each she hoped to be in some way effective. She did not drift into friendships: she accepted each relationship as it presented itself, thinking about it as seriously as she would consider a question in algebra.

Her closest friend during this first year was Gertrude Hildesheim, 'a German Jew by birth, but she doesn't seem to be anything particular by religion'. A little quiet anti-Semitism had been taken for granted in Margery's circle; several times she feels bound to account for this friendship: 'She is so awfully good *practically* and so really thoughtful that our not believing alike doesn't prevent my feeling I must respect and like her'—'I am sure she is not a girl you would mind my knowing, as she is really thoughtful, and very conscientious and honourable.'

As Margery came to terms with lessons and friends, her place in school remained basically precarious. Some girls came with the open intention of going on to Newnham or some other college, but no sure course lay ahead of Margery. She went on from term to term, never quite sure whether she was to return. It was a point of honour in her family to tell of the smallest ailment; it would be unfair, as one of them pointed out, to die without giving those who loved you a chance of saving or helping you. In her first letter home she told, as something of a joke, about the extraordinary rule that face, hands, teeth, and feet must be washed nightly. As to feet, said Lady Fry, Margery must ask to be excused unless the water was really hot, and even then it would not always be right. In fact, it was by now established that Margery must stay in bed at least one day a month. Miss Lawrence did not care for this arrangement. If girls wanted to rest, they were to lie for a few minutes on the floor.

The school was draughty in the spring. It was natural, though indiscreet, of Margery to invite sympathetic shivers from Lady Fry. Postscripts about warm underwear came in her sisters' letters. Later in the term there was cricket. They played 'Unionists v. Home Rulers—sorry to say the Home Rulers beat us hollow'. Lady Fry hoped the balls were not hard. One day, having gained a free hour by evading singing lessons, she lay with a friend 'in the sun on a flowery, lark-haunted hilltop overlooking the sea. Never, except in dreams, have I rejoiced in such a perfect picture of glorious flowers, poppies, ox-eye daisies, large deep blue cornflowers and crowds of white campion, mustard and other flowers.' When this letter arrived Agnes was told to offer to send a parasol.

The drawing-master accused Margery of being taught 'in a funny way'. 'I think Mother would back you up', Roger wrote, 'if you wanted to give up drawing but at present you must try to learn as little of the grub and smut in water-colour and as little of the swagger shading in the drawing as possible and then I will administer an emetic in the holidays.' Margery was also determined to elude the teacher of solo singing and the dancing-master who taught them to 'slaide their steps'. (Later she forgot him so completely that she complained that she had never been taught to dance.) These irritations removed, she could concentrate on the strangely thrilling voice of Constance Crommelin expounding mathematics or Latin grammar. At the end of her first term she was serving for the first time in her life on a committee, organizing cricket matches and teas. There was a play toward and she and Gertrude Hildesheim had a whole section of the scenery to paint.

After the summer holidays she was able to report that hot pipes had been 'laid on throughout', but with the first winds of autumn Agnes sent a solemn warning in her own words. If Margery did not positively fuss over the least sign of a cold, she would unfailingly be fetched home. It was a desperately important term. Somehow Margery had managed to bring back her parents' permission to sit for the Cambridge Junior Locals.

She was now a senior girl, feeling at liberty to snub any new girl who seemed 'interfering and familiar and impertinent'. She would have been mature beyond her years and indeed her century if she had recognized that those she snubbed needed her comfort perhaps even more than the shy people to whom she opened ear and heart.

That autumn she first mentioned Dorothy Scott, whose influence was to be important in setting the course of Margery Fry's life. 'She lives in Hampstead but I can't find out that she knows anyone we know. She is a chapel girl, but I think her people are very nice people from all I can hear, I mean not at all careless or flippant.' Dorothy's uncle was C. P. Scott of the *Manchester Guardian*.

Excitement was high among the women teachers of those days as they offered up their victims for the hard-won ordeal of public

(c) Aged about ten

(b) Aged about eight, with her sister
Ruth

1. (a) Aged about six

2. Aged about sixteen
Portrait by Roger Fry

examinations. The candidates must not get their feet wet, they were nourished with invalid food cooked on the teachers' own gas-ring after the other girls had gone to bed. To Lady Fry examinations were unwomanly. To Sir Edward Fry they were harmful: for girls, unnecessary. He had noticed how quickly the carefully memorized details of a legal case fled from his own mind after the hearing: from this he concluded that a short-term objective was an enemy to learning. Margery felt for the first time bewildered. 'Of course it doesn't really matter but I shall mind failing less if I know that you won't be expecting me to pass.'

In the second week of December 1891 she sat for her three papers —Algebra and Trigonometry, Arithmetic and Astronomy, Euclid and Conics. On the eve of the examination Sir Edward Fry wrote: 'We shall not be at all troubled if you do not succeed. Sir Robert Peel was plucked when he first tried for his degree.' But more was at stake for Margery than for Sir Robert Peel. Hardly knowing what she was doing, she was fighting her way to an independent life in the only way open to her. A week earlier she had written to her old governess, who was still teaching Ruth, to ask her to use any opportunity to influence Lady Fry in favour of Newnham. A few years later the same governess wrote to a rebellious Ruth: 'Some dear and precious lives are growing older, we shall not always be able to please them dutifully and lovingly.' To Margery she now preached the same gospel, the only one practical for her profession. 'It may be your lot to go to Newnham, who can say! If not, the Great Renunciation would scarcely find you wanting, I am sure.'

Margery failed in Euclid, but she came safely back to school for the next lap. It was settled that she was to sit the Locals again in June. She had her own room, considered too small for a bath, so that she had to use the bathroom (even in the 'twenties Lady Fry held that bathrooms were only for servants). The room was nine feet by seven feet, but Margery herself was not very big, though she was solidly built: according to Miss Lawrence's records (carefully tabulated and sent to an eminent physician), Margery Fry weighed three months after her eighteenth birthday '7 st. 11½ lbs. net'. She put up her parents' photographs, a photograph of the family pet Jock (the only dog she ever loved), and one ornament. When the other girls inspected the room they exclaimed at its bareness. Margery said that she could not work among knick-knacks. She was neither tidy nor austere, like some of her sisters, but whatever the state of her bits and pieces she could produce a beautiful uncluttered surface.

She was the school orator, the leader of the drama club. Some of the plays the girls made up seemed pretty silly when she wrote them down, especially one about the modern woman going out to 'mind politics' while the husband stayed at home to look after babies and mend stockings.

The school was prospering. As the numbers grew Miss Lawrence made the study girls prefects, or 'keepers' as she chose to call them. Each had a group of three or four junior girls in her care. Margery thought there was much to amend in the system. Girls came to school with different educational standards and as all promotion was by academic achievement it sometimes happened that the 'keepers' were younger than their charges. And, says Margery, 'Those who have least real influence are the most inclined to fuss around and irritate their charges.' By the time Margery was eighteen the school had given her all it could. Some of its ways began to seem absurd; she was not even sure whether all the teaching was thorough. But she was irradiated by a strange pleasure. She was enjoying being herself, Margery Fry. Several times her governess had scolded her for introspection: now a terrible question arose. She knew she was critical—was she also smug? This time she consulted, not her mother, but Roger, who wrote at once from Paris:

I like to hear a good growl . . . if the grain of the world is cross . . . why the devil shouldn't we say so to one another . . . and not add to our unhappiness by the pretence of happiness. As for your conceit of yourself perhaps it's justified by the facts and anyhow it's a fault on the right side because it makes you able to work and go ahead whereas if you're always bothering about your weakness and feebleness and badness and generally playing the worm, you'll probably end by doing like a worm and only make a little heap of mud.

She took his words to heart, and generations of conscientious young women were to profit by his advice.

In the summer of 1892 Sir Edward Fry had finished fifteen years on the Bench. He had always said he would retire as soon as he had qualified for a pension, and his children knew he would keep his word. He was sixty-five, but in full vigour; in fact, he was to be recalled to various government employments until he was over eighty, and his retirement occurs less than a third of the way through Agnes's biography. But in 1892 London ceased to be his home. 'I longed with a great longing to possess more leisure for thought and reading, and to pass the last years of my life in the midst of country sights and sounds in that daily intercourse with nature of which I was always thinking in the midst of my busy life in London.'[2]

When Lady Fry wrote in May to say that her husband's resignation had been received by the Lord Chancellor, Margery asked to borrow *The Times* from one of the more accessible of the Misses Lawrence. She could find nothing about her father, but soon afterwards a letter from Failand described the place as a desolation: the workmen had moved in to enlarge the old house to provide that 'union of simplicity of life with the benefits of cultivation' which Sir Edward had planned for them all.

Before the removal there was to be a long family holiday in Switzerland. Excited by the general upheaval, Margery at first accepted that she was to leave school the day after her examinations ended, omitting the ceremonies suitable to so poignant on occasion. But as the end of June approached panic seized her. Isabel wrote: 'I feel as though the world were falling about my ears.' Outside the narrow world of the schoolroom and the drawing-room London had always lain, its strange echoes and promises of greatness breaking through the Thames fog and shining in the frosty sunlight. What sort of a life would it be in the soft, sad winters by the Bristol Channel? Nothing definite lay before Margery, except that her parents had not positively denied that she could go to Newnham. Suppose after months they consented, would she obtain admission? She begged to go back to school. 'In a little while more I could get started on my maths. in a way which would make it easier for me to do them alone for a while.'

It was unthinkable; for the removal to Failand, Lady Fry needed her full muster of daughters. Yet, in the end, one was missing. Margery took Constance Crommelin back with her to Bayswater for a day or two. It was a somewhat distraught household, yet Constance found time to talk to Isabel, whose quality she had recognized on a visit to Brighton. In the autumn Isabel went to teach at Miss Lawrence's school; soon she and Constance had a school of their own in Marylebone; after Constance became Mrs John Masefield, Isabel continued to work out her educational ideas in schools in the country. Isabel lived for the rest of her life under her own roof. There remained at home Mab, Joan, Agnes, and Ruth, whom Margery was now to join, possibly as a permanent inhabitant of Failand.

[2] *Memoir of Sir Edward Fry*, p. 77.

IV
From Somerset to Oxford: 1892-1894

As he looked over his two hundred acres at Failand, sloping towards Portishead and the Bristol Channel, Sir Edward Fry wondered that in the limited acreage of England it was possible for a man of his moderate means to gratify the taste for landowning. Though his income had been very large by modern professional standards (a judge's stipend being the same in 1877 as in 1954), he never considered himself rich. He had not inherited great wealth and was then a pensioner with a large family to provide for.

He had grown up at a time when a young man of talent and integrity, coming from a home where food, warmth, and reasonable living-space were supplied without anxiety, had every chance of becoming wealthy. Ostentation was worse than wicked, it was vulgar: economy remained a high virtue. Translated into everyday terms, economy meant for daughters at home a carefulness about gloves and cab-fares. For the head of the household economy permitted those kinds of expenditure which his daughter Margery, as she came to know the world and the conditions of its people, did not hesitate to call intellectual luxuries. He could buy scientific apparatus and books: the four thousand volumes in the library at Failand were weeded periodically. Travel was not only permissible but commendable. Since the mid-seventeenth century, when George Fox had ridden up and down the country in his leather breeches, bidding Friends to 'spare no place . . . . Go through the world and be valiant for the Truth upon earth', travel had been part of the Quaker way of life. The children of Friends were encouraged to learn languages and travel fearlessly, long before the present spate of school journeys and exchanges. It is true that Sir Edward Fry's travels were not particularly original or adventurous: Switzerland, Italy, even Egypt were well-trodden ground, where the wants of English tourists were well understood. For Lady Fry even the shortest journey was an exercise in apprehensiveness (Margery's own word for the quality conveys her mother's robust fidgetiness, better than the more corrosive 'anxiety'). The sisters were supposed to inform the station-master beforehand if they had to change trains, and Joan, who looked the Gestapo full in the eye when at the age of seventy-seven she visited the German Quakers in 1939, is said to have observed this precaution all her life. But Sir Edward Fry's children grew up with the idea that whereas spending on clothes was suspect, spending on foreign travel was (with due circumspection) acceptable.

In retiring to Failand the ageing Fry parents did not withdraw gratefully to a country cottage. The paraphernalia of a judge's household in London were transferred to Somerset, set out, in fact, more spaciously in the open country. The old farm-house, bought originally as a holiday home, was extended over the years until it became, in the words of Sir Edward Fry's granddaughter, 'a very large and rather pretentious, rambling, pinky-grey stone house with a vaguely Georgian front facing north, a high porch with a flight of snowy-white steps leading to it, a clear view across the Bristol Channel and the Welsh hills'. The neighbourhood was thinly populated. Over lunch one day three of the sisters found that they had severally visited the same cottage in the course of the morning: the object of their visits had kept a tactful silence, sensing the predicament of these ardent young women with little to do. The nearest 'calling' neighbour (as distinct from those whom in Florence Nightingale's phrase the Frys 'poor-peopled') was a retired colonel some miles away. The intermediate stratum of tenant farmers, blacksmiths, carpenters, and so on, which must at that time have lain richly over the land, was open as rarely to their excavations as to Jane Austen's.

Portbury railway station was seven miles away. The only shop within three miles was the tiny post office, selling a few jars of boiled sweets. The London carriage was still used for calling, and Gibb the coachman, who had been with the family since Highgate days, was as happy as his master to be driving between country hedges. For family expeditions, such as the six-mile drive to Meeting at Portishead, an oval vehicle with seats around it, known as the 'whorlicoat', was presently acquired. Over the years a donkey-cart for Mab and a pony-cart were added. All these vehicles had to be shared among the family: Lady Fry's grandchildren remember the 'carriage fight'—a fierce contest in unselfishness—as part of the breakfast-time routine.

At an early stage in his occupation of Failand, Sir Edward Fry had built a schoolroom in his grounds. This was intended for the villagers, but was quite independent of the village school. Such private pioneering in adult education was not uncommon among rural Friends. At Failand the whole family shared in the activities of the classroom, though in time they became Ruth's special charge. She held classes in basketry and leatherwork, and conducted a highly successful 'band' of both wind and string players.

Joan Fry found means to work farther afield. She was a good horsewoman. She had exercised regularly in Rotten Row, but at Failand riding became a serious means of locomotion. When the Local Government Act of 1894 regularized the appointment of women to be Guardians of the Poor, she had qualified by a year's residence in Somerset to be one of those chosen. It was a service encouraged in the Society of Friends, and among the two per cent of Guardians in that year who were women, twelve were Quakers. Joan was then over thirty, upright and distinguished in bearing, exceedingly handsome apart from the disfigurement of her eye. Her voice was like Margery's, but in early life, it is said, more commanding in tone. Margery recognized the physical and mental likeness between them, but was apt to be irritated by those qualities in Joan which in her parents she was bound to revere. Yet the tenderness between the sisters, which was to have so many years to grow in, was never wholly out of sight.

To see Joan ride off down the lanes, sitting side-saddle in her grey habit on her grey horse, was part of the Failand life, arousing no particular interest as to whether she was going to visit the poor in their cottages or to turn up at the workhouse when least expected. But with her Margery certainly saw the inside of Flax Bourton workhouse. Joan Fry, who herself loved working with her hands, was among the Guardians who concerned themselves with finding employment such as basketry and sewing for the workhouse inmates. Margery must have remembered this when a generation later she held a similar concern for prisoners.

To ride out on errands of chivalry was one thing, to ride for pleasure another. There is a story that when Joan, in her thirties, disappeared for the day with some cousins, including young men, she was told on her return, 'It was not wise.' We are still too near those times—the survivors are too deeply involved or too settled in their loyalties—to understand how it was that in family after family

—and these among the most gifted, physically and mentally—sons married, daughters did not. To claim that the nineteenth century bred a race of selfish and tyrannical parents only begs the question. There was often real love and sympathy between these parents and children. Perhaps the fathers, tenderer though less realistic than those whom Shakespeare knew, believed the suitors were not good enough. 'Of sex', said Isabel Fry, 'I had until nineteen years old, not vague or hazy ideas, but no ideas at all.' Margery, having satisfied much of her curiosity from the Bible as soon as she could read it, thrust the subject out of mind. The most shocking claim of Freud, just after the turn of the century, was that children had sexual impulses. For sex was bad, though at the same time romance and marriage was represented as ideally beautiful, as remote from everyday life as the state of paradise. Yet these parents had been reared, happily enough, in another climate. Lady Fry had married young: she is unimaginable without husband and children. While she, and many like her, looked on complacently as her maiden daughters grew middle-aged, she somehow gave her daughters a sense of failure. Occasionally there was even an open gibe—appalling to a later generation—about old-maidish manners and lack of grand-children.

Her father, in Margery's view, handled the theme more constructively. He taught her that for women, as for men, there were other things in life besides marriage. Later she passed on his teaching to the generation from whom war had removed the hope of marriage. Many of her cousins married, but many of her friends accepted from girlhood a general expectation of celibacy. At nineteen Dorothy Scott wrote, on the birth of a brother's child, of 'the sense of added richness to life which an infant in the family gives . . . you'll envy me my maiden aunthood! Cheer up, you'll probably attain to that position sooner or later.'

Margery, now in her twentieth year, had been as far as she knew perfectly content with the society of a girl's boarding-school. She asked only to be free to organize her own friendships, to learn interesting things, and to be on occasion 'wicked', chiefly about stupid pomposity. In the first weeks at Failand she tasted a new pleasure, as she looked at plans and measured up window-seats with a carpenter's rule. If she had been a boy, she thought, an architect's life might have been the thing. Roger came down to design the woodwork: he even painted a fresco of Plato and Socrates at one end of the veranda. Margery was, in her mother's words, 'a great part of the sunshine' at Failand. Roger saw that she was becoming indespensable at home and Cambridge was receding. It was too far away. It bred agnostics like Roger's friend, 'Goldie' Lowes Dickinson; it had even dissipated Roger's own faith.

Really if this Newnham plan fails [wrote Roger on his return to London] we must make a huge fight for something else—I think painting under me after Christmas when I shall have settled down to a regular studio will be the thing. I don't think you need to be afraid of too early specialization on art because you've got broad interests to keep you awake to what's going on. . . . So far I haven't interfered . . . but if there is a danger of your being permanently mewed up why I shall have one big pitched battle because I could not do any *harm* and might do good.

But after Christmas there were relatives to be visited and in February Mab had influenza. Margery, being the least occupied at Failand, was sent down to Weston-super-Mare to nurse her: 'very much enjoying having something to do that really wants doing'; for people did not in those days shuffle off their minor illnesses with a few hours' rest in bed. Some woman relative was always available to ply the invalid with attention. At last, in May, she was in London, watching Roger paint portraits and spending a day painting in a studio 'a model in evening dress, flopping over the back of a chair to pick marguerites'.

When her parents took her to Rome a year later the city seemed no more than 'a parcel of uglyish ruins'. 'Don't pump the emotions, I think they begin to come at the end of a fortnight,' Roger advised. But by her uncles and aunts, those cultured mid-Victorians so heavily weighted with time to stare, her emotions were constantly pumped—particularly by that Aunt Sarah who had seen only moderate charms in the rock-pools at low tide.

I must be hopelessly deficient in some sense which enables all 'cultured' people to keep up a perfectly continuous conversation upon the peeps, glimpses, gleams and lights that go on. . . . For one thing, if the driver waves his whip and says, 'Now it's beautiful on your left hand looking backwards', or if Aunt Sarah says, 'Oh, look at these shadows, really they are quite an intense blue', half of the joy of the thing, which is the feeling that it hits you and nobody else can see it just the same is gone, and besides that my soul hasn't got energy enough to be going on all day jumping up and down with a fit emotion for every view.

But she could not live by writing off her scorn in letters to Roger. That dislike of herself which was always ready to pounce now came upon her and shook her. 'Why in creation can't one get rid of this beastly cynical criticalness? I'm always hungering for people, and when I do see any, however hard I try I can't seem to get on with them or like them.'

She wrote to her old governess, Mrs Wharton, who had moved on to that last refuge of governesses, a post as companion to an old lady.

In your varying moods, Margery dear [Mrs Wharton replied], I feel and think for you. My hope is that introspection may diminish and a larger hope be yours. To me, you seem to be just heaving your way through a silva oscura; but you will, you must, thrust [it] aside and make your way to an opening, a clear pathway, lying in full sunshine. My conviction is that many will see you with my eyes as you pass through life, that many do even now, and that if you only *could* leave self-distrust (or sometimes even self-approval?) to fall out of the scheme of observation and take things—for a time—in less bitter earnest, you would fare better.

The way through the dark wood opened in June, with a letter from Dorothy Scott to her 'dear Fry'.

When we were at Oxford we were taken over Somerville Hall by one of the students. It was awfully nice and I'm seriously thinking of going. Of course it's not so 'fine and large' as Newnham, but I like it none the less for that. The students have a boat on the river, play hockey and tennis and are altogether a sensible collection of people I think. There are various advantages to my mind in going there instead of to Newnham. Newnham is out of the question for you, isn't it? I have sent for the entrance exam. papers—perceive they are as easy as one could possibly expect. You could walk in easily.

Within a month Margery had charmed from her parents permission to sit for the examination. It was high summer, and Failand had to put on a round of funereal garden-parties. Margery escaped, and rode round and round the estate on 'the yellow pony. . . . She has the most delicious gallop imaginable.'

News of success came when she was staying with her Aunt Bessie at Yattendon Court, near Newbury, the house which Sir Alfred Waterhouse had designed for himself. 'Uncle Alfred', after winning his first success in the competition for the Manchester Law Courts, had gone triumphantly from Manchester to Liverpool, from Liverpool to London, charging the skyline with the pinnacles of the Imperial Science College at Kensington and University College Hospital in Gower Street. It was Alfred Waterhouse who planned those dark roofs of Whitehall Court which, seen from St James's Park behind the paler offices of Whitehall, became an essential part of the London scene. It was he who shocked not only Holborn but the main streets of provincial cities with those fiery insurance blocks which are said to have created the terracotta industry. This aggressive and exuberant talent sprang from a Quaker home; for Alfred Waterhouse was a birthright Friend, reared in the same traditions of plainness as the Frys and the Hodgkins. Stranger still, the quality which the young Frys most disliked at Yattendon was an effete aestheticism—'that restrained artistic gentleness', Isabel called it, 'which though it is gentle bars in one's natural man with an iron force'. 'Pink cotton-wool soaked in milk-and-water' was Roger's phrase.

Poking fun at the Waterhouses was obligatory, especially as the Frys were in awe of the grand Yattendon establishment. 'I can't help thinking', Margery wrote home to her mother, Lady Waterhouse's sister, 'how if this was the Summer Palace I should enjoy looking at it . . . because I should like to destroy one half of the things as much as I should like to run off with the other half.' Lady Fry enjoyed a little laughter at the expense of a sister whose brilliance had always overwhelmed her. Having done her duty by the family attitudes in writing thus, Margery could sit down to enjoy Aunt Bessie's reading of *Hyperion* for the benefit of her son-in-law, Robert Bridges, who was writing a critical essay on Keats—'I hadn't any notion it was such a really fine thing.' Though Robert Bridges had married Margery's first cousin, he was already a handsome poet of fifty with a greying beard, seeming to Margery immensely tall and intimidating. One evening there was a dinner-party. Aunt Bessie and her eldest daughter had spent an hour and a half arranging the seating, but at the last moment there was some hitch. Margery gathered that Robert Bridges was refusing to take in the Italian lady assigned to him, and in the ensuing confusion she found to her terror that he was having to make do with herself. His conversation was surprisingly pleasant, 'not at all cannibal-like'. According to family tradition the awkward situation had arisen because the poet flatly refused to take in anyone except Margery Fry.

She stayed on at Yattendon even longer than was strictly necessary and took her leave only because her blouses were out of hand; in fact, the only garment worthy of the place seemed to be her new frilled nightgown. Before she left there was a disappointment. Dorothy Scott had failed in arithmetic. She could not join Margery at Somerville until January.

So Margery Fry went up to Somerville Hall unprotected. There, in the second week of October 1894, still shaken from the long, quiet struggle with her parents and 'all the beastliness of going off', she fell asleep in her narrow bed in the West Building. The glow from her own small grate that night was a great comforter.

V
Mathematics at Somerville College
1894-1897

MARGERY FRY went to Somerville to read mathematics. Though Roger Fry declared she was not a mathematical genius and he was ignorant enough of the ways of a women's college to hope she might use it as a base for painting in London, the choice of subject was never in doubt. The Fry sisters shared more than one gift, but in their close family life each felt it important to specialize. Mathematics belonged to Margery as botany to Agnes and music to Ruth. She turned to 'sums' in any slight illness as others would turn to light reading. She would even write out a problem on a postcard as an offering to an invalid.

Her parents sent her to college reluctantly, but with the purest of motives: to give scope to their daughter's spontaneous desire for knowledge. No social, professional, or academic ambition moved them. Vaguely they wished her to be of use in the world, for service was part of their religious tradition. But outward concerns were not to cover the whole of life: inward retirement was also a duty.

Sir Edward Fry saw his legal career as a life of service. He demanded from life a field commensurate with his talents. The material rewards of his service, the consequent style of living and segregation from the lower middle classes, were taken for granted. Praise counted for nothing, publicity was despised. After a due period of service he was prepared, though he was not permitted, to disappear completely from public life. In this withdrawal his wife supported him. Once, pouring cold water on one of her daughter Joan's philanthropic projects, she remarked that in her youth in the Society of Friends she had seen far too much of 'running about after concerns'. The cultivation of the mind, or as Mariabella Fry more simply would have conceived it, the study of God's creation, was as obligatory as the service of society. It was indeed purer, less corruptible. As life in the nineteenth century became larger and more secure for talented, industrious, clean-living persons, hopes of life after death became less obsessive. In libraries and gardens, in Italian galleries and Swiss landscapes, the paradise of retirement was attainable this side of the grave.

To this paradise of study and contemplation the daughters of men of science and letters were now to accede in the fresh innocence of their early twenties. In the new women's Halls of Oxford and Cambridge these fathers would see talents like their own shine again, untarnished by the necessity of making a career and supporting a family. Their girls could become exquisite amateurs of scholarship. 'They were beautiful, in their Liberty dresses,' said an old Somervillian who had climbed to Oxford by a stonier path, remembering the leaders of College society in the 'nineties. The word 'amateur' had overtones of contempt from the moment it drifted into the English language, for not every leisured Victorian brought to his cultural pursuits the seriousness of a Fry. But Edward Fry was middle-aged before the horrid hybrid 'amateurish' was heard. Nearly a century later his daughter found in the word 'amateur' a title she could respect, defining among its attributes 'this hunger to use the faculties which no one asks us—or pays us—to apply . . . this energy of mind which cannot find its outlet in the flow of everyday life, but overflows into other channels and fertilizes its surroundings'.[1]

But not all the Somervillians of 1894 were amateurs. Miss Maitland, who had succeeded Miss Shaw-Lefèvre, the first Warden, in 1889, outfaced the class distinctions of her time as firmly as Miss Buss in her schools in North London. Teachers sent themselves to Somerville in their mid-twenties, supplementing the savings they had scraped together by loans which they hoped to repay from the salaries, larger but still meagre, which the reputation of Oxford would bring. Girls went up with scholarships from the ambitious day schools of the Girls' Public Day School Trust or from independent foundations in the big cities, returning to teach in similar schools. These, academically, were the pace-setters: the 'regular Miss Buss's girl' reading for the Honour School of Mathematics in the room next door did not even try to look like a lady, but, wrote Margery in one of her first letters from Oxford, 'she sort of turns the sums upside down and there you are'. On the walls of the girls' schools the

---

[1] 'The Essential Amateur', address (unpublished) delivered to the London Branch of the Federation of University Women, 1956.

honours boards were going up. At first a place at Durham or the new co-educational college at Aberystwyth would win three inches of gold lettering full in the headmistress's eye as she took prayers: in a few decades an open award at Girton or Lady Margaret Hall would have to be squeezed into a dark space over a doorway.

Sir Edward and Lady Fry brought their daughter to Somerville College in July 1894, explaining to Miss Maitland that, now that their daughter had qualified for entrance to Somerville, they wished her to sit for no more examinations. Sir Edward Fry recognized that for a professional career examinations were a regrettable necessity: but his daughter had no need to consider a career. She could study without distraction. The long fight for women's degrees at Oxford was just opening up in deadly earnest. Yet when Miss Maitland looked from the indomitable face of Sir Edward Fry to the bright anxious gaze of the young woman who sat beside him, 'rubbing a hole in nervous agitation through a perfectly new glove', as Margery recalled later, she decided to take Margery Fry on her parents' terms.

It was said of Miss Maitland that she 'quite literally wanted Somerville to inherit the earth'.[2] It had, in fact, inherited a simple house and outbuildings, humbler than the homes of some of its students, and a buttercup field hemmed in by the Radcliffe Infirmary, the Clarendon Press, and the new yellow Byzantine mass of St Aloysius' Church. But the gatehouse built in 1893 was an outward sign that Somerville Hall, hidden formerly behind garden walls, intended to become a college, and in the year that Margery Fry went up Somerville College became its official name. Miss Maitland was not indifferent to bricks and mortar, but she cared still more for people. Her own publications had ranged from instructive novelettes with titles such as *Ella's Half-Sovereign* to *The Afternoon Tea Book*, but it was she who gathered into Somerville a body of tutors who formed its scholarship during the next forty years and left a permanent impress on its character. Up to 1884 lectures and examinations for women at Oxford had been provided entirely by the Association for the Education of Women. Some of the tutors of the A.E.W. still visited Somerville in 1894—including Miss Annie Rogers, who knew the University Statutes backwards and in her girlhood, it was said, had been inadvertently offered an Exhibition by Worcester College on being placed first in the Oxford Senior Local

[2] Dr Woods, quoted in V. Farnell, *A Somervillian Looks Back* (privately printed, 1948), p. 22.

Examination. The A.E.W. survived until 1921, when women became members of the University, but in the 'nineties Miss Maitland realized that the College would reach maturity only when it had its own tutors in every school. In 1894 Miss Mildred Pope, who had left a country rectory to teach in a grammar school at seventeen, became Tutor in Modern Languages. By appointing Miss Pope librarian after she had taken a First the Warden kept her about the place until the new tutorship could be created. There she was to remain, one of Somerville's best-loved tutors, unhonoured by Oxford University, but winning a European reputation, until in 1934 she left to spend her last five working years as Professor of Romance Philology at Manchester.

It was in 1894 also that Miss Maitland called back to Somerville as her secretary the Hon. Alice Bruce, a daughter of the first Lord Aberdare. On her retirement in 1929 Miss Bruce could claim that she had held 'by appointment or deputy, singly, or in pairs, or in accumulations of three or four, for periods varying from three weeks to thirty years, every office in the College except Tutor of Science or Classics'.[3] At the same time Jane Wallis Kirkaldy, a Somervillian who had gained a First in Animal Morphology in 1891, became Tutor in Natural Science to all the Women's Societies.

Now I'm going to tell you how the day goes [Margery wrote to the family at Failand]. When you go down in the morning you go and shake hands with Miss Maitland and then everyone stands round the room while she reads the Bible and then prayers. Then you have breakfast and everyone just goes and gets what they like at a side-table, and goes and sits anywhere, only that you're supposed to go to Miss Maitland's table about once a day. Then after that the new girls generally sit in the library and work and the old ones in the drawing-room (of course you *needn't* work at any particular time but they most of them seem to work there till one, unless of course you have to go out for lectures or anything like that). Then at 1 is lunch . . . a help-yourself meal and you get up and come away as soon as you've done without waiting for anyone else. Then everyone goes out in the afternoon, either out for a walk or to shop or play hockey or something else, and at 4 there's tea in the drawing-room. . . . Then till dinner time is another work time and for dinner you have to be very punctual because they wait in the drawing-room until everyone comes and then go in in a very solemn arm in arm procession. After dinner you have to go into the drawing-room again where there is tea and you're rather supposed to stay there as long as Miss Maitland does. I hate

[3] *A Somervillian Looks Back*, p. 57.

these drawing-room times a good deal, it's so horrid *trying* to stand about and chat. Then after that this week there has generally been a meeting of one or other of the clubs, for electing presidents and so on. . . . Then you go back to your room and work (if you like) till 10, and then either you go to a cocoa, or sometimes people come and call on you in your room. . . . It's rather hard to get to bed early, as the correct time for visiting is between 10 and 11, but you have to be in your room at 11, or else I think they would go on later.

Margery had a room with an oriel window and a window-seat in the West Buildings, an impressive pile in red North Oxford Gothic, built a few years earlier in the north-west corner of the meadow. Its inmates were admonished day and night by the melancholy chimes of the Clarendon Press. At the other end of the field was the House, once Walton Manor, a square stone villa hung with wistaria. There, said tradition, Mrs T. H. Green, who had learnt to scrub as a hospital probationer, had helped with her own hands to clean the place before the American walnut furniture and the beds specially made by Heal's were carried in, and the first five students came into residence in 1879. There Mrs Humphry Ward, Matthew Arnold's sister, had arranged blue and white vases in the drawing-room. There Ruskin had come to tea with the first Warden, Miss Shaw-Lefèvre: and there the Warden herself, graceful and worldly-wise, a living presence even today as she looks out from her portrait in the College Hall, had steered the earliest students between the extremes of fashion and dowdiness, even, it is said, lending her own hat when the head-gear of one of the students seemed unlikely to help the women's cause in Oxford.

A new spirit of asceticism blew through the corridors of the West Buildings, different from the elegant economies of Miss Shaw-Lefèvre's time. A rope coiled at one end of the upper landing was in case of fire to be hung from a student's window and provide an alternative escape to the canvas tube down which bodies could be impelled to safety. A gymnasium at one end of the building was to keep the students in trim for such ordeals. A bathroom at the end of each long corridor took the place of the zinc bath-tub which each resident of the House kept cosily under her bed. The rooms were pleasant enough, heaven indeed to those who had shared an unheated bedroom with sisters and tried to read amid the prattle of a family sitting-room.

There was still no question of women being given any University

3. About 1895
(*Left to right*) *Dorothy Scott, Margery Fry, Constance Crommelin, Isabel Fry*

4. University House, Birmingham, 1908

qualification, but for ten years they had been allowed to sit for the examinations in certain Honours Schools. During the first five years of this concession thirteen of the fifty Somerville students who sat for Honours gained Firsts. By 1894 women might sit for every Honours School in Oxford, though English Language and Literature, and Modern Languages, in which Honours papers were set for women, were not recognized by the University. Girls came up variously prepared for university work: a few had been reared, like Lewis Carroll's Alice, entirely on the old governess dialectic, others had been taught in highly organized schools by teachers fresh from Oxford. The students went at their own pace, some taking Honours after two years, some after four years or more.

To Roger, as always, the tone of Margery's letters was different from that of letters to be handed round at Failand. Anxieties shared with him would be met by animating sympathy where her mother would meet them with nagging solicitude. There was a touch of self-consciousness, too, in writing to a man of thirty, living among artists in London or Paris or Florence, from a community which must in his eyes seem essentially bizarre in spite of his determination to get her away from home. There was also from the beginning that ambivalence towards Somerville without which in the end her love for the place would have lacked its creative power. She was not made or nurtured for blind devotion to institutions. 'This is a very holy place,' she told Roger. 'Everyone seems to work all day, as if creation depended on it and I've been working like a slave and slave driver combined in a fury of despair.'

It would have been wicked folly to complain to her parents, but in her early letters her distaste for the Promised Land penetrates even her letters home—for the brick-red curtains hanging against the yellow wallpaper of her room, for the knick-knacks which established students scattered over theirs, for the ill-blended formalities of cocoa parties, when she sat with other Freshers in a row on a bed, while some condescending senior in a grand dressing-gown made small-talk. Margery had never found conversation so difficult. For weeks she was a nobody, even to herself, for the work, as she had feared, was beyond her. Her tutor, Mr Gerrans of Worcester College, gave her twenty 'sums' in the first week and she managed to get out only three. 'For once in my life,' she wrote to Roger, 'I'm feeling tolerably small, it's consoling to feel how wholesome it is. All the same I'm sure I shall like the place.'

Like nearly every able-bodied Somervillian, don or student, Margery played hockey in the little hired field or even on the sloping lawns, disturbing the peace of Nobby, the fat pony which in more leisured days had been bought to draw the College basket-cart on expeditions to Witham Woods. Hockey would toughen their wills as well as their bodies, combat the invalidism into which so many girls were tempted at home. It would provide an antidote to study. It would draw away their thoughts from silliness, from the pre-occupations which perhaps gave the Burne-Jones maidens their 'yellow-jaundicy' look. Of the twenty-four women who entered Somerville with Margery Fry seven would marry. Her contemporaries at Somerville, coming mainly from large and vigorous families, would bear between them fourteen children. The majority who remained single would make their way in a world where, in her own words, 'it is usual for people to find something inherently funny about celibacy'. Yet, she was to add in 1950, 'going back over the last fifty years try to think of them without all the work, paid or unpaid, of single women. You will find that in transforming nursing and education, in changing the whole status of women, in bettering the position of children, they have supplied, not only the leaders, but the rank and file and the enthusiasm. They have addressed the meetings and they have addressed the envelopes.'[4] In 1894 the twenty-four fresh Somervillians knew only their own luck in escaping from the parlour or the private schoolroom to a study bedroom within a mile of Carfax.

Like most of the women's colleges and public schools of that time Somerville College was entirely a community of young people. Even the Warden, 'so great and so remote' as she seemed to Margery at first, was only forty-four. 'Miss Maitland *was* Somerville':[5] her relations with her College were, for the time, perfect. The portrait in the College is a posthumous copy of a small photograph. Her letters are dull. Yet everyone liked her—even Lady Rhondda, who had found college life intolerable. Margery Fry accepted her—as perhaps she accepted no other person in her life—as a great woman, without definition and without comment.

Few girls then entered Somerville under twenty. Many of them were older than Miss Pope and Miss Bruce. Yet in 1894, apart from Miss Maitland, no one living in Somerville College was over thirty-five. The Warden held the College together as a family community,

---

[4] *The Single Woman* (Delisle, 1953), p. 32.   [5] *A Somervillian Looks Back*, p. 22.

but a new phase was inevitable when the West Buildings were opened. The separateness of 'House' and 'West' gave a sense of maturity: savouring their quasi-independence after years of climbing into the carriage after their mothers to pay calls, some of the richer students walked across the garden on sunny afternoons from House to West, from West to House, leaving cards on one another.

One of Margery's first callers was a fourth-year student, a Miss Pease, a member of a North Country Quaker family connected with the Frys; she came to arrange for Margery's attendance at Meeting, with a second-year student, Miss O'Brien. A few days later Mary O'Brien sought Margery out to explain that her own adherence to the Society of Friends was uncertain. For the first time, apart from the allusive by-play of a Quaker family, Margery discussed Quakerism. In many things, she informed her mother, she disagreed with Miss O'Brien—'for one thing, she's an ardent Socialist'. Since 1871 Quakers had been able to take their place in academic life and Margery must have set out to Meeting in hopes of finding at last a ministry which spoke to her condition. Oxford Meeting proved, however, to be an evangelical group which sang Moody and Sankey hymns.

She soon began, as the fashion was, to make the round of the famous preachers. She was impressed by Mr Inge, not at all impressed by the verbose ostentation of Canon Farrar (better known then for his sermons than for *Eric*). She liked to go with Unitarian friends to Manchester College Chapel. But she could not ignore in Oxford the supreme experiences of music and architecture. She went to New College Chapel with Eleanor Rathbone, to the Cathedral with Hilda Oakeley. She heard the Anglican social gospel preached in their diverse ways by Canon Gore and Canon Barnett. But how far, she wondered, did religious emotion take her, as the choral amen rose to the Cathedral vaulting and the service ended?

I never quite know how far it's quite right to go for the very beautiful music and service [she wrote to her mother]. It gives one a kind of semi-religious emotion, which I rather dread, because when you feel in a very good and benevolent frame of mind you almost persuade yourself that the excellent things you propose to do are already done. . . . I've been thinking a lot that I must be more charitable and not so horrid, supercilious and critical about people, but I really hardly know how to begin. If people are vulgar or absolutely self-satisfied, it seems so much easier to just avoid them.

The older students took her to the play centre they helped to run in a poor part of Oxford and to visit the hospital on Sunday afternoons. Such works of charity they had learnt at home from their mothers and now their educational privileges laid on them a special sense of obligation. The bridge between their actual studies and the service they could give to the world was still rudimentary. When someone had the bright idea of giving a tea-party for the girls who worked at the Clarendon Press over the way, the guests peered giggling through the windows at those students who had preferred to stay at their books, and the harsh Victorian class structure seemed more rigid than ever.

Margery envied the other girls their ease with humble people, but she was not, like Mary O'Brien, deeply concerned about them. It was hard enough to be kind to people you did not understand, and she wanted more than kindness in her relations with other people. She chose her friends among her own sort, people who might be better dressed and smoother spoken than the Frys, but who fundamentally shared their outlook and way of living. Love was no forced, untimely growth, overleaping affinities and tinkering with social divisions. It had to spread at its own pace, slowly extending the family love she had learned in her own childhood. At home she had slipped by with only casual participation in the family's good works: in general her happy presence at a school treat or a committee tea had been service enough. So now, in her first months at Oxford, she was not drawn in by 'causes'. She had her 'sums', her physical activities, and above all the chance of listening to talk.

For the daughters of country parsons, provincial shopkeepers, or schoolmasters, the outline of Oxford life given in Margery's first letter home was comprehensive: the round of study and communal meals, walking or hockey in the afternoon, cocoa in the evening, sermons on Sunday. The sympathetic and often witty companionship of the other girls, the ease of being waited on and of seeing good plain food and buckets of coal arrive as inevitably as the day: this, and the spires of Oxford, free browsing in bookshops, cowslips to pick, the vague sense of living near to greatness, made up an experience wonderful to look back on: irradiating a lifetime divided mainly between lodgings and classroom, with sometimes a walking tour with a colleague in the Lakes, even, after the Burnham Award, an Easter in Florence, before the complications of old age set in.

For Margery Fry and her friends Oxford had another dimension:

they had University connexions. Everywhere she was received either as Sir Edward Fry's daughter or (by Quakers) as the child of one of the Bristol Frys who had married a Tottenham Hodgkin. 'What is the proper answer to make when a person tells you how much they admire your relations? It's a question I often require an answer to.' Entertaining was generous and formal. Her cousin Monica Bridges came down to tea from Boar's Hill, though Robert, after all the trouble Margery had taken to get him admitted 'as an uncle', forgot to come. She dined with the Tylors, a family considered by her parents admirably suited to receive her. For Edward Tylor had sat with Alfred Waterhouse, Thomas Hodgkin, and the other boys of the Grove School on the men's side of Tottenham Meeting House, while Mariabella and little Bessie sat with their nurse on the other side of the gangway. He had left school at sixteen to work in his father's foundry, but travel in Mexico had later turned him to anthropology, a science which he founded at Oxford. He took Margery to his museum, to the physics laboratory at Trinity, to the Radcliffe Observatory. Through his eyes she saw Oxford not merely as a storehouse of antique dignities but as a place of discovery and excitement. Within the space of a fortnight, in her second year, she was attending logic lectures 'by the author of "Alice in Wonderland"' and an illustrated lecture on X-rays: some, she reported, had actually been of help in slight surgical operations.

Other students watched Mrs T. H. Green, tripping like a young girl with her cape swirling as she crossed the Woodstock Road on her way home from visiting the Infirmary. Margery could study her 'splendid face' across a dinner-table. At the house of Professor Romanes, 'feeling hopelessly infantile and in a society too high for me', she met Miss Moberly of St Hugh's, Mary Palgrave, and the widow of Arnold Toynbee. Some of these Oxford ladies were alarming: their esoteric gossip seemed to offer no doorway to intimacy. Margery Fry dreaded setting out with her card-case on a raw Oxford afternoon, and by the time Dorothea Scott had passed her arithmetic test and joined her at Somerville, Margery confessed that her calling was in arrears. The practical Dorothea offered to lend a fashionable black spotted veil to keep Margery's hat anchored in the February squalls. Veiled and spotted Margery walked over the snow, gaining assurance from disguise, 'like a Christy minstrel with his face blacked'.

Even at Failand her sisters were tobogganing with the Hodgkin girls that winter of 1895. The Somervillians played ice-hockey on Port Meadow, but after a week of this rapture Margery realized that she was falling asleep over her work every evening. She left her skates at home and walked up to Godstow to watch the others. In her second term Mr Gerrans had dropped his other Somerville pupils and was coaching her two hours weekly. She was going to start the integral calculus. 'I wish I could tell you without all the boring explanations how interesting some of the things are. It makes one feel how horribly small the part one knows or ever will know is in comparison with the whole thing.' On her twenty-first birthday she read a paper to the Somerville Mathematical Society.

No doubt Margery Fry was clever, but it was difficult for the others to take her work altogether seriously when she was not working for Honours. It was Margery who was available to visit the sick in Lent Term. She was the obvious choice from the First Year when a committee was formed to arrange a garden-party in May 1895, to precede a great meeting of the Association for the Education of Women in the Examination Schools. The battle for degrees had opened. The President of Magdalen (Mr T. Herbert Warren) was to ask that justice be done to the intellect of women. Professor Richard Lodge came from Glasgow to suggest compromise. Mr A. L. Smith of Balliol wanted to wait for Cambridge. Miss Wordsworth of Lady Margaret Hall wanted Alma Mater to be kind but strict: to demand from women a standard which would deter them from coming up to 'have a good time', but to shield them from the excitement of University prizes and public recitations: a speech which drew from Miss Annie Rogers several private snorts of derision. In the end Professor Pelham, one of the founding fathers of Somerville, moved a resolution to apply to the University for the granting of degrees. His resolution was carried by eighty-three votes to ten and the case for women's degrees moved on to the next slow stage of committees, memorials, and counter-memorials.

The occasion left Margery cold. 'A duller function I never in my life beheld,' she said of the garden party, and of its aftermath, 'Miss Maitland and a good many of the girls were hugely excited about it. . . . Personally I think it's quite nice they should ask for it. I don't suppose and don't much hope or wish that they will get it, for a long while at any rate, but I was awfully sorry that they wouldn't let us in to the meeting. I should have liked above all things to see all the Oxford swells, or many of them at least, in full battle array.'

One evening as they lined up for dinner Eleanor Rathbone asked her to sit by her. 'She was of middle height, she had beautiful soft dark hair and splendid eyes. But what struck me most (in those days girls didn't make up, so good complexions were the more noticed) was the beauty of her very white skin, and her clear, almost vermilion cheeks.'[6] So Margery described her sixty years later in a broadcast to schoolgirls. Eleanor Rathbone had so far seemed inaccessible: she was a year Margery's senior, she did not play hockey, and it was rumoured that she never troubled to listen to the first part of a sentence. Her mind was said to move among philosophical abstractions, and her thoughts could not be communicated even through writing, for it was illegible.

I remember very well [Margery continued in her broadcast] the first time we walked together. I suppose I was rather a prig, and I certainly had expected to find all sorts of interesting people at college, and was rather disappointed to find my own year were just school girls like myself, immature and perhaps rather silly. . . . I saw at once she was far ahead of the rest of us. She began to talk about women's suffrage. Until then I had accepted what was a pretty general view of the time, that all the talk about votes was rather a silly stunt. So it was a very new point of view that was opened up to me of the difficulty for women to make full use of their abilities in the service of the country, and of the difficulty of getting Parliament to attend to the special needs of women and children.

Soon after this dinner-table conversation Margery was invited to join a small 'society for discussing things in general', calling themselves the Associated Prigs. Eleanor Rathbone and Miss Pope were members and Mary O'Brien kept the records, calling herself by the Quakerly title of clerk. When Mary O'Brien went down she was replaced by Hilda Oakeley, who came up at the age of twenty-seven —'very clever and if she *ever* was frivolous she would be quite delightful, as it is I feel I have to dilute her with more ordinary people'. The A.P. discussions began to take a philosophical turn. Someone read a paper on Positivism—'an awfully limited hopeless creed,' thought Margery, 'besides which I never can understand how anyone can feel an enthusiasm for humanity in general—I can't form any conception of what it means except as an enormously large number of separate individuals'.

At Michaelmas 1896 Margery returned to Somerville for her third year to find the old House changed: the wistaria had been hacked

[6] 'Eleanor Rathbone', broadcast 18 March 1952 in the B.B.C. Schools' Service.

down, new rooms were added, electric lights shone out on the old cedar tree. 'Cherub' (Lucy Kempson) and Lettice Ilbert between them conveyed to Margery that she was said to be 'very haughty . . . a proverbial third year student, snubbing the innocent little self-confident Freshers at "sharp practice" debates, etc.'. Among the Freshers was Nelly Hodgkin, her favourite cousin, 'one of, if not the, most promising, neither shy nor bumptious'. Margery was proud of her cousin, yet when Nelly was elected to the A.P.s she admitted 'I've just an atom of not wanting her left in me'. In this period of sudden growth she wanted her family out of the way, even its most congenial members. She begged them to visit her less often. Mr Gerrans had twice scolded her for working so little in vacations.

Hilda Oakeley, shy almost to tears, read the A.P.s a paper on 'Sacrifice', with her eyes directed under the chair opposite. The sacrificial theme, so often presented to Victorian childhood, had been much in mind during the wretched winter of 1897, when Margery's feet were 'a couple of martyrs and chilblains' and for the first time she paid a scout to wash up the cocoa-cups and light her fire. When the thaw began she wrote to Dorothea (convalescent in Switzerland): 'Oxford covers in all its smells with a wet blanket of fog. May [Staveley] and I stodged through mud and mist and dreariness and half vanished snow for three mortal hours on Boar's Hill.' From her mother she hid the perilous circumstances of the talk, but revealed its content: 'how far it was right that it should be painful to do the moral and virtuous thing. I am so utterly convinced that morality is imperfect so long as we don't really enjoy everything that's right better than what's wrong, just as much as good manners are distinctly incomplete until one prefers the use of a knife and fork to one's fingers and so on!' But even with the worry of cold feet omitted, this decline towards hedonism alarmed Lady Fry. Margery clarified: 'All I meant was that the unpleasantness of doing what's right is no more an integral part of morality than stiffness is of strength—it comes from its incompleteness, and not from its nature.'

Her three years at Somerville would soon be ending. Mary O'Brien was already teaching in a board-school, where there was a class of a hundred three-year-olds all 'new' at once. Eleanor Rathbone had half a dozen tasks waiting for her in Liverpool. Margery had hardly begun to discover the springs of action, of 'doing what's right'. She did not, she felt sure, experience in Meeting or elsewhere that spiritual communion which was supposed to nourish 'concerns'.

Could acceptance of a creed provide an alternative? But how did one begin to believe? 'I've wondered a good deal lately how one is to get the force and motive which seems to come of almost any very definite and exclusive creed, without its arbitrariness: for certainly when you've once seen the thing to be arbitrary your chance of believing it is gone.' But no uncertainty seemed to hang about her as she walked up and down the garden with Eleanor Rathbone: Margery Fry, who knew half the great people in the University, who had played hockey twice for Oxford, whose wit set her table laughing every evening, whose tutor sent her books all the way from Germany, and whose eloquence was already a legend. She and Eleanor 'were discussing whether there was anything worth while to be ambitious about'. Eleanor thought it might be worth while to wish to be Warden of Somerville; 'and I said, "No, that wasn't good enough." And we came to the conclusion that Parliament was shut to us, and practically everything was shut to us. There was nothing that it was worth while to be ambitious about.'[7]

As to her own immediate future, Isabel's suggestion that she should return to Brighton and teach was unattractive, Roger's suggestion of painting in London too controversial to be worth fighting for. She wrote a letter of thanks to her parents for her years at Somerville: 'I think that the feeling of having belonged and in a way always belonging to a college, and of sharing common aims and responsibilities and a common pride in it with a number of people utterly different from oneself is bound to make a difference to all one's life, besides all the more personal influences of one's immediate friends.'

She took down her books and the curtains Roger had given her for her twenty-first birthday, leaving all bare and tidy for the next comer. From Oxford the train took her to Bristol, where she changed without mishap for Portbury. At Portbury, Gibb was waiting to drive her home between the fields of new-mown hay to Failand, once more to be reunited with her parents and with Mab, Joan, Agnes, and Ruth.

[7] 'Personal Call', broadcast 26 March 1956 in 'London Calling Asia'.

VI

Daughter at Home and Librarian at Somerville: 1897-1904

'YOU'VE gone on all this while thinking après ça le déluge and here is the deluge upon you', wrote Roger. Word came also from Margery's own species, like her aimless in the flood: from Lucy Kempson, busy in a country house where servants as well as family were down with a fever, not wholly able to conceal her pleasure in sweeping and cooking as she tuned her complaint to Margery's: 'Oh Margery!—the future does lie so nakedly before us. . . . I care lots for your woe, Margery dear, it is a real one and the hard fact is that there is no cure but waiting and grabbing at everything that turns up!'

To the servants' hall Miss Margery was a flibbertigibbet. Miss Mab was looking after the babies in the village, Miss Joan was a Guardian. Even Miss Agnes, poor thing, deaf as she was, taught embroidery and helped the master with his studies. Miss Ruth played the piano and beat time for the boys' band. Miss Margery was here, there, and everywhere; pleasant, talking and laughing, though she could be sharp, like the mistress. Every few weeks Gibb would be round early with the carriage and off she would go to the station, visiting relations or a college friend. Now and again she would come back from London in a smart hat. There was not much else to show for her college training.

Margery could invite her friends to Failand, one or two at a time. The two Somerville philosophers, Eleanor Rathbone and Hilda Oakeley, were reunited there in the summer of 1898. Hilda was socially harmless, but Eleanor's impending visit had filled her hostess, she told Dorothy Scott, 'with qualms of dread. You know I'm never absolutely free from fear of her and I know she'll bring conversational bombs to the family dinner-table (i.e. if she ever gets there herself wh. considering her un- and our hyper-punctuality I rather doubt).' Margery's fears were groundless: she found in

Eleanor 'a sense of what is good-form and gentlemanly which often makes me blush for my own obtuser perceptions'.

By this time Lady Fry could have become a notable hostess, like the American Quakeress, Hannah Pearsall Smith, entertaining the Webbs, young Shaw, and 'Bertie' Russell, at Friday's Hill in Surrey, or like her own sister Bessie, holding court for writers and artists at Yattendon. Sir Edward Fry was being drawn back into public life. The Bill which led to the Prevention of Corruption Act in 1906 was being drafted in the library at Failand. His own scientific and legal acquaintance, Roger's growing circle of artists, and now the friends whom Margery and Isabel were making everywhere they moved, would have made up a noble if dangerously blended company.

When the British Association was meeting at Bristol in 1898 Margery was presented to Lord Kelvin at her Uncle Lewis Fry's house. 'For almost the first time in my life', she wrote to Dorothy Scott, 'I had such shyness that I could hardly sit on my chair because it seems to me that a mind as big as that is a thing worth being afraid of.' Next day, when the great scientist was brought to see the library at Failand, he sought out Margery in the drawing-room and asked her whether she could solve a cubic equation. 'So I've felt a feeling I've never felt before of what people mean by "a great honour".' But except at the most dutiful of garden-parties, those 'groups under the dreaming garden-trees', which to Matthew Arnold typified the 'high midsummer pomps' of Sir Edward and Lady Fry's generation, were unknown at Failand. Lady Fry is said to have been timid in conversation, a conventional hostess, neutralizing any trace of controversy: but her daughters knew she had 'unused selves'. The warmth and efficiency which could have brought a house-party to life were used in fretting over daughters' ailments, locking cupboard doors, and counting jam-pots.

Margery's invitations poured in: she was involved in the struggle, painful as long as her mother lived, to reconcile the demands of parents and friends; but she kept her friendships in repair and laid the foundations of significant future relationships. It was during a visit to the Vernon Harcourts in the Isle of Wight, for instance (a party she nearly missed, her parents being abroad and her elder sisters feeling it unwise for her to join without parental leave a party including several young men), that she first met Champion Russell, whom twenty years later she was to rediscover as a fellow worker.

As Margery moves through the last Victorian summers from one bountiful house to another, where most of the dusting was finished before she came down for breakfast, where grass was cut and strawberries brought in by devoted gardeners, dishes washed unseen and almost out of earshot: we may well ask, as she expected us to ask, what she or her friends had to complain about. Looking back from 1950, Margery Fry compared George Eliot's Dorothea Brook in *Middlemarch* with Eleanor Rathbone,

two characters essentially similar, one frustrated, the other fully used. The clue to the difference lies in the changed position of women in the century that has passed. For the people of today it is difficult to feel either gratitude or enthusiasm for the men and women who helped to make these changes possible. There are middle-class girls who would gladly, for a life of elegant leisure, forgo the career which is now assured as a matter of economic necessity as much for them as for their brothers. There are many women who, struggling with professional work as well as household chores, must feel that they could gladly put up with a few weeks of Dorothea Brook's gentlewoman's world 'where everything was done for her and none asked her aid'. These younger woman may ask whether this century of effort has, in fact, been worth while; I who have lived through three-quarters of it, reply emphatically that it *has*.[1]

She would quote the words used by Florence Nightingale in an essay so bitter that her friends had persuaded her to print it only for private circulation (it was published in 1928 as an appendix to *The Cause* by Ray Strachey). 'If a parent were to say "No, you must not eat your dinner", or "you must take no exercise because I cannot spare you, you must stay and read to me, and only eat at odd times", the whole world would be amazed at the selfishness of such a parent. Yet the moral starvation which parents inflict is just as great. What has society done for us? . . . It affords us neither interest, nor affections, nor employment.'

These words were written before Margery Fry was born. She herself went from a mentally stimulating family to a progressive school and a residential college. Yet from college she returned to experience in her own mind and body, as few women will remember experiencing by the end of the twentieth century, the fearful enervation of the grown-up unmarried daughter living at home. Parental demands for affection, company, attention seized precedence over all other demands, even where daughters as well as servants were numerous. In the intimacy of school and college Margery and her

[1] 'Good-bye to the Parlour', broadcast 12 April 1950 in the B.B.C. Home Service.

friends began to speak out to one another. At home, all was respect and compliance. Parents gave in return an anxious tenderness which today we should consider unhelpful even for little children. No interest must be followed to the point of fatigue. No risks must be taken, except, for many women, the risk of being left, in middle age or later, alone and without resources. In old age Margery Fry believed that an occasional feeling of childish inadequacy was common among her contemporaries, though she alone seemed ready 'shamelessly to confess it'.[2] All this Roger feared for his sisters. He chose as his wife not a family acquaintance, but an artist, a young woman who lived independently in London. Roger and Helen were married in Margery's last year at Somerville. For her the marriage was full of hope: in her brother's house she would share the freedom from convention, the creative excitement she would have found in a home of her own. But in the first years of their marriage Margery saw little of them: a restlessness, only gradually to be recognized as mental unbalance, kept Helen from wishing to return from Italy or France. At last Roger took a house in Surrey. Margery, as the least occupied daughter, was sent down alone in November 1898 to prepare the house for their homecoming.

It was in this dead place that she received a letter from the Warden of Somerville asking her to return as Librarian. 'It sounds so tempting that I hardly dare to let myself think about it seriously,' she wrote to Dorothy Scott. Margery Fry certainly felt no vocation as a librarian. Years later, when she was helping to found another library, she remarked that books came to her as cats went to people who liked them least. Simply, the choice of returning to Oxford must not be missed. Margery went up to Somerville for the second time at the beginning of Trinity Term, 1899, feeling 'rather like a fresher without the excitement'.

There were 6,000 books huddled on shelves in the dining-room and in various corridors. The nucleus of the Library was a bequest of 500 volumes from the library of Mark Pattison, Rector of Lincoln College, who had died in 1884. Gifts came in constantly. The College itself was spending £100 a year on books from its penurious income. Miss Maitland's vision ranged farther than Margery at first realized. Miss Pope showed her how to set about the books. They were up betimes, beginning work at half past eight. For part of the morning she helped the secretary, copying letters by hand or even taking

[2] *Old Age Looks at Itself* (National Old People's Welfare Council, 1954), p. 5.

money to the bank—foreseeing, in fact, a certain danger of becoming the 'general errand-boy'. She had a rather dismal, isolated room on the ground floor of the House: Lady Fry had to be reassured about fire and burglars.

Work at first was merely the price of being in Oxford. Then some Elizabethan reprints were found to be 'quaint and amusing'. Turning out a drawer crammed with old newspapers, she found the unbound copies of Ruskin which he had sent along after his tea-party with Miss Shaw-Lefèvre. By the end of a month she noticed in herself a 'desire for more good *editions* of books, because it does seem rather well worth while to have curious and original copies in a library that's likely to go on for a very long while in some form or another'. A few days later, 'the books seem to want more and more going over the more you do to them, but there's a sort of satisfaction in getting them quite accurately done, with their dates and sizes and all put in on the cards'. Margery Fry's handwriting in books and catalogues is still part of the beauty of Somerville College Library.

At the beginning of Michaelmas Term, 1899, Miss Sheavyn, the English Tutor, read aloud from *The Times* Mr Chamberlain's speech on the outbreak of the South African War, while Margery marked some new hand-towels. A light wind of excitement, not altogether disagreeable, passed over the College: 'those with military relatives can't help feeling joyful, however much they want to prevent war'. Agnes, always a willing handmaiden to other people's intellectual exercises, sent cuttings for a debate on American diplomacy. 'The war', wrote Margery in November, 'grows more and more terrible. Of course it is the first time in my lifetime that anything like fighting against a civilized nation, and on this scale, has happened and I can't help working a continual proportion sum between this and a really big European war.' But to remember the South African War required an effort of the mind: as to remember the famine in India, about which the Somervillians also collected facts and debated.

In the pages of the *Friend* the war came near enough to reproach Margery for her callousness. Lady Fry and Joan were both on a committee of women Friends for the relief of war victims. The *Friend* was not an exciting publication, but it generally contained at least one item of family news—that Uncle Joseph had spoken as usual in Meeting for Sufferings, that Joan Mary Fry had read a paper on Ezekiel, or that Edward Fry had given an address on Corruption at Birmingham Town Hall. Margery also read that Mary O'Brien had declared in public the arguments against public ownership which she had already developed in a letter to her fellow Quaker at Somerville. She had even traced the causes of war to materialistic greed.

The first phase of the war ended with the relief of Ladysmith in February 1900.

The whole town, and Somerville too, went half crazy with the comfort of it. . . . No one could have helped feeling as if an almost personal anxiety had been relieved, but the Quaker in me with its natural tendency towards the minority made all the flags and policemen's rattles and bonfires and cheerings seem very far from a seemly expression of relief. It all seems too appallingly real for that kind of thing and I was very glad that I was dining out that night, as the whole college dined together and jollified, and I didn't want either to join or to hold off.

The Fry family maintained an unbroken Quaker front against the war. The Quaker Queries (by which Friends still examine their conduct, corporately and individually) had been in the eighteenth century practical and specific about military activity. 'Are Friends faithful in our testimony against bearing arms and being in any manner concerned in the militia, in privateers or armed vessels, or in dealing with prize goods?' When the Queries were revised in 1860 this was changed to 'Are Friends faithful in maintaining our Christian testimony against all War?'—to which was subsequently added, in the evangelical phrasing of 1875, 'as inconsistent with the precepts and spirit of the Gospel'.

This nineteenth-century version of the peace testimony—at the same time more easily evaded, and more searching if accepted, than the less sophisticated Queries of the preceding century—had now to be tested for the first time in Margery's memory. The Society of Friends was not at that time particularly associated in the popular imagination with pacifism, nor had there been any influx—as after the First World War—of members who had left other churches over the issues of war and peace. The children born into the Society each year outnumbered 'convincements' by ten to one. These children, instead of proceeding straight from a Quaker academy to a Quaker business or, after 1828, joining other Nonconformists at University College, London, were now free to enter Oxford and Cambridge. They were not only permeating the professions but were active in every new movement, scientific, social, even artistic. The sober testimony of Friends, after a period of aloofness, was heard again in the world: it was not surprising that the world modified some Quaker judgements.

When Robin Hodgkin, Margery's undergraduate cousin, wrote to the *Friend* just before the relief of Ladysmith, his main concern seemed to be lest hundreds of young Friends, uncertain worldlings like himself, were hiding behind the few leaders who, with absolute sincerity, were proclaiming pacifism. Of war he had no first-hand experience: the Goliath then was hypocrisy. Margery commented on his letter on 16 February 1900, the day of its publication:

Robin has written to the *Friend*, rather a good letter, explaining his point of view. . . . The more I think of it, the more perplexed I become, it seems impossible to cut off the particular exercise of force which we call war from all other cases of its use, and if I should not hesitate to call in a policeman to protect us from a burglar why should I object to the use of force against an invader? The fact seems to me to be that the Christianity which rejects war—(what one feels inclined to label as Tolstoi Xtianity)—with its clear sense of absolute right and absolute wrong which can always be disentangled by the illuminated soul is a doctrine which one must either accept throughout or leave altogether as impracticable, and I suppose if one were to accept it one would have to maintain that it was a creed not only for those of spiritual genius but capable of being held by the most commonplace and mundane people too, and one would have to give up all lingering hopes that it would in the end work as well even for this world as commonsense. On the other hand, if you are not prepared to sacrifice commonsense to mysticism, and if you feel that the utmost one can do to further the Kingdom of Heaven is to compare without flagging the shades of grey and always to choose the one nearer to white, I can have no doubt whatever that war will sometimes (I do not think probably in this present case) seem the lesser evil, and then, as Robin says in his letter, if you admit that it is inevitable the least thing you can do as a good citizen is to take your part in preparing for it and bearing the burden of it.

For Margery 'the inevitable war' had not yet arrived. She wore the 'Peace Testimony', as Penn is said to have worn his sword, as long as she was able. She did what she could for the victims of war, as for the victims of all violence, and when at last she accepted a war as just, she accepted with anguish. She never 'jollified' over any military victory.

When the last of the Associated Prigs went down the gap widened between students and staff. More and more of the students came straight from school and the dons grew no younger. But students and staff were still remote enough from the rest of Oxford for some of their activities to be communal. The 'Prigs' were replaced by the Somerville Parliament, open to anyone in College. Not yet in sight of the vote, these young women felt it worth while so to master parliamentary procedure that twenty years later, when seriously concerned with legislation, Margery Fry claimed to have learnt more of definite use in life from the Somerville Parliament than from any direct instruction at Oxford.

Some of Margery's contemporaries were already learning about these questions at first hand. Eleanor Rathbone in Liverpool had taken her hereditary place as a voluntary public servant. May Staveley, who was eleven years older than Margery, was Warden of a new women's settlement at Birmingham. Dorothy Scott was with her. The settlement movement, originated by Canon Barnett when he was a curate in Whitechapel, was at its height. Twenty-five settlements were founded in London and the provinces between 1890 and 1900. University graduates and undergraduates, living communally in the poor districts of the cities, aimed through personal friendships at understanding those social problems to which they were not satisfied to apply a superficial charity. Having learned the needs of the poor, the settlers hoped not only to give personal service but also to use their privileges of birth and education to influence legislation. The battered dignities of Toynbee Hall and the *art nouveau* grace of the Passmore Edwards (afterwards the Mary Ward) Settlement still recall a confidence in the upper-middle-class way of life which contrasts with the modern nostalgia for what are supposed to be working-class values: a confidence which enabled the settlers to live undisguised among streets greyer, smellier, even noisier than we know in England today. Some of the workers, like Dorothy Scott, lacked the simplest kinds of experience: they had rarely ridden in an omnibus and never shopped in a market. They did not even expect to like the work or be particularly good at it. They only felt constrained to make some return for the materially easy lives they had inherited. Seeing for herself, subjected at meals to the endless shop-talk of dedicated workers, now and then inspired by a lecture from Beatrice Webb or Eleanor Rathbone, Dorothy plodded on. Hilda Oakeley, drawn into the educational programme of some settlement (probably the Passmore Edwards, to which she returned as Warden in her more confident middle years), felt as unsuccessful as the boy who tried to bring back the golden balls from fairyland. 'I am discovering a little better each day that there is nothing on earth I can do except lecture or write to people who don't exist, or don't want to hear things which I shall very soon think I don't want to tell them.'

Somerville College had bought a canoe. Margery paddled it up the Cherwell, glad for once to be alone, for she was looking for a kingfisher's nest. News from her friends moved her, but did not lead her to mistake a ruffled conscience for a sense of vocation. Her own achievements were trivial enough: her labours with the books seemed only to show her ignorance: sometimes she wanted to wear a placard inscribed 'I know nothing', though Lucy Kempson (once more smiling, cherubic, teaching and learning in France) wrote soothing words: 'I believe very honestly you can and do do something there. You've waited so long and arranged so many flowers that you really do deserve it. I think some day I should like you to be Warden.'

Besides her work in the Library, Margery had other small functions, 'opening the freshers' minds like oysters', according to Hilda Lorimer, the young Tutor in Classics, or welcoming returning Somervillians. 'I sometimes feel as if one got mechanical and half-sham in one's attempt to take an interest in the lives of a great many people . . . some of whom one only knows very slightly, but I console myself with the feeling that it would be horrid to come back to college and find no one who ever seemed to want to hear and generally at the moment one is genuinely interested and anxious to hear about it all.' She even took on a pupil in mathematics, asking advice from a family acquaintance, a Mr Bertrand Russell, whose *Principles of Geometry* had come out in her last year with Mr Gerrans. But it was when she rose to speak to an audience, with a few notes written boldly on a little card in the palm of her hand—with perhaps a couple of allusions only to be used if the temperature of the audience was exactly right—that Margery Fry felt joy and mastery. After a College dinner at the Randolph, when Professor Dicey, Vinerian Professor of Law—one of the wittiest speakers in the University—had replied to her proposal of 'The Distinguished Guests', their performance was described as a duet.

At the beginning of Margery's second Hilary Term it was clear that the Victorian era was ending. Lady Fry advised her daughter that everyone would wear mourning for the Queen and she had better buy it as cheaply as possible. The Somervillians crept about in the ubiquitous gloom, depressed by the liverish chills peculiar to Oxford at that season—'extraordinary how closely boredom follows digestion

—and when everything seems stupid and dull you can perhaps keep yourself from actually snapping but you can't force yourself to interests'.

Whole mornings passed on such chores as ruling the College wages-book and marking on the University lists the lectures open to women. On Sunday the sermon at Manchester Chapel was long, dull, and orthodox. Yet somehow, on the way home across the Parks, Margery and Miss Sheavyn got into conversation on one of the least orthodox subjects—that of social class. Miss Maitland had known, when she appointed Phoebe Sheavyn, that she was not a lady born. She had been brought up over a draper's shop in a small Midland town. As happened in many families (even among Frys), the younger daughter had the better chance: Phoebe was allowed to teach in a board-school, after her hemming had passed the scrutiny of a male inspector with a magnifying-glass. But another inspector had not considered her suitable: she went from one private school to another, exploited and defenceless. At last she became governess to the children of a kind architect who taught her to draw and encouraged her to sit for the Oxford Locals. There followed a scholarship to the new College of Aberystwyth and another to Bryn Mawr, U.S.A., a post with Professor Wright, working on the *English Dialect Dictionary*, and in 1897 a tutorship at Somerville College.

Margery and 'Phoebus' had been friends ever since Margery returned to Somerville. That mysterious fuel which produced in the Frys a radiance and sometimes a dangerous flash of fire nourished a homely warmth. Margery was incapable of the cool reserve which normally clung to the late Victorian young lady like her well-cut neutral-tinted clothes. She had an openness about her own little troubles which, combined with an interest in theirs, made her accessible to people of a different origin, though she did not yet know this. She had made friends with 'her own sort', she had a proper ease with servants, she had made tentative and artificial relationships with a few of the 'poor', but now for the first time she realized she had come close to one of the others—the vast, mysterious lower middle classes. 'It must be extraordinary', she wrote to Lady Fry, 'so completely to have changed your point of view by education as to feel that half the things that interest you are Latin and Greek to your own sisters. And yet she says she feels sure that people of that position would immensely enjoy more intercourse with educated people.'

Margery's parents took her in the spring of 1901 to Italy. At an early meeting of the 'A.P.s' Margery had chosen for her theme 'Beauty is truth, truth beauty'. Now in Florence, though on a conventional tour, staying at conventional hotels, she was in the heart of the worship of the beautiful, led by the Berensons with the fervour which Mary Berenson's American Quaker parents had once devoted to evangelical religion. English-speaking aesthetes were buying up Tuscan villas to which they fled from the ugliness of the industrial regions which had founded most of their fortunes. Italy was also part of Roger's world. The dusty books at Oxford, the sermons, the discussions about society and duty, soon seemed distant and alien. Margery seemed at last to have found reality: she was, as she wrote to Dorothy, 'took rhapsodical'.

I've been looking at one of the finest towns that ever man imagined and at pictures that set all sorts of long gone asleep things and never woken up things, twitching restlessly in one's mind and wanting to express themselves once more from oneself as they've expressed themselves over and over again through all these absurdly human painters and builders and sculptors. It's rather rot to be a librarian after all and to go back from Italy in the spring to mug at my books, and oh! what rot it is to be a girl and travel round properly at hotels instead of taking a knapsack on one's back and tramping off into those Appenines that call to you to come, and oh, what rottest rot of all to be a great galumphing Englishwoman and only to see how it would feel to have a mind that lets utility go to the devil and chooses the simply beautiful at all costs. . . . I'm in one of those rare but painful states of mind when Art and the World say 'come' and one may only shudder and say, 'if I could', before one goes back to hurry up the getting old process and seem an embodiment of the prudent virtues to the young.

Somewhere in Florence the Frys met a Fellow of New College, in his early forties. He was travelling with a student, who noticed that his tutor's absence of mind that Easter was extraordinary. He was constantly losing his way, and in the galleries of Florence often failed to see the picture he was looking at. His companion concluded that the Renaissance lacked interest for a medievalist. Soon after term began Margery received an invitation to the annual supper-party given by the Fellows of New College. Lady Fry was asked to applaud her discretion in refusing it, for a function in a man's college was a rare pleasure. It was probably the first invitation she had ever received from an unmarried man outside her own family. 'I am always pleasantly surprised when I find a man-friend,' she said to a friend at

Somerville. 'I take it for granted that women will take to me if I like them.' With the encouragement of one or two of the most revered hostesses, it did not seem improper for Margery and her new acquaintance to meet from time to time in an Oxford drawing-room.

He grew less comic, more likeable; possibly even lovable. She soon knew that he wanted to marry her. He was fifteen years older than Margery, but her father would prefer a man of proved worth. He was in orders, but her cousin had lately become engaged to a clergyman without the skies actually falling. He was a churchman of a kind the Frys could best approve, disliking the specifically religious attitude which loosened the connexion between religion and morality, insisting on a decent, traditional worship, but abhorring sacerdotalism. Early in the year Margery had become, as Dorothy had long foretold, a maiden aunt, sharing the privilege with five other maiden aunts on the paternal side alone. Now at twenty-seven she had the chance, not only of being loved as Helen was loved by Roger, but of having children to initiate into all the joys she had known as a little child, as well as those which she believed could have been granted more freely in her girlhood. She was being offered a position of some dignity and power. When most of the professions were still closed to women, marriage with a liberal-minded man who recognized his wife's maturity (and she knew several such men among the founding fathers of Somerville) could be the fullest outlet for her talents. But by the end of the summer she had decided her affection for her friend was not 'the real thing' and refused him.

'How good it is that women's instincts are so sound,' wrote Roger in a letter of the utmost tenderness. Isabel also, whose fierce judgements had often brought her younger sister to tears, now understood 'the sort of feeling of sinking back into an insignificance— conventional of course, but none the less sensible to one's tenderest feelings'.

Margery's suitor took his rejection hard. In the depth of her inexperience she had not understood her power. She had tried consciously from her schooldays to mitigate her natural sharpness. Now she found herself obliged to hurt a good and sensitive person. She had to go on seeing him in the small, observant society of Oxford and it was soon clear that he continued to hope. Her guilt was not eased when his crabbed handwriting began again to make her laugh instead of cry. Lady Fry reported with some annoyance, after a visit to London, that 'the faithful friend' seemed in good form, had preached an excellent sermon, but it was several years before Margery had the relief of hearing that he was happily married.

'How bitter it is when the very thing you long for is offered you in a form that you can't accept,' she said to a Somervillian of her own age. Later, in *The Single Woman*, she wrote:

Even for the level-headed unmarried woman later youth is a time of interior disquiet and frustration which a reasonable pride hides from the outside world. There are the love affairs which come up against hopeless obstacles or those that just fizzle out in disillusion. There are the friendships which just don't ripen as love affairs. The possible husbands who are just impossible. And perhaps the worst pain of all—simply watching the things taken for granted in other lives passing you by.

During the summer of 1901 her sense of personal significance had also been heightened by plans for the new Library at Somerville. The creative zeal which had inspired her as she followed the builders around Failand now returned: she scribbled elevations of libraries in her idle moments. At the Gaudy a cheque of £50 from Sir John Evans made up Miss Maitland's Library Fund to the full £2,000 needed. Soon Margery was called into consultation with Mr Champneys, the chosen architect, famous for the John Rylands Library at Manchester. Earlier in the year an important gift had come from the bequest of Amelia Blandford Edwards, a distinguished Egyptologist. She had made an awkward condition, that her books were to remain together in their original bookcases. A special room was to be made for them in the new building. There it remains, a place of mysterious sanctity to Somervillians brought up to read books rather than to look at them behind glass, but increasingly valued as a beautifully preserved mid-Victorian library. In the spring of 1901, Margery Fry turned from her dustier labours to handle these fine bindings and to unpack a Shakespeare folio of 1632, a black-letter Chaucer of 1545.

Peace was signed at Pretoria at last. It was Coronation Year. A woman at the Settlement told Dorothy Scott that the King would never have ordered a holiday if he had 'known what it was to be short'. More fortunate people, as usual, had the sense of a new era beginning. Lady Fry wondered what people like herself would do if the twentieth century brought, as predicted, 'automatic servants'. With no human servants to fuss over, would not their souls be arid? Or would they be able better to concentrate on 'isolated poor people and needy relatives'? 'Oh, Margery, I would like to know how the universe looks to you,' cried Hilda Oakeley across the Atlantic. In Montreal there was a man called Rutherford who set 'the physics building constantly trembling with excitement. . . . The chemical atom is not incapable of subdivision.' Hilda recommended a scientist of her own year, studying radio-activity, as the first Mary Somerville Research Fellow (a medieval historian was, in fact, chosen). But the terms of the Fellowship had still to be drafted. Knowing that the attitudes of Victorian parenthood would persist far into the new century, Eleanor Rathbone wrote to Margery urging that the Fellow should be given at least a moral obligation to stay her full three years —'I don't think the Council realizes quite the position many women are in towards their families, nor what advantage to the Fellow herself strict regulation may be, to enable her to resist domestic pressure.'[3]

These words, perhaps, were behind Margery's resistance to her parents' suggestion that she should take a term off to visit Egypt at the beginning of 1903. Isabel needed a holiday and Margery, her mother thought, would be none the worse for a respite from her 'squirrel-cage'. For the first time Margery asserted her duty as a professional woman: 'If I once begin to let pleasure—even such a mighty one as this—come between me and my work, what usefulness I have will be largely lost, because even if what one does is not of any supreme importance, it *is* important that people may feel that one is to be relied upon . . . knowing as I do how a "substitute" means a little extra burden on everyone. . . .' The brave plea ended in anti-climax. After much manoeuvring among the sisters, it was decided that Margery was the only possible companion for Isabel. With very little pressure Miss Maitland admitted that Margery's absence would cause no inconvenience (there was indeed an almost bottomless reservoir of intelligent, unoccupied young women to draw on) and Margery went with Isabel to Egypt. They saw the usual tourist sights (with perhaps more than usual tourist perception of the beggars who crowded round them). Like other travellers, they found their private griefs diminished by the shadow of the Pyramids, though 'it would be very dreadful if everywhere we lived under the shadow of all the past as one does here'. The next term Margery decided to keep Hilda Lorimer company in learning hieroglyphics from the Reader in Egyptology at Oxford. Being 'counted as

[3] Letter to Margery Fry, 1901.

University', they got in free—'and the privileges one gets in that way are so few and far between it seems wrong not to save money even by learning hieroglyphics'.

Through Mildred Pope she was at last appreciating the bitterness of a woman's status in Oxford, which in her own life had troubled her little. The Honours School of Modern Languages (hitherto only a 'Women's School') was now being established by the University. 'Mildred Pope is the only person in Oxford who knows about considerable parts of the subjects (she has been coaching the Reader in French, himself a Frenchman, on some of them)—but she can only be consulted in a back-stairs way.'

The women's colleges continued to build. Slowly (for the weather was appalling that year) Champney's neo-Jacobean arches were rising between the West Building and the old House. In the roofless Library passage, Margery told her mother, a robin was nesting at eye-level.

'But tell me,' Lady Fry insisted, wanting to hold her sixth daughter to her heart for ever, 'what are you really thinking about all the time, far away in Oxford?' A variation on her old theme came back from Margery:

I have been wondering very much lately whether there is really any way of turning the force with which one clamours and longs for things for oneself, for happiness, satisfaction—even for fame, or knowledge, or excitement—into channels broader and less selfish. If one *could* it would be a motive force with a vengeance. But probably this isn't clear. Anyhow, the only way of doing it is obviously love and it's so hard to extend love beyond the very few people one cares for by nature.

Returning after the Long Vacation in October, Margery rushed into the College garden to see her new Library. There it was, complete, as she had pictured it: except that across the warm red façade, picked out in white bricks in the bulging script then in ephemeral fashion, was the mysterious Somerville device, *Donec rursus impleat orbem*. In a rage she ran up the stone stairs to 'that most dignified and well-proportioned room' where the shelves she had helped to design would receive the books she had sorted and catalogued for three years. Mr Pelham, the Chairman of the Council, was sympathetic but too diplomatic for Margery's taste: 'Mr Champneys the architect came down but Mr Pelham after all his fulminations about the motto was as meek as Moses over it when it came to the point—

never even stipulated that the swellings of the letters should come off. . . . I could weep at the sight of those horrid white words.'

Before the affair could be settled there was worse cause for weeping. Only a few weeks earlier she had left Roger and Helen. 'They were charming to me and there is a certain uncommonplaceness about their whole way of life which makes the rest of the world seem a little tame and unromantic by comparison.' Now Roger wrote that Helen had been taken to a mental hospital. 'I can't stand *anyone*. You would understand and help more than any other.'

Miss Maitland saw to it that Margery slipped away so quietly that few noticed even in that close community. In Hampstead there were practical things to be done: charwomen to be found, winter clothes for the children to be bought (a job to keep Lady Fry occupied): above all, a mother-substitute to find for the children. Margery said it must be Joan. Lady Fry said it must be Mab: she was the trained nurse, the lover of babies. Margery insisted: she understood the love and trust between the distraught young mother and the middle-aged uncompromising Quakeress. So Joan arrived at Hampstead and Margery went back to her Library. When all hope for Helen failed at last, Joan moved into the fine house at Guildford which Roger had built for Helen's recovery, and stayed there as long as the children needed her. She never again made Failand her home. 'I find it difficult to describe how happy and secure we felt in her care,' says her niece. '. . . She gave us for the first time the feeling that we mattered, that we should grow up to be "people".'[4]

Margery went back to Somerville. By the end of November the 'horrid white words' had come down, though Mr Champneys was furious and Miss Maitland regretted the expense. Looking at the Library, 'simple and jolly' as she had wanted it, Margery saw the loggia and the steps as a stage. The young Frys had never gone to the theatre and by the time Margery broke the ban it was too late for her to become an habitual theatre-goer. But though the London theatres, most of them built in their childhood, were as remote from the Frys as the London pubs, Isabel at least was a confident actress and producer. Margery was now prepared to put on a show for the official opening of the Library, before a critical University audience.

Moreover, she asked Robert Bridges to compose a special piece

[4] *Joan Mary Fry*, p. 26.

for the occasion, in the form of a masque. He had written quantities of verse drama but it took him several days to recover from the idea of his lines being mouthed in public by human actresses, even by Somervillians, who, Margery assured him, could 'probably be relied upon to perform simply and without any stage-tricks or vulgarity'. Presently he asked what his masque was to be about. Margery said it was to be the myth of Demeter and Persephone. Demure hesitations followed, but by the end of March two-thirds of the masque had arrived, 'a great deal really charming and the whole of it very good'.

It was a trying summer for both poet and producer, though the students, even the girl who could not say 'anemone', found rehearsals delightful. Margery had the responsibility of arranging the Library as well as the masque. She corresponded 'freely and fiercely' with the poet. Though he refused to attend a rehearsal, having no experience of stagecraft, he interfered in details of the production. Margery, on her side, was tiresome to the poet. She did not like his description of Hell; he replied that it was not his idea that Persephone should go there, and, if Hell was not fit for her girls to know about, Margery had better close her 'Academe', of which he seemed already to see her as Principal. She quibbled about phrases: the 'electric beams of the sun' offended her somewhat conventional taste in poetic diction. She even tried to pick holes in his meticulous prosody and had to be referred to Milton.

But by and large this dramatic collaboration went more smoothly than anyone could have hoped. In early June the books were on the shelves, arranged by cheerful helpers, among whom was a new acquaintance of Margery's, Rose Sidgwick, who was coaching in history that term. The Piranesi engravings presented by Sir Edward Fry were hung between the bays. The portrait of Amelia Blandford Edwards accompanied her bookcases as she had wished. On 11 July 1904 the Vice-Chancellor and Proctors attended a function at Somerville College for the first time. John Morley declared the Library open. The Somervillian nymphs appeared in the costumes approved by Lady Evans. Scholars applauded their Greek dancing, though nobody now remembers who can have been the choreographer. Persephone (later Mrs Leyton Richards) gave Demeter (Miss H. C. Escreet) a modified account of Hell. Dons and their wives who had clamoured for invitations were not disappointed. 'Even the grey weather', Margery told the author, 'was not a drawback, as too bright a sun made the actors grimace.' Everywhere Miss Fry was complimented on her production.

But now Sir Edward Fry, so universally kind and judicious in Agnes's memoir, appeared in a strange light. He had never cared for Robert Bridges, whose pipe-smoke on visits to Failand had seemed an unwholesome rival of the gardener's bonfires. Now he conveyed to the poet that the audience had found the carrying-off of Persephone rather funny. Sir Edward Fry had just been made a Doctor of Civil Law at Oxford: he was not a person to be answered back. To Margery the poet admitted sadly that he did not 'pretend to understand the Oxford audience'. He had hoped also that she would have provided for the entrance of Hades 'something of the nature of darkness or smoke to give the touch of awe'. This point, however, was amended in the preparation of the manuscript for printing.

The sound of well-bred clapping had died away, the loggia steps where so many books would be read on summer mornings were empty. In the long Library above Margery Fry had left, in Dorothy Scott's words, 'some physical impress, however slight, on Somerville'. John Morley had called her 'the perfect librarian'. But when, at his suggestion, 2,000 books came to the College from the library of John Stuart Mill, she was no longer there to receive them: for on 29 June 1904 she was appointed Warden of the new residence for women students at Birmingham.

VII

'Taken by the Hand by a Man by the Name of Beale', Birmingham: 1904-1908

THE prototype of English civic universities had been granted its charter in 1900. With a speed astonishing to some of the more timid academics Mr Joseph Chamberlain had collected £500,000 and was convinced that at least half as much again would be forthcoming when there was something to show for it. A vast building programme was planned for a site in Edgbaston. Halls of residence were discussed and in general judged desirable. There were visions of adjacent halls for men and women, sharing kitchens. When it became clear that no money could be spared to build them, a committee of women, under the chairmanship of Mrs Beale, the Vice-Chancellor's wife, decided to go ahead with some project, however small, for a women's residence. Within a year funds had been raised by subscription, a house in Hagley Road had been bought, and by 1904 it was time to look for a Warden. Mrs Muirhead, wife of the Professor of Philosophy, was a member of the Hostel Committee. The Muirheads were close friends of Dorothy Scott, who once again played her part of destiny in Margery Fry's life. The Professor called on Margery at Somerville; in the end she agreed to apply for the Wardenship if it was advertised. The advertisement immediately appeared in the *Athenaeum* and the *Spectator* and within a month she had accepted the post.

'The salary is *very* meagre,' she wrote to her father, '£60 a year. . . . I think they ought to raise it as soon as possible, not, as you know, because I should need it, but because it is such an unsound principle to trust to getting good people from un-mercenary motives.' Her parents approved of the appointment. Perhaps they saw Birmingham through their daughter Joan's eyes, as a centre of Quaker enlightenment. At Woodbrooke, the former home of the Cadburys at Selly Oak, a college for Quaker study and research had been set up in 1903 by John Wilhelm Rowntree and others of Joan's friends. For Lady Fry there was a wistful satisfaction in seeing her favourite daughter as the mistress of a household, caring for a group of five to ten girls, hardly more numerous than Lady Fry's own daughters, in what Margery herself described in a letter to a friend fifty years later as her 'lifelong role of St Ursula (who, you will remember, went about with 11,000 virgins)'. It was better than teaching or slumming. 'I think', wrote Lady Fry, 'you are in your right place.'

Margery Fry went to Birmingham in that deep melancholy which, for more than half her lifetime, was to cloud her approach to any new work. She believed Birmingham to be almost wholly unlikeable: one of her male cousins told her frankly that 'to housekeep over a hencoop in a provincial suburban villa' was 'just like a Fry with a swelled conscience'. Obsessed as always by the passing of time, she had an irrational dread of leaving Oxford. Only one or two people in Birmingham would remember her as a really young person, for she had just passed her thirtieth birthday and 'said goodbye to anything that has a right to be called youth'. University women were extending the frontiers of youth, marrying and even bearing children in their thirties: but in the popular view thirty was still the end, the age at which a working-class wife tied on the remorseless little floral bonnet which was remain for decades the badge of old womanhood. Ellen Bosanquet, who was already a mother when she visited Somerville that year, remembered a curious flash of anger as Margery glanced at the ringed left hand holding a piece of sewing: 'Mending rags with jewelled fingers!' It was the only encounter of the kind in eighty years of close friendship. The Fry conscience would not yield to that day-dreaming which, Florence Nightingale declared, was absorbing the mental energies of Victorian daughters even when they seemed most attentive to their parents. At thirty it was time to put away any thoughts of marriage and motherhood. The aching lack would remain, would even be confessed when confession seemed helpful to other women, but the lack would be her own: nobody else would have to pay for it.

'The question is no longer, as in the cared-for course of education, "what is best for you?" not even, unfortunately, "how can you best serve the common good?" but "what have you got to offer that the world will buy?" . . . I do not think older people always remember that this moment of decision, of choice, of exclusion—this discovery that one can't have all the toys in the shop, is a critical and difficult one in the lives of young people.'[1] For Margery Fry the choice, through the circumstances of her time and the slow tempo of her family life, was delayed until she was thirty. The tasks which had already come her way had been carried out with single-minded efficiency: but no one ever showed more clearly the difference between the single and the one-track mind. At every turning-point in her life she faced the pain of exclusion. In every situation which she chose for herself her energies spilled over, like those of the 'essential amateurs' she loved to contemplate.

The young women around the dinner-table at 215 Hagley Road were enchanted by the Warden, who, although no older than some of their sisters, seemed to preside with complete confidence in herself and in her students. They had no idea that she was finding Birmingham 'a horrible place', was feeling at times 'like a caged beast'. They liked the look of her. She was neither tall nor elegant, not even fashionable, but there was warmth and brightness in her southern colouring, in the ornaments which she wore with dignity, bits of gold and lace, jewellery set with glowing, semi-precious stones. They were fascinated by her talk, as she led but never monopolized the conversation, the strong and varying music of her voice, the scope of her interest and wit, and at the same time the ease and homeliness, as of a woman talking over the garden fence to her neighbour.

Mr G. H. Kendrick, who had first moved the resolution for the founding of the University, had urged the senselessness of class divisions in state education: he believed the University should include both secondary and elementary teachers in training. At the Hostel degree and certificate students were to live together: it was open also to students of art and cookery. Miss Helen Wodehouse, University Lecturer in Philosophy, later first Principal of Bingley Training College and Mistress of Girton, was one of the first residents, who usually included in addition to members of staff one or two professional women from outside the University.

In a residential institution the students had expected lists of rules, even longer than those found necessary in their day schools. Miss Fry asked them instead to show that consideration for the staff which they would show for their parents. It was an appeal perfect for its time. In 1904 a girl whose parents were able to pay a minimum of twenty-five shillings a week for her keep could only relatively be

[1] *What Life Has Taught Me*, p. 56.

called poor, but many parents were educating their daughters at great sacrifice. As at Somerville, duty and responsibility weighed heavily on some of the students. The Warden believed it more useful to evoke youthful high spirits than to suppress them. As she gained experience and the Hostel grew in numbers she hardly modified this opinion. 'The principle of trusting to their honour', she told Lady Fry, 'may be rather demoralizing to the poorer type of student. But it's so completely justified with the better ones that I incline to thinking that the weaker . . . must just get along as they can. It's worse to spoil good material than not to improve bad.'

Shyness, of a depth now rare, and recognized where it occurs as a problem, then almost universally eclipsed the young people of the lower middle classes when they met people outside their own age or social group. Students who could not travel in daily to Birmingham came mainly either from secluded parts of rural Warwickshire, Oxfordshire, or Staffordshire, or from the overgrown villages and small towns already surrounded by slagheaps and untidy railway sidings. They came generally from homes where thrift, industry, piety (religious or political), and even intellectual curiosity formed the pattern of family life as surely as in the Fry home beside the Bristol cocoa factory two or three generations earlier: but few of the families who sent their daughters to Hagley Road had enjoyed those fruits of leisure which industry was then bestowing on its favoured grandchildren.

So, wearing their 'best little frocks',[2] eating the plentiful and well-cooked food under the eye of maids, impersonal in long starched aprons, some of the students believed it safest to mind their manners and hold their tongues. They left the conversation to their elders and betters. Then suddenly Miss Fry was upon them, demanding an opinion by a question or only by a smile. She made it clear that to keep silent was to dodge a social responsibility. Some of these early students still look back on their first weeks at the Hostel as 'purgatory'. One evening a week they could go, if they chose, to the Warden's sitting-room, where she showed them books and pictures, talked to them about places and people she knew. One student, then another, would begin to share her own small treasure of thought and experience: for it was not so much anything which the Warden had put into her students' minds which seemed to be emerging, but something that had been there all along: 'hidden dreams and desires'

[2] From a letter written in 1962 by a student of 1904.

—unknown often to their parents and even to their most gifted teachers. No one had ever listened to them before with such eager attention: as if their fumbling contributions were needed for her own being.

Fifteen, twenty years later, when the memory of these shadowy little novices was already obliterated by the acquaintance, renewed at Hostel reunions, with the mature and genial women they had become, Margery Fry would hear that one had become a magistrate, another the chairman of a local council, another a college principal.

'One goes plodding on, doing less than a person's work', Margery wrote to her mother in her second term at Hagley Road, 'yet always bothering about utility, and oh! I get so bored with it all. I wish all the young were at the bottom of the sea and that my conscience were amputated.' Her functions had been set down as the superintendence of housekeeping and the maintenance of discipline. The separation of discipline from academic responsibility had seemed to set the régime of the Hostel far below the true collegiate life she had known at Somerville, but she had been advised to accept the conditions offered—'If Miss Fry asks for nothing she will get everything,' she was told.

At first there were gaps in her day which, being unable at any time of her life to bow to Parkinson's Law, she filled in small ways: giving a hand at the Settlement with applications for a fund to relieve unemployment—'likely to do at least as much harm as good. . . . I wish they would give in work and not in charity', gaining honourable mentions in the *Westminster Gazette* competitions with competent verse in the fin-de-siècle manner, learning Italian with Dorothy Scott and the Muirheads, writing an essay on 'Sentimentality in Art' —now chiefly notable for the effect on her later teaching of Roger's criticisms, when he urged her to argue from concrete examples.

She was distressed by the quarrels of servants. Margery Fry and her sisters accepted perforce, but with uneasy stirrings, that utter dependence for material comfort on a lower order, born to servitude, living under the same roof but at a baser level, which her mother and aunts had taken completely for granted. She once warned a colleague that the worst job in running a hostel was 'combining the incompatible in servants' tempers . . . roughly speaking, ill-temper and cleanliness are always united'. Hagley Road was blessed with a genial cook who fed the community on an ample, starchy diet (sausage and mash for Sunday breakfast), but Lilian the head maid was a woman of intimidating refinement. When the students outraged her sense of propriety she turned 'a peculiar shade of mauve'. She had 'mysterious emotional yearnings' which the Warden tried to assuage by the loan of her bicycle. One vacation, when the students had left, Miss Fry kept the servants from moping by getting out the old costumes and scenery and producing *The Rose and the Ring*, performed by the students a year earlier. Miss Fry herself took part, and the show was put on at a Settlement social. 'Lilian's acting was grotesquely indistinguishable from her ordinary manners and altogether it was odd to see how antagonistic to each other extreme respectability and any dramatic talent are.' When all else failed, the Warden suggested that the maids should write and keep by them a letter of application for a new post, a suggestion which immediately produced a mountain of buttered toast for tea. Perhaps Miss Fry brought out the hidden dreams and desires of others in that house besides the students. Lilian left to do 'rescue work' with the Salvation Army, and ten years later Margery Fry visited her in the Dr Barnardo village where she had become a house-mother.

The Warden's torment did not end with the loosening of her students' tongues. She watched anxiously the reactions of robust Midland Protestants to the young Catholic lectrice, Jeanne Lepetit, whose strength she had not yet estimated. The schoolmarmish dogmatizing of certain student-teachers next tried her patience. With Helen Wodehouse, who, as Apollo, improvised her part, she devised a Grecian entertainment called *The Quacks*, about four nymphs turned to ducks for daring to advise the god. Margery Fry played Midas.

From her first day in Birmingham it was impressed upon Margery that Sir Oliver Lodge (the Principal of the University) was the one who counted. She found him 'kind, and in a way, not inaccessible, but he is one of the most formidable people I have ever met. But I feel sure he would be reasonable and easy to meet, whenever one wanted to make him understand about things. . . . He proposed my being upon some Educational Council for the district.' Apart from the academics, the people of Birmingham were as alien to her as the scarred landscape. She had been used to splendid talkers, her own family, Roger's friends from Cambridge—men like Lowes Dickinson and Arthur Clutton-Brock, whom she met too rarely but always with delight—her own old Oxford friend, the Vinerian Professor of Law, cousin of Leslie Stephen, Dr Dicey, who, though he thought it 'better to be flippant than dull', could soliloquize for

MF—F

an hour without flippancy. Mr Beale, the Vice-Chancellor of Birmingham University (a solicitor, retiring by nature, but drawn inevitably into civic life), seemed 'pompous and rich and dull'. Eight years later she wrote to a colleague on his death: 'Rather disquieting, isn't it, to find out how unfavourable first impressions often are when one reflects with how many people one gets no further. . . . A great power, and in some ways even a great man, I think.' More than fifty years later, when Margery Fry was asked in a broadcast interview about the crucial years in the formation of her experience, she said: 'I had great luck in being taken by the hand by a man by the name of Beale.'[3]

It was Mr Beale who decided that Miss Fry, a woman in her thirties with no official academic status, and a comparative newcomer to the city, should be a member of the University Council: it was he who recognized that her talents could be used on the Finance Committee. With Mrs Beale, she became a governor of the King Edward's Schools when the Board of Education made it a condition of grant that women should be represented on the Foundation.

These responsibilities came later. By the end of her first term she had entered the public life of the district as a governor of the Handsworth Pupil-Teacher Centre. A few months later she was co-opted to the Staffordshire County Education Committee, as one of 'two women of Experience in Education'. Now those journeyings began which were to eat up so much of her life, as she travelled through the harsh Midland winter or waited on a scorching platform while the sun shone benignly on Oxford and the gardens of Failand. Sometimes she was asked out to tea after a meeting: to nurse the youngest of the vicar's many children on her knee in a turbulent living-room, or to be regaled more splendidly over a draper's shop. Once she was escorted to the station by 'a strange old man like a tom-cat' who told her his grandmother had accompanied Elizabeth Fry on her visits to Newgate. The three women on the Staffordshire Education Committee divided the territory between them: Margery's share was the industrial southern region. It was a country absolutely unknown to her, and although she had got up the facts for the Somerville Parliament her first-hand knowledge of popular education was limited to the family patronage of the village school at Pill, near Failand. She schooled herself to patience and humility, hardly speaking in committee for a year.

[3] 'Personal Call', 26 March 1956.

On leaving Somerville College she had been elected to its Council. Now, from Oxford to the provincial university and its teacher-training, from the endowed grammar school to the new county schools and the old board-schools renamed, the whole archipelago of English education lay in view, though the bridges between the islands were still too tenuous to exist even in Margery Fry's keen sight. Yet in 1893, the year when Margery Fry left Miss Lawrence's school, young Michael Sadler, brought face to face through University Extension work with the destitution of popular education, had called a conference at Oxford which brought pressure on the Government to provide secondary education. In the year she went to Birmingham, Sir Robert Morant, Permanent Parliamentary Secretary to the Board of Education, issued the Code for Elementary Education which for the first time looked beyond the bare equipment of state-educated children to perform the humblest tasks: inviting in its opening words some comparison between the objectives of state education and those of his own Winchester, 'to form and strengthen the character and to develop the intelligence of the children entrusted to it', suggesting more specifically as a duty of the elementary school 'to discover individual talents to be further developed'. The new county and county borough authorities, replacing the school boards only two years before Margery Fry joined the Staffordshire Committee, had power to develop such talents by secondary and technical education.

When we look at the yellowing photographs of school groups in these early years of the century, in which rows of children, exhibiting signs of undernourishment and many kinds of mental and physical defect, sit gloomily under the gaze of their shabby-genteel teachers, when we hurry past the sombre neo-Gothic brickwork of the schools where children are still being taught, it is not easy to re-create the excitement of the times. We must, in our imagination, repeople the Victorian town halls, the narrow asphalt schoolyards and forbidding staircases, with administrators like Graham Balfour, first Director of Education for Staffordshire, cousin and biographer of Robert Louis Stevenson, whose father, an army doctor, had been described approvingly by Florence Nightingale as a 'dangerous animal and a great innovator':[4] or with humbler officials like the one who wrote to Margery Fry: 'I felt always that none saw my serious limitations more clearly than yourself and none gave me greater credit for trying

[4] From a report of Mr Graham Balfour's retirement in a Staffordshire newspaper.

to do my best': with committee members like Margery Fry herself or like that alderman whom she sent down to Failand to see the methods and achievements of Ruth and Agnes in the schoolroom, commending him to the mercy of her civilized family who had not had her opportunities of appreciating modesty under a disguise of bumptiousness. Above all we need to remember the teachers, the gifted children of the poor, who found in the training college or the pupil-teacher centre their own chance of education. Some, capable of the highest academic distinction, were cruelly miscast as teachers of the three R's to huge classes of widely ranging ability, yet are still remembered by old people who left school at twelve.

Margery Fry turned her attention to needlework, of which she knew herself a competent judge. The schools kept up the tradition of exquisite plain sewing which the sewing-machine was already making obsolete. Margery found it absurd that little girls should wear out their eyes on samples of fine stitchery while their clothes were in rags. She was delighted to find a teacher who set her class to work on remaking old garments. (The combination of utility and beauty, in which teachers after the First War became skilled, had to wait for a more lavish expenditure on school equipment.) Her condemnation of the traditional methods was not in vague terms: she took home the pathetic little scraps of calico and counted the stitches.

There was no school medical or optical service and serious eye defects, due to neglect at birth, were common. In 1906 the Local Education Authorities were empowered, not compelled, to provide medical inspection: they were not even empowered to give treatment. When Birrell's Bill to establish medical inspection was discussed in the House of Commons it was estimated that in a poor area at least half the girls would have nits in their hair and only three per cent of the children could be said to be 'clean'. (It must be remembered that the reluctance of even lower-middle-class parents in some areas to send their children to council schools could until quite recent times be put down not to sheer snobbish perversity but to a real fear of infection.) As usual, the opponents of a school medical service spoke of the pauperization of the lower classes. Margery Fry found she had to 'badger' to get the permitted inspectors, and 'the aristocracy bands together to hamper and hinder one's own pet views' (there were two peers and a baronet in the Education Committee). But, she wrote to Dorothy Scott in April 1908, 'The Walls of Jericho give me great and constant comfort; today we've amicably appointed the first of a brace of school nurses for Staffs, over whose existence we have torn out each other's (official—most of us haven't any other) —hair by handfuls.'

Soon she was scolding over school drains: 'after all I have a nose in my head and I know when it's offended. . . . You can't think what a powerful and unpleasant female I was. I dealt with Mr. Balfour and the architect like as if they were bad boys and firmly laid down (out of my head) just what and where the drainage should be.' Or she was trying to abolish caning (of which Roger had appalling memories) and being told that caning would only be replaced by undesirable and surreptitious methods of punishment, or fighting (unsuccessfully, it seems) for the reinstatement of a married teacher whom the Board had black-listed on discovery that she had been pregnant when she left the service to marry. In the words of a doggerel 'ABC' handed round the Education Office she had become

> F for Miss Fry whom none can aroint,
> Who always is talking, and ever with point.

'I wonder', she reflected, 'if anybody else in the world—barring the cheap-jacks—talks as much in the week as I do.'

In the holidays she could still listen to Professor Dicey ('miles and away the best talker I have ever met'), endlessly soliloquizing. A few days later she was hearing a different accent (and 'Brum', not Cockney, would be for the rest of her life the accent of her proletarian stories). Yet, in the sitting-room over the draper's shop in Staffordshire, she was startled to hear allusions to Aristotle and Pepys, even a quotation from Renan. A few years earlier she had listened to the choirs of Christ Church and New College: but she had '*never* heard singing anything like so beautiful' as that of a choir of working men and women from Barrow-in-Furness, led by 'a little elementary schoolmistress . . . with just a gesture of her finger and thumb'.

'Vulgarity'—a word then close in meaning to its source—was a word she still used pretty often. Today, when snobbery is something of a joke except when justified by the greed for power and prestige, it is difficult to imagine the acute pain caused at each level of Edwardian society by the manners of the stratum immediately below. Even Margery Fry was surprised by the trend of her own sympathies. 'I think', she told Dorothy, 'Brummagem is making a first-rate democrat of me'; and later, after some 'squalid committee worry':

'I think the Black Country is as black in mind as it is in mud—and yet I get more of a red radical every day.'

The transformation was speeded when Rose Sidgwick, coming to Birmingham as University Lecturer in History, joined her in 1905 at Hagley Road. Margery fought for justice. Her ease in communication made her appear more socially adaptable than Rose, whom Margery described as 'gentle, dignified, with a slight but ineradicable touch of the academic', but it was Rose at this time who had a more spontaneous liking for 'common folk'. Seeing in her friend a Wordsworthian dependence on natural beauty, Margery feared for her happiness in Birmingham: but Rose found in Margery herself 'a kind of spiritual seaside'. There is no doubt that on Rose's side the friendship was strongly emotional: but her upbringing as a sensitive member of a brilliant, liberal, and even iconoclastic family had given her toughness. Soon after she came to Birmingham she wrote down rules of life for herself: 'Thou shalt not cling, thou shalt not clutch' was the first clause of her Decalogue.

The students accepted Miss Sidgwick immediately. She made the life of the Hostel even richer than before. She brought home to Hagley Road friends like Bishop Gore, with whom she shared enthusiasm for the new Workers' Educational Association (said by Sir Oliver Lodge to have been first so named, by himself, in Birmingham). Margery now found much in common with the ecclesiastic who, in Oxford, had dismayed her by his insistence upon the necessity of a creed. As the first bishop in a solidly nonconformist city he was showing the necessity, and the possibility, of co-operation between the sects for the achievement of any kind of reform. It was Rose also who opened the Warden's mind, somewhat sternly trained by her father and brother, to the lighter pleasures of literature, even persuading her to write, perhaps misguidedly, a paper on Meredith, which Margery believed awoke her audience 'at intervals from an uneasy sleep to an acute sense of boredom'. It was in Rose's company that Margery began to look at the district, not only as a field for endeavour, but for its own sake, as a sensuous experience. They went down a coal-mine, they visited a blast-furnace under the guidance of a student's brother, who tended a turbine. 'You know I grow more optimistic as I grow older,' she wrote to Lady Fry when recovering from the chill which followed this visit. 'The only beauty I long for is the beauty that's hidden in things as they are, not some rainbow illusion which is just the effect of distance. And even in a grubby place like this there is a lot of that to be had for the looking, though I wish a little more material beauty would clothe the naked fact sometimes.'

Until the coming of Rose Sidgwick, Margery's letters home had cast a steady light on the events of her life. Now Rose shared her interests, received the first-fruits of her comments. On the other hand, as Margery's visits to Failand became shorter and less frequent the conversations begun in Lady Fry's boudoir were sometimes continued in writing. When some of the older Frys and Hodgkins of her generation began to slip away, Mariabella Fry spoke often of death to Margery. At first, Margery felt, she had not responded as she ought.

I was a prig. . . . You know better than anyone how all the cowardlinesses and mistrusts cling round me. Perhaps the strongest thing one has to cling to after all is the thought that the real seers and saints have always, however much they differed, seen through fear, and I suppose to some extent, as we should take Lord Kelvin's sense of what was probable in physics as worth more than our own, so their vision of life stands for more than our blurred one.

When the May evenings brought melancholy to Mariabella Fry instead of the joy she had hoped for, Margery wrote:

If the whole is greater than the part the meaning of it all must be not only better than, but actually include, that wonderful 'significance' which I think is what gives a sting of pain to all beauty. . . . You know we are much alike in the insistent sense of the end to come to *this* goodly life, anyhow. And I don't think I can be more conscious of mortality if I live to be 100 than I am now. It always seems as if beauty and happiness can't be looked at full face—there's never time, or if there is one can't use it for some odd reason so that it's only out of the corner of one's eye that they are to be 'glimpsed' (as Agnes calls it).

As a Quaker Margery passed the scrutiny of Birmingham, which knew all about Quakers. She went sometimes to Meeting and would perhaps have gone often if she could have slipped in and out quietly, as a seeker, instead of being greeted with the fervour some thought due to a successful woman and a Fry. When Yearly Meetings came to Birmingham she saw with pride and wonder the place that Joan had begun to occupy in the Society.

It really is nice to see how *tremendously* Joan is valued by all these people.

They evidently rely so much on her judgment and wisdom about things and she is so completely in her element amongst them that I long for a perennial Yearly Meeting for her to live in. It is as if a sea-anemone had but one tide a year. And, after all, one hasn't much say in choosing *what* shall be tide and what ebb to one's soul. One can live contentedly in a pulp while the waters are away but no amount of will power will float one's tentacles like the real thing. But I think Y.M. would be *very* low water to me, which is odd, since Joan and I are much alike in many ways.

One of the leading Quaker families gave her 'a sense of negative exhilaration, like extra-non-alcoholic drinks. They are good souls, but they make you so anxious not to be a good soul yourself that the anxiety is almost a pain.'

The fact was that, in spite of her own indestructible roots in the Society, Margery Fry could not bear Quakerism. The Fry children had not been sent to Quaker schools, and outside the schools nineteenth-century Friends made no concession to childhood except for the provision, here and there, of a tall hassock for small dangling feet. The lively little creature had been expected to sit for two hours with nothing more interesting to look at than the familiar faces of the Elders. ('I thought how well you must have known the pattern of the panelling,' she wrote to her mother after speaking in the old Meeting House at Tottenham, which Mariabella Hodgkin had attended as a child.) Moreover, her London childhood had coincided with the Evangelical influence on the Society. The Quaker silence was broken by long preachings and prayings of a fervour less spontaneous than the 'stirrings' of the seventeenth century.

Yet other birthright Friends (including some of her own sisters) came through boredom and embarrassment to a mature membership of the Society. Margery's longing for a spiritual certainty, often expressed, remained unsatisfied and had in the end to be abandoned. In her allusions to Friends there is an irrational tone, as in a child scolding its mother: the sense of justice permeating her other relationships here fails her. Even the anecdotes of childhood—as of the uncle who, instead of decently reprimanding her for a piece of pertness, fell on his knees and prayed for her—were recounted in old age with a strange fierceness. Perhaps Roger and Isabel, those emphatic and greatly loved adolescents, seven and five years her senior, had brought Margery's childish judgements to a critical precocity. Whatever the cause, her comments on the Friends hint at some deep hurt concealed even from herself.

'Burning with suppressed wickedness' after an exposure to 'old Mr. Cadbury's pieties', she conceded, in a letter to Lady Fry, 'one can forgive them much for their practical goodness'. She had indeed been brought up among Quaker beneficence, though not on the scale of Bournville. The prompt formation of committees, the collection of funds which followed every disaster and even sought out unpopular causes, merely bored her: she gave her contribution, then brushed aside these 'tidy drawing-room things'. In the cut-and-thrust of statutory committees she began to find in Staffordshire and Birmingham a more satisfactory field of operations than in the most enlightened paternalism. Interpreting experience through Rose's historical and political judgement, she became convinced that a decent life was better assured through rights of citizenship than by chance proximity to well-concerned riches. Yet later, when in her travels up and down the world she made the acquaintance of unmitigated greed, ruthless ostentation, she discovered a tenderness towards what she called Franciscan Quakerism.

In Birmingham her commitments increased. A house at the bottom of the garden had soon been added to 215 Hagley Road. A third house was taken in 1905. She was teaching mathematics to a matriculation class, meeting male students for the first time: fearing before she met them that they would riot, and when she faced their silent ranks that they were bored: reassured at last by the gift of a pair of home-made blackboard compasses—'I sometimes wonder whether those stages of mistrust are really necessary.' A rash invitation to Sir Oliver Lodge and Professor Muirhead to see the students in *The Rose and the Ring* led to her being co-producer for several years of the University play. As she watched her unpromising young men become graceful and responsive actors she concluded that geese were perhaps 'only swans that had not found an owner'. In the Hostel also dramatics continued to flourish: the Warden was the chief of 'rather too many cooks' who painted a scene of a Grecian bay for a production of *Andromache*. This production occasioned as earnest a correspondence with the translator, Gilbert Murray, as with Robert Bridges over *Demeter*. Some still remember Miss Fry as the Duchess in *Alice*, 'thumping her baby with vigour': to some purpose, for it was in aid of the building fund of that 'phoenix among hostels' for which Mr Beale had sanctioned plans 'before there was a ha'penny to build with'.

VIII
University House, Birmingham
1908-1914

'I WONDER what it will all turn into as I sit here at the little beginning of it,' Margery Fry had said at the end of her first week in
Birmingham.

The new University House, opened at Edgbaston in 1908, showed
that she had convinced herself and the University of the rightness
of the residential system. She compared her house to a garden-
frame, 'extraordinary valuable for the more delicate, the sensitive
and the rarer plants. . . . What one wants to see done is to give
people the best of possible conditions to grow up on their own lines
and help each other—a place where they know they are invited to be
themselves and are not going to be criticized all the time. . . .
Shelter from their own families is often what they need most of all.'[1]

When Miss Maitland died in 1906 some people—Mrs T. H.
Green among them—wanted Margery Fry as Principal of Somerville. An older woman was chosen. Somerville College was to have
twenty years of Miss Emily Penrose's statesmanship. Margery Fry
was to have the chance of creating her hostel in Birmingham.

University Hall, lately reconstructed as a hall for men and
women, looks fresher than a building which has passed its half-
century. It was designed to fit what Margery Fry believed to be the
needs of fifty women in 1908. Though she hated pretentious architecture, she believed that women must be taught not to 'pinch'
(a word which in the Fry vocabulary meant the practice of frugality,
not theft). She wanted large windows, well-proportioned rooms,
kitchens where servants could work happily, good bathrooms. The
building was to be at the gates of the new University, where the
huge clock-tower, a reminiscence of the watch-tower at Siena which
Joseph Chamberlain had admired, rose as his memorial. His son

[1] University House Association bulletin, 1929.

Neville, secretary of the canvassing committee for the new hostel, was left in no doubt that all that Miss Fry wanted was a 'decent plain building'.

She learned all she could from Liverpool and Manchester, she went with a deputation to the Board of Education to ask for a building grant. 'You would have laughed if you could have beheld Sir Oliver, Professor Hughes and me like country cousins lingering longingly outside the Horseguards to watch the soldiers drill, or Professor Hughes, Neville Chamberlain and me solemnly meandering round the National Portrait Gallery, Mr Chamberlain rather unhappy at my insisting on treating it as an expedition to choose a place for his portrait as premier.'

'I love bricks and mortar and plans and tracing paper and all the rest of the fuss of building.' She hung over plans with Rose Sidgwick and Helen Wodehouse and every student shared the excitement. The Cadburys offered to pay for the garden: some old trees were preserved and Margery Fry watched the Cadbury gardeners laying out the rest with shrubs and variegated holly 'like a cemetery or public park'—neither of which the gardens in the least resemble today. At last the walls of warm sandstone, with the row of great windows facing the garden, began to rise. She kept a steady watch on Mr Buckland, the architect. 'I say how very good one feature seems to be, what a pity it can't be repeated in place of some atrocity.' The plain window-headings she also asked for go up to the first floor, but the dormer windows have the curved architraves she disliked, curiously repeated in the tiled eyebrows of the fireplaces in the study bedrooms.

I want you dreadfully to see this place [she wrote to Roger], though there are things—the fireplaces for example—that will make you howl with misery. Those wishing to build should not have to work through committees and obstinate architects and above all those intending to furnish should not have to do it on the dirt cheap. All nice colours cost, and all nice textiles cost and nice shapes aren't to be had simply. But when all is said and done it's a much better place than most of its kind, and is good to live in.

On the last Sunday evening at Hagley Road the whole company carried a picnic supper to the new hostel. They drank a toast to the new home from chipped cups. Then with shouts of triumph they smashed these symbols of penury against the new walls. The

removal took place early in the autumn of 1908 in time for Hal-
lowe'en and fireworks, 'which tried to the utmost my determination
to let the students run all reasonable risks'. In 1912 Jacqueline Merle,
arriving in Birmingham from Provence as a lectrice, came in from
a grey September evening to find lights and music in the hostel
common-room, men and women students dancing. Among them she
caught her first glimpse, never to be obliterated, of the Warden: a
youngish woman who might herself have come from the South of
France, with one white lock in her dark hair. As Miss Fry came
nearer, listening to the boy she danced with, the French girl saw
that her eyes shone with interest and enjoyment.

The life of University House up to the 1914–18 war must be
viewed not through our own conventions but through those of 1908,
when Miss Fry was considered advanced in allowing students to
invite their men friends to dances. Even she dared not allow them
to go to the theatre together. As well try to identify ourselves with
a medieval peasant, or even with Wordsworth on 'the first mild day
of March', as with those girls who carried the breakfast-tables out
on to the garden terrace early in the splendid summer of 1911: at
home, some had never seen the living-room window unfastened.
University House bred enough wardens, principals, and tutors to
spread its ideas of freedom and happiness, even across the Atlantic;
in a decade or so they were no longer unusual.

University House is best judged by those magnanimous and
creative women, now ageing, who believe it was there that their
powers were discovered and set free. They remember the smell of
grease-paint or hyacinths, Miss Fry and Miss Sidgwick cutting
flowers for the tables, the great earthenware pots of herbaceous
flowers which the students taught one another to arrange for the
corridors. They recall the visitors who came and went without pomp,
as in a friendly home: Marie Curie lunching with the Warden during
the Birmingham meetings of the British Association, Sir Oliver
Lodge coming over on a Sunday afternoon, to read aloud, slap-bang
through *Macbeth*. They remember the personality of the Warden,
'round, round as the world' in the memory of one of her ablest
students, her voice reading prayers in the morning, perhaps those
of Robert Louis Stevenson, to a voluntary and fluctuating group;
her fine rage when someone infringed the courtesies of the house;
how she threw everyone into confusion by appearing as a Spanish
parent, veiled in black lace, and demanding to see the Warden;

turning back, while a distinguished scholar waited in her room, to finish her set of tennis, convinced when the maid summoned her to meet 'Dr Fraud' that someone had arranged a retaliatory leg-pull.

In 1917, Marion Richardson, a young teacher from Dudley who lived at University House while holding a scholarship at the Birmingham School of Art, spread out before Roger Fry at the Omega Gallery the children's drawings which had that day failed to get her a post in London. He recognized at once a teacher who could (and later did) transform the art lessons in schools. 'She's very remarkable,' he wrote to Margery, 'she really has found out how to *educate* and not to teach, which I thought was impossible. She's a very nice creature and we always talk a lot about you. In fact I recognized in her a piece of your bread on the waters come back bearing its sheaves with it or something of that kind and realized a bit what you'd been up to all these years at Birmingham.'

Miss Fry was human: she felt the attraction of an interesting face or a touch of what was then called 'breeding'; but she was just, unsentimental. Everyone was safe with her. And perhaps the most remarkable thing was that people living at University House were not aware of an overruling personality. The rest of the staff were not shadows. Nor was the hostel more than 'a great part of her life'. She forgot it completely when she was in France with Mildred Pope, in Florence with Dorothy Scott, where Geoffrey Scott took them to visit the Berensons; or at The Hague in 1907, when her father, in his eightieth year, attended the Second Peace Conference as First Plenipotentiary Delegate for Great Britain. One or two at a time, the sisters stayed with their parents on the second floor of the Hôtel des Indes, 'the Americans', Sir Edward Fry explains, 'having anticipated our Government and secured the first floor'. Margery's turn came in the summer vacation. A letter to Roger shows this sometime 'housekeeper of a provincial hencoop' in a setting of international diplomacy.

. . . If what I write is rather disjointed stuff you must understand that we're never uninterrupted here, and this is being composed in the intervals of Father's feelings about an Admiralty letter on a policy which he considers to be 'insular and insulting'. . . . A constant stream of discussion goes on here, very distracting but immensely interesting. I know you'll be interested in knowing how Father does. Honestly, I'm amazed to see how well (as far as I can judge) he does the extraordinarily complicated and difficult work there is to do. Of course the job itself is almost absurdly hopeless, if you had absolute wisdom and omniscience it wouldn't be easy. With the infinitesimal freedom of a 'plenipotentiary' moving in a maze of international jealousies it's rather a marvel if you can make yourself felt at all than wonderful that you don't set the world in order. As a matter of fact, a lot of what Father has done will never be known for his, perhaps his best work, but I suppose it's rather petty to wish to claim credit. . . . The regular Peace people, rather naturally, are so sore that nothing revolutionary gets done, that they take a good lot of trouble to minimize the things that probably will result. But this general talky-talk you can get from anywhere. What I want to tell you—for I know it'll please you—is that Father has personally shown that extraordinary power which he still has of adapting himself to new things. . . . We're a very odd party here and perhaps the quaintest thing of all is to see Mother, a very piquant mixture of her usual self with some quite new personality out of that store of unused selves which she has even more of than most people. It was really worth while eating through a long dinner (even if it bored you and they amuse me)—to see her acting hostess for the old Turk, a great beau of hers, just as it is somewhat startling to see . . . Father gallantly lighting the cigarette of an Ambassadress.

The set of students who came, through the Warden's conversation, so near to the councils of Europe went their way and a new generation heard of her travels in Crete. Some of these women later made their own way to the Greek islands, long before they became generally known to tourists. Margery had shown an almost old-maidish timidity before this journey with her cousins, Ellen Bosanquet and Edward Hodgkin, and their spouses. Professor Bosanquet wanted to press on to the British School excavations at the east end of Crete. Mrs Hodgkin wanted to sketch, and their paces proved incompatible. In the general tension the details of life, then unmodified for tourists, provided constant irritation. 'Life is complicated by the fact that the water jugs of the country are amphorae and need careful propping before they will stand, also a good deal of flea-hunting is a necessary of life.' After a night quartered on Greek soldiers when, in Mrs Bosanquet's words, 'for all sanitary arrangements we had to be escorted across an open courtyard by a soldier carrying a torch', and in Margery's, 'The amount of fierce commands which it took to get three cups of tea would easily have carried us through a battle', the women decided to make their own way back to Candia on mules while the men pressed on. It was on the journey back, with a polite but feckless guide, that Margery found she could jolly along Greek peasants as well as Staffordshire councillors and that her cousin saw the 'diplomatic humorist' of Somerville revealed as the 'humorous diplomat'. They rode, Margery said, 'like the Canterbury pilgrims', and on Easter Sunday, in a church twelve foot square, she took for the only time in her life an outward element of the sacrament.

The whole thing was, I suppose, very superstitious, but the rudeness and remoteness of it all, and the seriousness of the people, and the feeling that to be Xtians at all had, till lately, meant such danger and hardship to them made it all incredibly moving, and when at the close of the service the old archimandrite motioned us to come up just to take the Communion it would have needed a very superstitious Quakerism to have refused from his hands the little bunch of rosemary and geranium and the piece of bread (just the same rough country bread which he had brought us—also in his hands!—for our supper the night before).

Each year that passed seemed to her acquaintances a cornucopia of interests and friendships and work well accomplished; so also it seemed to her, when she forgot the passing of the years. Just after her thirty-fifth birthday she went down to Failand for her parents' golden wedding. 'The parents' *own* circumstances and surroundings in a way are so singularly fortunate,' she told Dorothy Scott, 'but as a family we seem rather a poor result of so many hopes, with Portsmouth and Roger both so checked in all that counts for happiness and with the rest of us so unlike what anyone could have foretold.' Six of the nine children of Edward and Mariabella Fry were with them on this fiftieth anniversary, two others not far away: but there were, and would be, only two grandchildren. 'It is difficult, that life of the old and middle-aged together, and the fact of their all being very good about it doesn't really make easier a thing which doesn't depend on affection at all, but is simply a case of paces like bicycling by a walker.'

These were terrible and wonderful years for Roger: years in which he had to give up hopes of his wife's recovery and in which he became, in Sir William Rothenstein's words, 'the only English critic with a European reputation'. In 1910 he brought the paintings of the Post-Impressionists to London. The sisters converged on the Grafton Gallery. From Roger's own exhibition in January 1912 Margery bought one painting and borrowed another: Edgbaston was not far behind London in feeling the impact of the Post-Impressionist explosion.

'I suppose everyone's life looks rather prosaic to themselves and so you could never imagine how much of something that is less dull and ugly and utilitarian than my own working-young-woman existence you stand for,' Margery wrote to Roger. Committees were absorbing more and more of her days. Some gave unmixed delight, like the Somerville College Council where the great hall, opened in 1913, was planned as a memorial to Miss Maitland: a project financed at Margery Fry's suggestion partly by an issue of debenture shares. In Staffordshire also she had 'the fuss of building' to delight her. Once, in committee, seeing her absorbed in architectural plans, Mr Balfour paused, continuing with terrible emphasis, 'I particularly want Miss Fry to attend to this.' She did not want her family to have exaggerated ideas of her importance—'Committee-ism is a very elaborate system to check and supplement officialdom. It's evidently so beautifully British that one could never bear to give it up, but often it means nothing more than railway journeys and a silent presence or perhaps two remarks without effect.'

Rose Sidgwick had joined her on the Staffordshire Education Committee: Margery Fry had also introduced her mother's friend, the Dowager Lady Farrer of Idlerocks, Stone, a Wedgwood by birth. She was a woman of wit, good sense, and unpretentious culture: yet Margery half regretted the presence of a lady of an older generation when she herself had things that were 'not pretty' to say—'I never know whether it's a blessing or a curse to have one's thoughts come out helter-skelter like mine . . . but I do know that it leads to a lot of wondering if you've shocked people afterwards. Not that I care about most of 'em.'

In 1909 she became one of the first two women governors of King Edward's Foundation. Though she believed that women were not really wanted but had been forced on the Foundation by the Board of Education, they came in useful when Miss Creak, the splendid old tyrant who had built up the King Edward's Girls' School from its small beginnings in New Street, had to give place to Miss Major. 'Mrs. Beale and I escorted her [Miss Major] up and left her, if a precipitate flight can be described so mildly.' In less than three years Margery Fry was Bailiff (or chairman) of the Foundation.

She talked daily with teachers. Once she went for a picnic by a canal 'in fairly real country' with three of her old students, elementary teachers, who had joined forces in a little house, 'a 1000 times better than lodgings. . . . I sometimes think that little set is the best thing the hostel has produced.'

A warm and unremitting sense of concern was a precious gift, but not altogether a rare one among the leisured women of Margery Fry's generation. A great many could speak up for their causes, though not many so attractively. It was her legalistic mind, joined to her humane and rhetorical gifts, which was now in the Midlands recognized and developed. She was one of a committee of four who in 1912 drafted the by-laws for the regulation of children's employment in Staffordshire. In the same year she joined the County Insurance Committee to administer the National Insurance Act, 'just till the machinery is started'. A year later she was appointed to the County Sub-committee on Mental Deficiency. She turned again to her father, who at eighty-six was still there, in the library at Failand, to guide her through the clauses of the Mental Deficiency and National Insurance Acts. In 1908 she had been appointed a governor of the Girls' Industrial School (later the Remand Home) at Lichfield. Soon she was being teased on the committees about her 'suffragette air': her father and friends were advising her to modify her vehemence. But penal reform was in the air: Dorothy Scott was on the committee of the new Penal Reform League and perhaps it was she who set her friend to read the books of Holmes, 'the police court missionary—rather interesting, though grim', as Margery described them in a tentative recommendation to her family. Holmes was then secretary of the Howard Association, another group dedicated to penal reform.

In Birmingham, Dorothy and Margery had been at the fountainhead of what they called the 'feeble-minded agitation'. Mrs Pinsent's husband had been one of the two men on the founding committee of the Hagley Road Hostel—perhaps because his wife was wholly absorbed by her concern. She was a member of the Birmingham Sub-committee for Special Schools and Classes. Finding these very sparsely attended, she went round the city elementary schools and found over a hundred children whom the medical superintendent of a local asylum said he would certify as mentally deficient without hesitation. Such children, Mrs Pinsent urged, were at the mercy of neglect and cruelty and grew up to be punished as criminals and alcoholics and to become the parents of illegitimate and often feeble-minded children. In 1901 Mrs Pinsent published in the *Lancet* a 'thorough and complete scheme' for State intervention in the protection of the feeble-minded, and in 1904 she became a member of the Royal Commission on the Care of the Feeble-minded. The nature of mental deficiency was little known: in the special schools it was often treated as curable, teachers spending most of their time trying to teach reading and writing. The case-histories Mrs Pinsent produced seemed to prove conclusively the need for protection. Yet the opposition was fierce, as Margery Fry well knew in Staffordshire: in January 1913 Lady Farrer handed her a cheque to pay for a campaign organizer (saying, with the irony Margery loved, that she knew no better way of spending Wedgwood money'). In March, Lady Farrer's relative and near neighbour, Josiah Wedgwood, was boasting that he had lived for two days on bars of chocolate to be in the House to champion the cause of individual liberty against the Mental Deficiency Bill. By the end of 1912 the Home Office had received 800 resolutions from public bodies, on one side or other of the question. Margery Fry had done her share of the chores which led to this awakening of public interest, though she was never certain about the spelling of 'deficiency'. 'On a humble scale', she would remind her admirers in later years, 'what reform doesn't at the bottom rest on hours of envelope addressing?' When the Act became law she was needed to serve at a higher level. So also with the National Insurance Act. Originally the County Committees had expected to deal with questions of hygiene and public health. In the event they had to labour over tedious and tangled administrative details. 'I don't think I shall be very good at it,' said Margery Fry; but she set to work.

Still there was time, between train journeys to Stafford or Oxford or Bristol, between the perusal of blue books and statistics, the problems of students and the requisitioning of fresh paint for the House, to hear the larks 'singing absurdly, and as they get up from the lawn I have seen the white crescents of their wings as never before'. One day in 1912 a flying-machine came over the garden: it was 'hardly like seeing a new thing, it is rather a form of movement one seems always to have known and expected'.

'You are so pretty still, there is so much of the eternal child in you,' sighed Lady Fry when Margery reached thirty-six. 'A thing that has been missed is somehow easier put right away from one's thoughts . . .,' Margery affirmed. 'Probably I'm extra well suited to a single life because I am *rather* of the jolly miller's type.' At thirty-eight she wrote:

I often think . . . that the knowledge of a sympathetic ear makes me not tell you the happiest side of life. . . . There are so few, if any, people I would really change with if I got the chance. For one thing, I think my work really suits me very well, for another, I do enjoy the feeling of freedom to shape my own destinies which after all is a big advantage. And I think with me life gets pleasanter as I get older, one gets more friends and more outlets, and perhaps more feeling of being wanted, tho', thanks to home, I've never had much experience of the opposite.

When she and Dorothy reached forty, Margery wrote, 'Ten more years shot off. . . . And nothing for it but grin and swear it doesn't matter.' But she had hung in her room, with the Roger Frys and the portrait of Thomas More given her by Emily Hobhouse in 1904, a reproduction of Blake's 'River of Life', her mother's birthday present: 'It is a great joy. It has more conviction of immortality than anything else I know.'

The 'ponies', as she called her pair of young deputies, Marjorie Rackstraw and Elizabeth Drew, made her begin to feel old. She no longer played tip-and-run with the students after dinner, as at Hagley Road. But the smell of grease-paint was still in the air: during six years at Edgbaston she had produced *The Knight of the Burning Pestle* for the University, *The Frogs*, *The Tempest*, *The Winter's Tale*, *The Playboy of the Western World* at University House. So, it seemed, she might go on for ever: and the students, accustomed as they were to a certain suddenness in their Warden, were taken aback when in June 1914 she told them she would be leaving at Christmas.

IX

Relief Work in the Marne: 1915-1918

MARGERY FRY had lived, with brief intermissions, an institutional life with other women for twenty-three years. She had resisted the accumulation of rules, she had kept in view the dignity of individuals, but nothing could change the annual disappearance of the people she knew, the compulsion to memorize new names and faces. Though she never admitted fatigue, she sometimes confessed she was bored. The bright welcome, the attentive ear were there for all comers, but she dreaded the seeping of integrity from her personal relationships. She did not at any time of her life ask for much solitude, but it was frightening to be never alone, even in a tram or a branch-line train.

In the autumn of 1913 she became, through the will of her bachelor uncle, Joseph Storrs Fry, financially independent for the rest of her life. She had known him from infancy as a very kind, very boring elderly gentleman. The charms of his gold repeater watch were soon exhausted and his pockets seemed to contain nothing more extraordinary than religious tracts. His nieces used to quote his typical reply to an invitation, 'I do not at present see any objection'. He was interested only in the business and the religion into which he had been born. He had collected none of the paraphernalia of the arts and sciences, not even a house or garden of his own choosing. He is said to have died in the room where he was born, in the old house in front of the original cocoa factory.

'For the people who are un-intimate by nature,' said Margery, hearing of his death, 'it is very hard to know what life looks like.' Yet Uncle Joseph had a memorable funeral: the factory choir sang at the graveside, and at the same time as Friends were holding a 'meeting for worship on the occasion of the death of our Friend' a memorial service took place in Bristol Cathedral. Though he had taken no part in local government he was called 'the foremost citizen of Bristol'.

'I think he must have had a power of touching the imagination of humble people which was rather difficult for us to understand, who

saw perhaps more of his kindliness and stainlessness than his power.'
The public image of Joseph Storrs Fry still eluded his niece, but she
took a cool look at her own: now a woman of means, whom people
were also calling a foremost citizen.

We all do such tidy drawing-room sort of things. . . . The things the
students tell me of their work in slum schools are hardly credible they
are so shameful and sad. And it seems absurd that these young creatures
should be handling them while I am like the ideal woman that a funny old
man once described to Helen Wodehouse, 'I shall like to see every female
in a good dress, fairly stout, with a comfortable mind and her feet on a
good carpet'. If this money of Uncle Joseph's really does in the end come
to us I feel it'll be necessary to stake strong precautions against mental
and moral fatness.

Though Uncle Joseph's interests had seemed strangely limited to
his niece, his will was a masterpiece. Night after night he must have
sat in his lonely room, parcelling out his huge wealth as if for a
Christmas treat. First came the gifts to his workers and the great
benefactions to Quaker and other causes. Then came the legacies,
as one after another this apparently lonely old man remembered
those who had shown kindness or need. In the autumn of 1913 his
largess fell like manna over a wider area than anyone had guessed at.
Perhaps, reckoned by H.H.H. (Hours of Human Happiness), which
Margery set up later as a standard measure of individual achievement, Uncle Joseph had not done so badly. Yet he had made one
miscalculation: he was nearly twice as rich as he had believed himself to be. When the residue of his estate was divided Margery Fry
found herself with a larger income than a university professor: just
ten times as large, by her friend Dr Fisher's reckoning in 1917, as
the pay of 42,200 certificated elementary school teachers, men and
women. She sent off donations where formerly she had squeezed out
subscriptions. She relaid the lawn at University House. 'I feel that
Uncle Joseph's money *is* after all (as far as I am concerned) being
spent on the turf but not quite in the way he feared—it is the kind of
interpretation to please a Greek oracle out of Herodotus, isn't it?'
Early in the summer of 1914 she sent in her resignation from
University House. She began again to dream of building, this time
for herself. 'It should mean London, not Birmingham,' Roger urged.
'I don't think you ought to be afraid of not having a job. It's time you
cultivated the power of living without doing. I see the fearful danger

of an active life.' ('I always feel that one has somehow gone very far from the ideal in letting oneself get rushed or hurried,' Margery herself had said a few years before.) If Margery found it necessary to have a job, her brother reminded her, she could manage the finances of the Omega Workshops, opened in Fitzroy Square in the year of Uncle Joseph's death, when Roger Fry decided that the immediate future of the arts was in the hands of people, like himself, 'with a few hundreds a year'.

Such a choice had become impossible. The mood of Florence in 1903 would torment but never direct her. Though to put her committal into words would be to make her a prig, one of 'the virtuous', categories she dreaded, no course of action was possible except to go on seeking justice for working-class children, for mental defectives, even for 'bad girls'. Of the Mental Deficiency Act (still misspelt) she says, 'Just that one thing seems clear, that this must be got going. Outside that life seems rather foggy. . . . I sometimes feel as if I'd muddled things badly to find myself with so indefinite an outlook at 40.' But she enjoyed pulling strings, winning people over, 'highly confidential wow-wow-wowing with everyone'. One small triumph carried her on to the next. Like George Fox, the first Quaker, she aspired to 'walk cheerfully over the world'. The sadness of mortality, of beauty only 'glimpsed', of a natural sympathy with pain, formed the setting of a gaiety shining from many facets.

The multiplicity of tasks which made her in Birmingham 'a rather elderly man' went on until the last days of the summer term, 1914. Officials concerned with the Mental Deficiency Act came to dinner, the hostel butcher was persuaded to put down in writing, to support the Warden's letter to *The Times*, his views on cruelty to calves. Then Margery Fry went off to enjoy, as 'a youngish woman', the long carefree summer which she and her friends had known from infancy as part of the natural order. She was with Roger in Capel Curig—a district she never cared to visit again—on 4 August 1914. Rose wrote from Hawkeshead the next day: 'It is like one great funeral: people meet their friends without a smile; and there is about the same "sure and certain hope" of a resurrection.' By September, University House was required as a military hospital. Margery Fry, with Rose Sidgwick and Marjorie Rackstraw, returned early for the removal to temporary quarters in an Edgbaston villa, 'such a grim hole, really, and all stinks of gas: entre nous', Margery told Agnes in a footnote to her home letter. They packed without ruthlessness: daily life was interrupted, but its values unchanged. The returning students found all their little possessions safe—the small vases, the pictorial biscuit-tins. In some ways, Margery found, life was pleasanter than before: everyone was on her best behaviour. Even committee members showed a new magnanimity.

In October, Margery and Rose found a 'little house' to rent for £60 a year: 'five bedrooms, two sitting-rooms and a decent servants' hall'. Furnishings were bought from Roger to equip the house, as Margery warned her mother, 'in a style at once too bare and too flagrant for your taste'. The Omega prints, the striped carpet in orange, grey, and green, the tall painted chair first made their appearance. 'I rather think of letting it for Belgians till Christmas.' A family of the locust variety immediately appeared, little square Rubens children with a pregnant mother, a nursemaid or two, and an unexpected number of adult relations. So, from the first days of her housekeeping, history was reflected in Margery Fry's hospitality.

Early in 1915 Margery met Dorothy Scott in London to discuss a scheme for housing refugees in disused army huts. The war was expected to end in a few weeks. She found her sister Isabel sewing great military waistcoats, 'very belligerent', her sister Joan befriending ostracized German families, her sister Ruth in a tiny office near the Angel, 'very busy and happy—one word down the telephone, two to me and so da capo'.

Aunt Bessie Waterhouse had once given little Ruth, the ninth of the Frys, a large manuscript book inscribed 'Ruth's Gleanings'. The title—which Ruth Fry later used for a published anthology—was prophetic of the subsidiary part she seemed destined to play. To follow nearly five years after the delightful Margery was not an easy role. In the nursery and schoolroom, when they were dressed alike and shared a governess, life was often amusing and exciting, but perhaps always too highly geared for the younger child. It was no easier for her to learn Margery's gay resilience through exhortation than for Margery to acquire Ruth's skill on the piano by having her knuckles rapped. Delicate health became for Ruth a barrier to education and to almost every activity beyond the Failand schoolroom. Yet she yearned for public life, for administration. She knew she had her share of intellectual power and a capacity for patient mastery of detail. In the autumn of 1914 she was called to London to join Hilda Clark and Edith Pye in their 'concern' for relief work in the devastated areas of France. The red-and-black Quaker star (first seen in 1871 when Mariabella Fry's brother, Thomas Hodgkin, had been one of the workers for the victims of the Franco-Prussian war) was rising again. No one guessed when Ruth Fry was appointed Honorary Secretary of the Friends War Victims Relief Committee, that she would have to become 'a sort of generalissimo-cum-quartermaster general . . . responsible for a vast programme of supplies, administration, personnel management, public relations, fund-raising, leadership and inspiration, on behalf of a complex of projects the like of which had never been known in Quaker history before'.[1] By 1921 she would have journeyed, over war-ravaged railways, to every field of her committee's work, almost as far as the Ural Mountains, burning herself out in a decade. In 1915 the London office seemed more suitable for this delicate and inexperienced woman than the 'good, tough job' which was offered to Margery: the organization of relief work in the Marne and Meuse area, and later in the whole of France.

The story of nine years' relief and reconstruction in Europe has been told by Ruth Fry in *A Quaker Adventure*. The Battle of the Marne had destroyed nearly every house in Sermaize, formerly a thriving little town of 4,000 inhabitants. Four hundred refugees were crammed into 'La Source', a disused spa hotel a mile outside the town. Here the Quaker team took up its quarters early in 1915, using the casino as a common-room and the little theatre as a store, where building equipment jostled the tawdry scenery 'I hardly know what my work *is*': at first Margery Fry seemed only to be writing requests for clothes and furniture 'in a horrid little book and then handing them on to someone else to see about'. This soon developed into the more positive occupation of 'catching unwilling people and forcing unwelcome truths upon them'.

A few weeks earlier the Belgian family had left the house in Birmingham to the two friends. Now, while Rose kept up the pleasant routine of 'visitors to nearly every meal', Margery was swept into the society of Quaker women and of young men, 'simple, transparent creatures addicted to hymn-singing and pillow-fighting'. As the leader of the group she had a cold little bedroom to herself, but she ate, worked, and wrote in the casino common-room. For the first time she was cut off from middle-class comfort, with the signs of domestic toil whisked out of sight and possessions laid spaciously

[1] Bernard Carter, in the *Friend*, 4 May 1962.

in order in polished chests and cupboards. The members of the *équipe* kept their things in egg-boxes.

Rumours reached England that the Quaker workers, especially the young men of military age, were living in idle luxury. A Red Cross Commission, sent out to investigate, reported somewhat sententiously that conditions at Sermaize would be 'absolutely unendurable were it not that . . . every member is animated by a single-minded idea of self-sacrifice and self-denial'. Perhaps even more important was the knowledge that the women of Sermaize, whose voices came through the floorboards every morning, were suffering the total loss of their homes. These were not the kind of 'poor' for whom middle-class women were accustomed to work. 'On était pauvre mais on était si bien': a few weeks earlier these Frenchwomen had been proud of their linen, rivalling one another in household skill.

Bare necessities were still to be distributed. There were 'some days of actual hauling and lugging of mattresses and blankets and pails. . . . Other days of squared paper and lists and computations'. When the owls or the nightingales kept her awake at night Margery knew that 'if not a man had been killed from first to last the misery of 100 years would still have been crowded into these 9 months'. On Sundays, when there was time to walk about in the warm sun and watch the swallows building in the ruined village, she became aware of 'a sort of throbbing dim bang' and felt the ineptitude of her own small labours in the face of the inexorable destruction.

Sometimes Margery marked a passage in her journal for Ruth's special attention—as, for instance, a commendation of the 'shovers', the young men who drove and maintained the team's motor vehicles: but she did not purvey romantic stories for Quaker Sunday reading. She found that war brought out, in others as in herself, the usual mixture of selfishness and generosity, of peevishness and courage. 'You order beds and they don't come and when they do you make such fearful bad blood by giving them you almost wish you'd left it alone.' 'The mere giving out of things,' she wrote a few weeks later, 'invaluable as a sort of first aid, is really not good continued indefinitely to people you're living right among. . . . I hate the relation of giver and receiver so much when it isn't the symbol of an already existing friendship.' Committee work in Birmingham had taken Margery Fry far beyond the 'charity' methods of her forebears: but still she had been working for the other nation: the grubby children, the unintelligent, the feckless and delinquent. People of her own sort had their responsibilities towards local and national government, in a broad sense they enjoyed its protection: but their education, their housing, their physical and mental health, their childbirth, and their old age were their own affair: only the poor needed help in the vicissitudes of daily life. Other people paid for what they wanted. The subtle gradations of hardship leading down from financial 'competence' to the want which could not be hidden had still to be explored.

One day in 1916, Margery saw an old lady sitting with dignity among the new refugees at Bar-le-Duc. 'I cannot help thinking how terribly you would feel, being turned out like this,' she wrote to her mother. Natural love, deeply channelled for parents, brothers and sisters, and a few close friends, was now breaking its embankments. Before she left France, Margery admitted that she and her fellow workers had given something, however inconsiderable when proportioned to the loss they came to relieve, beyond the material aid which she could plot on her graph-paper.

The rule of the 'cold brain' was not unseated by the overflowing heart. She seemed made for her job of negotiating with local authorities: she had her Staffordshire experience; like all Mariabella Fry's children, she spoke French fluently. Roger had predisposed her to like and understand French people. At her first coming she had seen France itself in 'a cherry tree flourishing tho' smashed by a shell and growing by a shred of bark'. When she went to Paris to visit 'high places' about the rebuilding of Sermaize, Roger was there to take her to see Matisse's studio 'with gold fish and balcony and other more or less recognizable items of his pictures'.

With guilty misgivings she bought some Parisian clothes to face the sharp looks of wealthy ladies who must be persuaded to work with rather than across the Quakers. But she was happiest in the villages, where the hammers rang as the workers put up 'asiles', temporary huts for the refugee families. Farms and machinery were destroyed, but the hay grew tall. Margery Fry had to introduce farmers to the idea of sharing the machines her committee was able to buy. Eighteen farmers (men and women) met the deputy-mayor, Margery Fry, and her young agricultural assistant.

The deputy-mayor explained a little, I uttered a few platitudes, then a wild storm began. One man in a Guy Fawkes cloak stormed round the room. . . . At intervals the deputy-mayor tried to pour oil—no one would serve on the committee, no one ever *had* worked with anyone else and it was no good trying to begin now—so for about an hour we went on with storm and occasional lull. At last we got a list of those who would use the machines if they were bought—another of those who had machines worth repairing—then a halting pi-jaw from me, an eloquent one from the deputy-mayor and some soothing hints from Mr. McLaren (aged 22!) —a Committee appointed, the rest turned out and in great peace we discussed possible horses and drivers and the number of machines required. About 3 borrowed remarks and a rapid calculation that 3 2-horse and one one-horse machine takes 7 horses established the belief that I occupy myself exclusively with agriculture at home.

Sous-préfets, mayors, *curés* learned to treat Margery with some deference, but to the ordinary peasant woman she remained an eccentric, well-intentioned foreigner. 'Elle fait ce qu'elle peut, la pauvre fille': the words rose above the babel as she tried to retrieve a wooden rake which had strayed from one group of villagers to another. No well-turned compliment from a university orator ever pleased her so much.

Around La Source the children, fussed and petted by 'les Anglaises', played with kittens and builders' planks, stayed outside when they should have been in school, to dig the garden plots *l'équipe* had made for them. When Margery returned from leave no one met her at the station, but a garland of leaves and 'Welcome Miss Fry' lay on her threshold. She begged the children to stop bringing in lilies-of-the-valley from the woods: there were no bowls left for porridge. She taught some of them to play shop and others tip-cat: she went to see their confirmation in the roofless church where Joan of Arc's uncle had been priest. She could not help noticing that, although fingers remained piously joined, the little boys' elbows were busy.

Joan of Arc stands bravely still—not such a *very* bad statue of her, but the church has got the better in the old squabble and she wears a neat petticoat with fleur-de-lys and not that too gallant boy's dress which she clung to so bravely in spite of all the parsons,—she stands with the back of her head and half her flag blown away and it is real sky she looks up at now and her flowers are arranged in the case of an unexploded shell. All the afternoon the sun fell full on her.

Among the children her favourite was eight-year-old Antoinette, whose story is told anonymously in *A Quaker Adventure*. When her elders were inert with misery Antoinette had 'pluck and hope for the whole family'. She had half a franc in her purse to buy wood for a new house: she had read the posters in the village and knew all about the possibilities. Margery led the little girl by the hand to the building supervisor and stood by while without prompting Antoinette made her request: 'Monsieur, je demande pour Maman le prix d'un abri de deux pièces, une cuisine et une chambre à coucher'—'as if one ordered houses every day'—and then struggled to write down the measurements all by herself.

Margery Fry never wrote more vividly of people, birds, and flowers than in her letters from Sermaize. Often she lacked intimate companions to share the moment as it passed—its value raised higher than ever in her reckoning by the distant sound of guns and the ruins at her feet. In October 1915, 'You can't imagine how flamingly splendid these stretches of country are, unbroken by hedges but all dressed out in poplars and cherry trees with bluest shadows among their fires.' In the following July she walked 'along the canal, most exquisite with poppies in the fields and the poplars in full green and everything absurdly peaceful-looking with kingfisher and turtle doves and I believe golden aureoles and quails'. As gunfire sounded unceasing twenty miles away she watched 'the young bats, downy and fleecy', the swallows chasing flies as she dozed in an aspen copse, the inflated cheeks of frogs croaking to 'the sobbing accompaniment of toads, like plucking the string of a 'cello'. In the grief and terror which no one could assimilate the small heroisms moved her—'One dish-cloth, patched with perhaps a dozen patches and with other holes neatly mended with an ornamental darning nearly broke me down.'

The maternity hospital at Châlons, opened by the Friends in December 1914 and directed by Edith Pye throughout the war, lay in Margery Fry's region. She had a distaste for professional nursing: 'a certain bright fatuity' seemed to her characteristic of 'a sub-medical atmosphere'. A personal whim could not, however, blind her to the quality of the work at Châlons or to the difficulties surmounted there. Though rows of cots bored her, she would in old age speak with a shining wonder of seeing a birth at Châlons: 'one moment, the mother the only person of importance, the next, the room filled with a new personality'.

In the spring of 1916, on her way to Corsica, Margery Fry called at Dijon to make a survey of the refugee population. She telegraphed for help to Jacqueline Merle, who had left her teaching post to work with her sister in a hospital. Mlle Merle was puzzled by the summons, until one wet day, when they were waiting for a tram under one umbrella, Margery suddenly remarked, 'Jacqueline, when the war is over the Quakers will have to leave La Maternité at Châlons-sur-Marne. But it will go on as a memorial to their work and you'll have to be in charge of it.' The suggestion seemed madness: Mlle Merle had no nursing qualification, and believed she was eager to return to teaching. 'We'll see,' said Margery. Nothing more was said until, eighteen months later, another telegram asked Jacqueline Merle to go the Châlons for three weeks to help during a shortage of staff. 'I did not guess', Mlle Merle wrote in 1962, 'I should live at Châlons for 30 years and for 28 of them should be in charge of "La Maternité Anglaise", later called "La Maison Maternelle de la Marne". So Margery had known better than I what I could do, and do successfully.'

Other familiar figures arrived: Marjorie Rackstraw was one of the first to follow Margery Fry, to remain under the Quaker star through the Russian famine and to be recalled, because of her immense experience, to the second liberation of Europe in 1945. Mildred Pope was there, 'a host in herself'. May Staveley came out to run a workroom for refugee women, Rachel and Jean Alexander, family friends from Bayswater days, were directing a factory for women skilled in the traditional fine embroidery. When the primary lack of shelter and clothing was supplied the need was for occupation, some financial independence, the retention of skill, even, as one woman told Margery, for 'un peu de poésie dans la vie'.

After the Battle of Verdun she began to experiment with a new kind of embroidery. In the following winter Edith Pye reported a deterioration of stamina in the women who, after bravely building up some sort of home for the return of their men, had now lost husbands and sons at Verdun. The relief workers had seen nothing 'quite so piteous', according to Margery Fry, 'as the crowds of tired, patient, mud-drenched people' coming into Bar-le-Duc. Time hung wretchedly, materials of the traditional kind were scarce. In her spare moments Margery began to devise patterns: 'doodles' on squared paper still fall from between the pages of her notebooks. She filled in geometric designs with bright wools worked on coarse linen or calico. She got Ruth Fry to send out wools in bold colours, such as the Omega Workshops used. At the refugee embroidery sales

in London her designs broke new ground: they were high fashion.
Naturally they were too advanced for all tastes: the young men of the
équipe teased her to the strains of Sullivan,

> And then we have the latest craze, it's broderie night and day.
>   (I've got a little list etc.)
> But what the fuss is all about is more than I can say.
> The lits-and-armoires books are lost in drifts of dust and ash,
> And in their place the room is strewn with post-impressionist trash,
> Yet e'en a weary shover's asked, when every moment's full,
> To drive the Govner 20 miles to drop a skein of wool.
>   Oh Margery, oh Margery we wish you would desist,
>   And your work would not be missed.

But she would not desist. She liked to remember (her features taking
for an instant a shrewd peasant look) one woman who said she
enjoyed the work so much she would do it even if she wasn't paid.
One of Margery's last letters from France in 1917 describes to Ruth
a visit to the embroidery depot. 'The women come in from neigh-
bouring villages, they ask each other—strangers till then—to come
and see them at home; they teach each other and they are *happy* in it.'

Needles and thread were among the 'soulagements' she carried to
the Serbian refugees on the quarantine island of Frioul, off Marseilles.
The Serbian Relief Fund asked in January 1916 for two workers.
Margery Fry, being 'more or less experienced', was one of the
volunteers. She and her companion Ka Cox awoke in Corsica one
January morning 'to find almond and broom flowering among the
white southern stones'. They faced for the first time the problem of
language and found nothing specific waiting to be done except the
distribution of 'millions of cotton pyjamas. . . . A lamentable
difficulty in co-operating . . . makes the job the least congenial I
ever struck.' But in a few days she made 'at least a dozen warm
acquaintances'. She left Corsica dissatisfied with her three weeks'
labour, infuriated by the quality of cast-off clothing—'so many odd
shoes and socks and stockings and gloves'—shipped out by the
Serbian Relief Committee. But she left 'a *very* shaky scheme of
cooperation . . . which is at least not the disgrace of open rivalry'.
From Corsica she and Florence Barrow crossed to Frioul in a squalid
little ship. Their cabin was in the stern, which 'seemed to have
independent powers of waggling'. They waited long in a room
decorated with instructive pictures of infectious diseases and were

then taken to see the wards, where refugees were herded with the barest equipment. One ward possessed only one towel. A party of stranded women journalists had been pressed into unwilling service as nurses.

Margery Fry again describes with the pen of a Nightingale the outrageous bales of clothing—'days' and days' work of that particularly unsavoury and trying sorting which the S.R.F. prefers to have done by foreign workers rather than by the cheapest labour in a decent warehouse at home'. Hopefully they opened a bale which might help to clothe the rows of ragged boys who sat waiting: it contained nothing but damp cotton petticoats. Some of the boys would be sent back to the army—she had made the acquaintance on the crossing of one who at seventeen wore the Croix-de-Guerre, and wondered at the innocence of his smile. Others were too young. She knew them for only five days, but according to Florence Barrow she saw to it that they were sent to England and given a decent education.[2] She wrote down also the name and address of the one competent worker on the island, a French nurse who sighed as she saw the two Englishwomen go, 'et moi, qui étais si contente de vous avoir'.

Under the 'rather dubious sauf-conduit' which she had made out for herself, Margery Fry travelled north with officers returning to the battle-front at Verdun, 'as carefully served with luncheon, tea and dinner as if they were off to a review'. She rejoined the refugees, 'sleeping together village by village', or sitting in a circle talking 'familiarly with a kind of pride of places that are now history, like people who have known a famous man in petticoats'. So Margery Fry went on, chronicling the miseries of war, concealing from her old parents its grosser horrors. The gunfire had become, she recorded in a private note in her journal, 'one absolutely steady roll without any sound of individual explosion'. The child who had screamed when the drums rolled in Highgate was always with her. She kept by her a detailed plan for the evacuation of La Source if a German break-through threatened.

At La Source she was in control as surely as at University House. 'Oh yes, she was all right as long as she was boss,' says one of her men, who knew Lady Fry later and recognized 'a lot of the old lady' in Margery. Yet she reproached herself for raging too fiercely, as much because of the jangling of her own nerves as out of compassion for the refugees, when some of the young men broke into a merry

[2] Verbal communication from Florence Barrow, who died on 3 March 1964.

sing-song. Margery Fry had at one time what seemed to her 'a singularly rough lot of men'. She set them to read Shaw on winter evenings. 'He knows how to give people a certain courage of irreverence,' she told Agnes. 'You are more an Aunt than a Mother,' wrote Francis Birrell when she was on leave, horrified by the rumour that older woman Friends were to be sent out specifically to 'mother' the workers: 'and Aunts, though more trying, are less deteriorating than Mothers.'

In Birmingham, Rose still kept open house. Margery's old students sat round the fire, their backs turned on the Omega carpet, talking primary-school shop. Rose lectured on history to the University and on social studies to the W.E.A., tried as best she could to fill Margery's place at the committee-table and in the lives of individual people, watched over her friend's finances. Ruth Fry ran the London office under increasing pressure. Roger Fry struggled on in the Omega Workshops, which were to have introduced the spirit of fun into furniture and into fabrics: even in wartime people had to buy tables and curtains, but unremitting work of hand and brain could not put off the knowledge that fun and everything else he cared for was being pushed into limbo. Isabel Fry had left the Society of Friends in 1913, believing its peace testimony to be untenable. Already in her mid-forties and suffering from an undiagnosed spinal injury, she was working out the bitter sentence conscience imposed on her, first as a farm hand, then as a munition forewoman. Finally, at the time of severest scarcity, she opened her farm school at Mayortorne Manor near Aylesbury. Julian and Pamela were away at school: Joan Fry, having finished her eleven years of mothering, was occupied as a Quaker prison chaplain and as a friend to 'enemy aliens'.

Mab, now in failing health, and Agnes were the only daughters left at home. 'This is a heyday for the true economical cheeseparing woman like myself,' wrote Agnes when rationing came in. Her little economies were a joke even among the careful Frys. It was in any case only in a figurative sense that Agnes could keep the home fires burning: years later she would wake in the night and think how strange it was that she had never been allowed, before she was in her sixties, to handle a piece of coal or stir the embers to a blaze without some advice from her mother. There was not much in the way of war work (or 'peace work', as the Friends conceived it) to be done by a deaf, middle-aged lady, tied to the slow elaborate life of old parents.

She could, however, organize sewing and knitting parties, sending out parcels of exquisite garments to Margery's children in France. She could also write letters. The mental energy of Agnes (she had perhaps the finest intellect of all the Frys) drove her into an outward busy-ness: but deafness, which imprisons some, produced in her an inward retirement into which others could be drawn. In her letters all tends to composure, to a sense of proportion, especially in these war years which presented so many mad incongruities.

In July 1917, before the rain began to flood the fields of Paschendaele, Agnes's letter took Margery home in the morning sunlight to the garden at Failand, 'paradise plus vegetables', where dew flashed from the cabbages in the former rose-beds. Weighing all, she was able to write without constraint to the battlefield of Marne about their father's distress over the coachman's illness, the calling-up of the butler: 'Some hard-pressed strugglers would say he had nothing to bear, and yet we know he has, and perhaps as much as he can bear.' 'How can you make your letters always so good to get?' her sister wrote from Sermaize. 'They're like the bouquet which stands on my table now in a marmalade tin,—orange lilies, rose phloxes, magenta sweet williams, with a border of the enclosed most lovely blue thing.'

Margery returned from Failand in June 1916 to the foothills of the Alps, in Haute Savoie, where homes were found for refugees from Verdun. Every day she wrote a card to her father, now physically helpless. Years before he had told her she would not go far wrong if she clung to a sense of the spiritual nature of the universe. On her last leave he had confessed to her that this sense was failing him. He grieved over the war, over the failure of his work at The Hague, over the ill health and unhappiness of his children, even over the little child lost fifty years earlier. One day she found time to write him a letter:

I think of you so very often and of what you said to me as I came away about the difficulty of realizing spiritual things that I do hope you won't mind my writing to you my thoughts . . . though I, who have always known that I could not think or feel as definitely as most people about such things, am perhaps the last person who should speak of them. Still, though I don't think it easy to make positive statements I do feel that at one's clearest moments one has to trust, only those clear moments come seldom and any kind of bodily pain or weakness is so very apt to obscure thought about that as about everything else. . . . It is, of course, rather

easier for people who have always been able to accept symbols and statements to embody the truths of hours of insight, because they can sometimes hold on to the form and find comfort in it, when they haven't the
vigour to refill it with meaning, but this has never been your way. We live
here under the very flanks of Mont Blanc and see nothing of it, as one
could do further off. I think it may be thus for you who are closer to the
great mystery and the great hope—just because of their nearness their
heights are hidden.

She was never more actively a Quaker than in these war years.
She is even remembered taking part in vocal ministry at least once
in the little thatched Meeting-House at Portishead. Though she still
made few intimate friendships with Quakers, she felt able to explain
their presence in France to those who asked: able also to explain to
the earnest young Nonconformists and agnostics of the *équipe* why
she had to go to endless trouble to arrange for masses in refugee
encampments, and why, even if the young men fled to the attics, she
had to receive the Catholic bishop as a friend.

On 18 August 1916 she began to tell her father a funny story of an
officer's horse tied to a rotten pole at La Source. Then 'I am very
sad today that a friend of mine has been killed. You may remember
a rather sad letter I had from him when I was at home. He was an
extraordinarily brilliant mathematician. It is horribly wasteful.' She
had known him for eight years. Her parents had met him at lunch
on their first visit to the new University House. Everyone who knew
his work considered him a powerful and original thinker, but he had
not rushed into publication or set about building a career. He
returned to his home in Australia in the summer of 1914 to lead a
section of the British Association, leaving the essay which had gained
an important prize still to be revised for publication. He enlisted
immediately on his return to England. He had written explaining to
Miss Fry that it was a step he detested, but felt bound to take. He
had died by accident, after trying vainly to save a pile of ammunition.

In France he and Margery Fry had corresponded. She knew of
his death several days before the announcement in *The Times*. She
sent his letters home to Agnes, who obliterated carefully, with Indian
ink, all of Margery's letter of 19 August, except the elaboration of the
story of the horse, the noisy car, the barking dog, the rotten post,
which she told with great spirit for her father's amusement.

Yet it seems clear that Margery Fry was one of the women who
came to the end of the war unconsoled even by a definition of their

loss. Grief, as far as we know, does not change: the attitudes of mourning, clear enough at any given point, are altered gradually as centuries pass and cultures mingle. But the tragedies of 1914 threw all observances into confusion. Sir Edward Fry lay at Failand, full of honour, and several lives were dedicated to his long dying. It had become the norm in his age and social class to die old, in one's own bed. A few weeks after he became bedridden, 60,000 young men died on the Somme in one day's fighting. In the early war years women wore black and the Last Post wailed all day from English cemeteries. By the end of the war everyone sang the soldiers' songs and even ladies took to the bright colours which the munition lasses bought with their dangerously earned pay. Reticence in grief became mannerly.

The ladies to whom Margery Fry wrote letters of condolence on her friend's death mourned in the old pattern: their replies did not spare her. She was at the vortex of a whirl of surmises, of dusty answers and reiterations of regret. The letters of this communal friend of University House had, it seemed, spoken only of Miss Fry. He had received from her presence that extraordinary stimulation of the mind, of the will to work, which many smaller talents knew before and after his time. His hopes of meeting her, she was told, had been more than once brushed aside by the demands of Failand or by her own preoccupations. Indeed, he had himself believed Miss Fry's work to be so important that nothing must interfere with it. A colleague gave the final thrust, 'You were so far above him, dear.' Thirty seemed young, looked at from forty-two. Yet at thirty, when she went to Birmingham, Margery Fry had become unmistakably a woman in authority. In spite of all the jokes, the tennis, the dressing-up and scene-painting, she had become, to some rare and sensitive spirits, great and remote, like Miss Maitland and the other stately figures of her own youth.

Rose Sidgwick, who went out to France, by long prearrangement, at the end of the summer holidays, was puzzled by her friend's mood. She had expected to share a common sorrow over the loss and waste of a friend. Charles Lamb might have called Rose 'an incomparable old maid'. For her the friendships at University House, where the senior women had talked with their male guests freely, merrily, and deeply, without regard to sex, had approached an ideal. In France, it was clear, Margery Fry was performing with grace and competence an even wider range of tasks than in Birmingham: as 'this

kind of man-in-the-street', said Rose, 'you are supreme'. Yet here
was Margery, who so rarely wasted energy in regret, obsessed by a
sense of lost directions. It was impossible for one of Rose's integrity
to lay claim to an experience she did not share. 'I still don't understand, right down to the bottom,' was her final word.

Margery Fry, at forty-two, had plenty of threads in her hands.
Birmingham was holding out many more, whenever she chose to
return. Pity was needed rather for those of her former students who
in 1914 had lived in almost certain hope of marriage and motherhood. Work went on unchecked. She went back to its crudities with
passion. Returning to Sermaize early in 1917, she swept aside the
tricolour which someone had thrown over her untidy table and began
calculating potato sales among 'Xmas treery and paper garlands'.
The woman paid by the hour to scrub for the *équipe* took an un-
reasonable time over the washing-up. One day Margery put her own
untried, chilblained fingers to the test, finishing the job single-
handed, pans and all. She had become, according to Jeanne Lepetit,
'maigre comme un chat'. Two years of pouring out sympathy un-
diluted by sentimentalism, of trying to rebuild within earshot of
destruction, had worn her down.

La Maternité at Châlons was crowded by the influx from other
hospitals in more heavily bombarded towns. But for Margery Fry at
Sermaize the first pioneering thrust was over. The Cité, the temporary village built by the *équipe*, had been officially opened, 'with
church and state hobnobbing wondrous to behold'. 'We must beware
of staying to interfere,' she had said from the beginning.

Dr H. A. L. Fisher (who had married her Somerville friend
Lettice Ilbert) was President of the Board of Education. 'For the
first time in our national history,' he says in his autobiography,
'education was a popular subject and discussed in an atmosphere
cleared of religious acrimony.' There was the shame over revealed
deficiencies, the determination to repair wastage as far as it could be
repaired, the obligation felt to those who were 'asked to pour out
their blood and mulcted in the high cost of living', which would
again affect the nation nearly thirty years later. Margery Fry read
Dr Fisher's speeches. In May 1917 she told the War Victims Committee she would remain after the summer only if she were kept by
'a large new district or the arrival of a big contingent of Americans
to place. . . . I feel obliged to it by the educational push in England.'
Soon afterwards she offered her services to Dr Fisher. 'I could speak

for keeping children at school till 14 with more power than on almost any subject on earth.'

Lady Fry's collection of letters for 1917 is so thin that it seems that the saddest may have been removed. Yet in the letters from Margery which remain there is a hint of the remaking that stirs in the darkness of tragedy accepted. She saw hope in the Russian revolution. She turned with a new sweetness and tolerance to the 'good young persons' who joined her *équipe* from America, wearing curiously unquakerly uniforms blazoned with spread-eagles, and expecting to learn French in three weeks. Yet she had no illusions about 'the awful chaos of ill-directed, ill-thought-out effort which [was] beginning to be poured out on the liberated regions' when she left Sermaize to take on the organization of an American Red Cross scheme. She moved into a magnificent palace in the Place de la Concorde and turned to 'gloomy office business'. 'I am quite clear my place is not ultimately with any organization as swanky as theirs, in France or England, but it's a chance of helping literally thousands of people.' In September she borrowed one of the gorgeous *salons* to receive sixty American Quakers.

Leaving Sermaize had been worse than leaving Oxford. The magic of Oxford wore away, but she never lost her almost savage nostalgia for her life among the people of the Marne.

It's this education business which makes me feel I *must* come home for good before long [she had written to Roger]. But that jams me back into B'ham and I sometimes feel I'd rather die than go on living there. . . . You know for most things it breaks my heart to leave France and also, in a way, to leave the queer, uncomfortable Bohemianism of this life. . . . The sheltered selectness of an old maids' establishment doesn't really suit me as well as a milieu where everyone lives and speaks with brutal plainness.

But by Christmas 1917 she was back in Birmingham with Rose. 'The psychic cult is in full swing': Sir Oliver Lodge's inquiries, which Margery and Rose had smiled about and Bishop Gore had preached against before 1914, had a new significance: crude amateur seances, of the kind which became an entertainment to the post-war generation, were the hazardous lifeline of many lonely women. At this time probably originated Margery Fry's fierce personal hatred of spiritualism.

Between journeys to Stafford and Dudley she toured the country appealing for funds for European relief. 'I don't raise the tears enough,' she said, but £5,000 came in from Liverpool after she had spoken there. 'There is no news inside or outside of me,' she said in May. 'I feel like a cumberer of the ground and yet don't quite know what I ought to be *at*. So I mess around at my old committees.' A conference in London on the feeble-minded was 'as boring as it would be'. The Fisher Education Act was passed without her help.

In October, when most people believed that the war would last for at least another year, Sir Edward Fry died a few weeks before his ninety-first birthday. His grave is now in Failand churchyard, but in 1917 this 'man of noble mind grave virtue and honest faith'[3] was laid in a rough meadow just outside the consecrated ground. Because of her father's condition Margery Fry had refused the one new opening offered her in the educational field: a visit to the U.S.A. as a member of the British Universities Mission. Rose Sidgwick went in her place. She was wonderfully successful. Margery was almost persuaded by the Bristol Union of Women's Suffrage Societies to stand as Independent parliamentary candidate for West Bristol. When the Labour Party refused support she withdrew. It was the beginning and end of the political career which still seemed to her the only career worth following.

But rich plans were forming for the future. Roger and Margery decided to share a house in London. His children were of the age she understood best. Rose would find work in London and join them. The house would be unpretentious and beautiful, filled with young people and their own and Roger's friends. Roger began house-hunting enthusiastically in Camden Town and Islington, putting convenience and economy before fashion, after the manner of the Frys. He had a splendid dream one night of a row of lovely houses on a green backed by hills like those of Provence. He had not realized before that London was bounded by such hills to the north, but that was because he and Margery had never pushed far enough up the Camden Road.

In November 1918, on the day that Roger Fry described his house-hunting, Rose Sidgwick died of influenza in New York.

[3] Epitaph at Failand.

X
Dalmeny Avenue and the Howard League: 1918-1926

FAR up the Camden Road, Roger Fry had found, not indeed hills grown with beech and juniper, but a satisfactory Victorian house, 'in a horribly good state of repair', overlooking Holloway Prison to the north, and to the south opening on to 'a beautifully designed garden that stretches away for ever'. A couple of dilapidated houses on the other side of the road remain of the Dalmeny Avenue of 1919, now rebuilt with blocks of council flats. One block, between Dalmeny Avenue and Holloway Prison, bears the name of Margery Fry Court.

The removal from Birmingham took place as planned, on the second day of 1919. It was a time of strikes, of cruel weather. Roger had to persuade a couple of drivers from Smithfield to move his goods from Guildford in meat-vans. Margery's chilblains gave her no peace. The enervation of postwar London, outwardly unscarred compared with France, was hard to accept. She had managed to persuade foreign railwaymen to convey hundreds of beds across a battlefield, but now she could not buy a piece of linoleum or get in a plumber to mend a pipe. Her mind was with the dead. By day she thought of Rose; by night her father, active and authoritative as in her youth, strode through her dreams. Margery and Rose were to have formed the stable element in the household where Pamela, Julian, and their friends were to find the undemanding security that growing-up required. Roger had been denied happiness: his freedom, the good that remained to him, must be intact. 'Roger comes and goes like a Cheshire cat,' Margery wrote later from Dalmeny Avenue, 'but now it's mostly going.'

'Freedom to shape my own destinies' had been one of the advantages which Margery also had schooled herself to take as compensation for her single state. Nobody had ever rated her destiny higher than Roger. He wanted to get her an interview with the

Ministry of Reconstruction. 'It would be a wonderful thing for the country', he wrote to Lady Fry, 'if they could harness her great ingenuity and practical wisdom to the job. I can't imagine any man who would have quite her kind of experience in such things. Really women are getting to be what I always said they should be, the great administrators. She and Pippa Strachey are both of the kind that if they were men would be G.C.B.'s and loaded with honour and glory.'

Already as she looked into the large, cold living-room she was warming it with thoughts of hospitality to those small societies, then looking hopefully to Geneva, which she was involved with: the Seven Universities Democratic Association, the Aborigines' Protection Society, that 'queer but plucky little body'. As the Post-Impressionist paintings, the Omega tables and cabinets were carried in, a new splendour was brought into her life. To live with Roger would be a home-coming: his kindness, his appreciation, his clever hands, his irreverent fun had enchanted her young days. She could not give him the happiness he had missed, but she could accommodate his friendships, respond to his work, deal with the countless excrescences of chores which impede creative man. Complicated instructions about the transport of canvases mingled in her diary with arrangements for her own committees. She went down to Fitzroy Square, while Roger was in France, to help Francis Birrell and Robert Tatlock to pack up the remains of the Omega products: for the Workshop was to be relinquished, at the very time, some said, when it might have flourished. 'I've never had such a pleasant and easy domestic life as in these years with Margery,' Roger was able to say years later. Pamela's college friend, who lived with the Frys for a time, noticed with what sweetness, when Roger was at home, his sister drew from him directions about domestic repairs and the number of guests to be expected, and with what light-hearted efficiency she ran the house. 'It is sometimes difficult to know whether I give too much time to outward affairs,' she told Lady Fry. '*Really* Roger would quite easily "do" with a person companioning and house-keeping most of the time, but I just harden my heart. . . . Sometimes I feel a brute.'

The first outward affair which took her away from Dalmeny Avenue was 'a rather vague and unofficial mission' to the Peace Conference in Paris. President Wilson had been strongly opposed in his wish to see women represented. Months of preparation, including an inter-Allied and American Conference of Women's Societies, led only to the allocation of half an hour's interview with the full Labour Commission of the League. The unenfranchised women were grateful for this favour and the publicity given to their cause, while the Americans and British saw no reason for gratitude in a short interview at the final session of the Commission, too late for any suggestion, however valuable, to be admitted to its report.

'A mission of this kind depends a good deal on first impressions,' said Margery, justifying to her mother a 'wildly extravagant expenditure on "tidy clo" ': a silk jacket for £3 5s. and, worse still, a black silk cloak 'which seems to give me a look of a "real lidy" with a dash of fairy godmother'. She sat impatiently through the Countess of Aberdeen's introduction, 'voluble, apologetic and woolly', deciding meanwhile that in spite of his graciousness to the women President Wilson had 'a face like an Aztec idol and a mechanical smile with no mirth in it'. (She did not know that he had recently suffered a cerebral thrombosis, diagnosed as influenza.) Into what was left of thirty minutes eleven speakers rammed five important subjects. 'I *think* I spoke well but it was a difficult job—one hadn't time to get used to one's own voice.' She had been allocated the subject of women's right to vote in any referendum deciding the status of their country, in her own opinion 'a stale old subject . . . which doesn't really come in much'.

The mission to Paris was a mere incident, but by then she had accepted the work for which she is now chiefly remembered in the world. 'There may still be a future in the world for S.M.F.,' she had written to Dorothy Scott just before Rose's death, 'but I would give anything for a little of the self-confidence I *seem* to have so much of.' She had already rejected a suggestion from a group of university women that her name might go forward if it were decided to appoint a woman to the Prison Commission. She had heard too much about prisons from conscientious objectors to wish to be a part of the system.

In 1917 Sir Edward Fry's sister Susan had died at the age of eighty-eight, in great peace, in her Regency house near Bristol. Her nephew Roger thought her the most beautiful character he had ever known—'though', Agnes added, 'a world of Aunt Susans would move to a slow measure, would it not?' Few now remember the 'wonderful eyes, the voice with the little ring of merriment', though some recall the bowls of strawberries, the pitchers of cream, the sunbonnets and laughter, when they were called as children to Mrs

Pease's paddock, after the custom of those days, to make hay while the sun shone. In her last days her thoughts went far beyond her children and grandchildren and the tenderly nurtured haymakers. She remembered hearing of a prison in the north of England where the waves could be heard in the cells and the prisoners never saw the sea. Her 'Message to the younger Members of her Circle when her Death was hourly expected' perhaps reproduces Aunt Susan's idiom no more personally than the recorded sayings of a dying Pope, but it found its way, printed on hand-made paper, to her nephews and nieces. 'We say that restraint must be put on the evil-doer for the sake of Society and that the fear of punishment must be used as a deterrent. Neither of these aims appears to have been reached by our present methods. . . . Let us admit our failures in our methods of reforming criminals. . . . Let us be prepared to support more enlightened and humane methods.'

'It's never wise to idolize the race of Frys', someone had chanted in the nursery. To decline ancestor-worship was a necessity of growth in such a family. Why should Margery claim kinship with that Elizabeth Gurney who had happened more than a century before to marry an undistinguished cousin of Margery's own great-grandfather? But when twenty-five years later she was questioned before the microphone about the origins of her work for penal reform she acknowledged the effect of Aunt Susan's Message.[1] Farther back, in prewar Birmingham, the seeds had been sown. She had become acquainted with Dr Hamblin Smith in his pioneer work in the medical classification of prisoners. She had met Cecil Leeson, the senior probation officer of Birmingham, who had succeeded Holmes as secretary of the Howard Association.

Aunt Susan Pease's concern was widely held in the Society of Friends at the end of the war. Through the imprisonment of conscientious objectors the prisons had been opened to the day-to-day knowledge of a great number of articulate men. Before then prisons had been almost completely isolated except for the entry of a few 'lady visitors' to women's prisons. In November 1918 Margery Fry reported that Stephen Hobhouse was 'getting to work on Labour Party research on prison reform' and that he was 'mighty pleased' about her probable secretaryship of the 'Penal Reform Association' [*sic*]. Stephen Hobhouse was a nephew of Beatrice Webb. She had disapproved of his pacifism, but was so disturbed by his account of

[1] 'Personal Call', 26 March 1956.

his repeated imprisonments that soon after the war the Webbs urged the Labour Party to set up a Prison Enquiry Committee. *English Prisons Today*, the book which Stephen Hobhouse produced in 1922 with the help of Fenner Brockway and Arthur Creech Jones, became in Margery Fry's words 'the Bible of penal reformers'.

Stephen and Rosa Hobhouse belonged like Dorothy Scott to the Penal Reform League. The first secretary, St John, was retiring. The Hobhouses were determined to get Margery Fry as his successor. The League, which had seemed moribund in the early war years, awoke to the general interest in childhood and education in 1917, when it called a conference on Juvenile Delinquency and published *The Child and the War* by Cecil Leeson. Later, in *A National Minimum for Youth*, it called for day nurseries, nursery schools, family allowances, and maintenance for secondary-school children. Early in December 1918, Margery Fry came away from the Hob-houses convinced that the League had 'a lot of good energy in it that ought to be kept going'. The Hobhouses and Frys had known one another from childhood. Margery had taught Stephen to play cricket at Failand. His refusal to compromise with his conscience or to mitigate by any family influence the increasing harshness of his prison sentences had won her respect, but she was repelled by his particular kind of earnestness. She still shrank from giving her main energies to the cause the Hobhouses were urging on her. The League was a tiny affair (the two penal reform societies between them had less than 500 members), but she knew that if she took it over it would grow. The recent activities of the League had come near her heart, but she would have to deal with other matters besides the welfare of children. 'You of all people!' a friend exclaimed when in her seventies Margery Fry was knocked down by a bag-snatcher. The reply was prompt. 'I never said criminals were nice people.' And indeed she never had.

She was unemployed, financially independent, a powerful speaker, and a proved administrator. (She took for granted another impressive asset, the high legal connexions of her family.) These qualities she realized were tempting to any struggling voluntary body, and she accepted the supposition that she was wanted for the sum of them, not for any identification of herself as a person with the cause of penal reform. Yet between leaving Birmingham and moving into Dalmeny Avenue, she had 'begun to see a little clearer about the Penal Reform League. It certainly is a sleepy small concern and won't be worth doing unless I can make something more out of it, but this I *hope* to be able to manage.' She was already 'trotting round and writing to likely people . . . rather a squalid job'. With the help of a 'little sentimentalist' she sorted the League papers. They were carried into the little room near the front door at 7 Dalmeny Avenue, where the documents of the Howard Association would later join them and remain for the next four years.

To bring about a marriage with the Howard Association was a delicate matter. Though the less active society, it was the older and richer. Cecil Leeson, its secretary, was paid £250 a year, whereas the League had to fall back on a person of means. Margery Fry had an old friend on the Committee of the Association: Champion Russell, whom she had met at the Vernon Harcourts' house in the Isle of Wight in those vacant early months of 1899. On 23 May 1919 she went off to meet him, in renewed spirits, for on the day before she had been invited to join the University Grants Committee, the new body formed (largely under the inspiration of H. A. L. Fisher) to preserve the independence of the universities by administering State aid directly from the Treasury.

'I feel so *settled* here,' she wrote a few days later. 'I sometimes felt in Birmingham as if I hadn't the capacity for letting down roots, but I rather incline to think now it's more a question of soil.' She had already given a dance for Julian, 'all very successful except that the fountain was choked with roots and flooded the scullery. The buns and sandwiches lasted out and the gramophone was just audible.' The prospect of a visit from Lady Fry reminded her that most of the floors still needed carpets, but there was no doubt that her own life was taking shape.

It was Sir William McCormick, the Chairman of the University Grants Committee, who first suggested that when she visited universities she could also visit prisons (to which the secretaries of the penal reform societies had been granted entrance). But the University was to support her penal reform work even more essentially than by paying her railway fares. It made prison-visiting bearable. Quite apart from the relative attractions of a prison and a university, the one rooted in despair and the other in hope, the prison staffs had for the most part in those early days a chilliness towards her function, whereas to the universities she carried a welcome in her pocket. 'They were very kind to me,' she remarked after a visit to a women's college. 'Probably would have been anyhow, but £1,000,000 behind

you doesn't make people less civil I discover—even nice people.'
'University today, prison tomorrow' became the pattern of her
travels. Letters to her mother became as eager and crowded as in her
early days at Somerville. 'I'm rather swamped at the moment, and
wish I was one of those hundred-headed hundred-armed divinities
who really *could* get things done—you'd think—at the proper time.'
A 'private note' follows about the swelling of her head through the
U.G.C. appointment. 'I do think Father would have been rather
pleased'. . . , then an account of an interview with Sir George
Newman about the Prison Medical Service: 'I'm afraid wire-pulling
is what I'm really born for, but if the bell rings at the end of the
pulls it seems worth while.' At this point Flossie opened the oven
door and a good smell of roast mutton reminded Margery that two
painters called Derain and Picasso were expected to dinner and the
table required her attention.

The other members of the U.G.C. were people of academic distinction and by 1919 there was plenty of choice among women with
high academic qualifications. Margery Fry had no degree, though her
experience of university administration made her acceptable even to
those who did not know her. This time there was no doubt, even in
her own mind, that she was being chosen for herself. This new
invasion of university life had to be conducted with the utmost
discretion and goodwill. It was Margery Fry who would be able to
gossip, snugly and profitably, over the tea-cups in a warden's sitting-
room: it was she who would find out, without offence except where
it was strictly due, the working conditions of a kitchen staff, the
privations of an ageing lecturer who by 1919 had somehow never
reached £200 a year. A. S. Kidd, the secretary of the U.G.C., and
Margery Fry soon recognized each other's qualities. 'I spent 3½
hours yesterday afternoon', she told her mother, 'going over the
form of enquiry, proposed to be sent to the various universities, with
the secretaries. I believe it's worth while to put in this behind the
scenes work, it's the one chance of understanding the job.'

In 1921 she 'visited' the University of Oxford. 'It gave me a queer
sense of whirligig to find a silver poker waiting outside to conduct
me in. I should have laughed when I was a student to think it could
ever happen . . . and felt a considerable humbug over it now.' From
the 'silver poker' waiting in the shadow of the Bodleian she went to a
provincial university college which spent £18 a year on its library.
One of the Scottish universities spent an average of £28 a year on a

student in 1921. The university population was inflated by ex-servicemen and the first full report (apart from statistical tables) issued by the U.G.C. in 1924 describes vividly the shifts to which universities were driven to house new departments and increasing numbers. Yet at Bristol, which had spent lavishly on buildings (through the bounty of the Wills family, the tobacco manufacturers), Margery Fry wished the money could have gone 'more on men and less on matter'. 'The War has taken the spring out of our year', said the U.G.C., lamenting the lack of university teachers. 'But', the same report adds, 'the universities must realize that if their service is to retain its attractions . . . the modest advantages which it professes to offer must actually be forthcoming.' Margery Fry's letters show that the inadequacy of salaries and pensions, especially for junior members of staff and for middle-aged lecturers who had no hope of a chair, was a personal preoccupation. Though she could never feel what it was like to have to earn her living and support others by her earnings, her imagination reached towards these people in the universities, men of intelligence and sensitivity who could afford neither books nor travel nor association with fellow scholars, except by taking on extra teaching and the marking of examination papers.

She served the universities at an unhappy period of their history. Before the last ex-serviceman had left, economic depression had begun to upset the balance of studies. Technology and agriculture languished. The pattern of Scotland and Wales, where a literary education leading to a profession had long been the only reliable investment, became the pattern of English academic life. Arts departments were overcrowded, there were long lists of applicants for the least attractive teaching posts. In 1948 she was still the only woman on the committee: she was also the only member who had served from the beginning. It was then, with a time of growth ahead which she would have rejoiced in, that she resigned, feeling that an amateur had no longer a contribution to make.

Within ten days of her session in 1919 with the secretaries of the University Grants Committee, Margery Fry spent a still longer afternoon

in a little stuffy lawyer's office . . . 3¾ hours of close concentration going over our Bill with the Howard Association secretary and a very helpful solicitor whom I've discovered. . . . Till now it has seemed rather like a bundle of shawls pretending to be a baby but I feel there's safety in the professional touch! . . . but oh! it's *horrid* hard work getting a bill into shape.

'Our Bill' was to embody the recommendations made jointly by the Howard Association and the Penal Reform League in *A National Minimum for Youth*. Nothing came of it immediately. Five years of steady work were to go by before the Criminal Justice Act of 1925 established probation as a national system, and the Departmental Committee on Young Offenders began its deliberations.

In the small front room at Dalmeny Avenue, Margery Fry applied herself to the chores of penal reform. Circulars were sent out to M.P.s, annual general meetings were arranged. Loathing meetings herself, Margery was always gratefully surprised when people turned up. Pamela and her friend Beatrice Green were initiated into the arts of multiple stamping and of tearing paper to size. Later Margery Fry employed a secretary, Miss Gorton, said to have been chosen because she assured her employer that she would not enforce tidiness in the office. Beatrice (now Mrs Dawkins) remained faithful to the cause and remembers the first penal reform meeting she attended. 'The audience, including those on the platform, yawned our way through an hour or two of tedious speeches, and then it was Margery's turn to speak, and the meeting suddenly came alive.' By the end of her first year Margery had collected a 'gang' of helpers and was refusing offers. The amalgamation of the two reform societies under the name of the Howard League for Penal Reform was announced at the Annual General Meeting in 1921.

Out of the 'large inchoate body' of the amalgamated committees an able executive soon emerged. Champion Russell and Gertrude Eaton, both in their sixties, remained. Margery Fry said later that she had always paid Gertrude Eaton the respect due to age. When she was really roused—as she was later, in the international field of penal reform—she would fight for justice, says Gordon Rose, 'with a persistence amounting almost to pig-headedness. This trait, combined with the unlimited talents of Margery Fry . . . and the help of Leonard Green's good sense, produced a formidable combination.'[2] Margery Fry had met Leonard Green in Birmingham as a part-time lecturer in Professor Muirhead's Department of Philosophy. After the war he had become secretary of an industrial federation. Mrs L'Estrange Malone was then private secretary to Lord Henry Cavendish Bentinck. She was a Somervillian of a later generation than Margery Fry. She became an Alderman of the L.C.C., a governor of the Old Vic and Sadler's Wells. A third committee

[2] Gordon Rose, *The Struggle for Penal Reform* (Stevens, 1961), p. 315.

member, Boucher, became increasingly helpful in the organization of the Howard League. These three, all probably Margery Fry's discoveries, were the kind of people, living in the world and on the whole liking it, whom Margery Fry enjoyed as colleagues. Champion Russell once wrote in the *Howard Journal*, 'It has been said that a man of quite ordinary ability may do a great deal of good in the world if he does not care who gets the credit for it.' In the Howard League those of extraordinary ability claimed no more credit than the addressers of envelopes. Margery Fry was the orator, the electrifier of audiences, but if she could she would have spoken anonymously.

In 1921, the first year of the new Howard League, Margery Fry became one of the first women magistrates. She described to her mother the confusion she caused by asking to affirm in the Quaker manner instead of taking the oath. 'It was very badly muddled and a most unimpressive affair. . . . Altogether I don't think I ever pledged my allegiance to George V at all.' A few weeks later, pledged or unpledged, she sat on the Bench for licensing cases—'Fellow-magistrates received me kindly and explained things to me in re-sounding undertones.' Mrs Bramwell Booth was chosen as the first woman justice to visit Holloway Prison, and Margery Fry had to wait another six months to get her foot in.

The Magistrates' Association was formed within a month of the appointment of women magistrates. The idea of such an association had been floating for some years: it was at last brought to land by Mr Wilkins, an ex-Mayor of Derby, who pointed out that statistics were essential to a local electricity board of which he was chairman, but that the Home Office seemed content to let the magistrates' courts work in the dark. He wrote to Cecil Leeson, before the amalgamation of the societies, and Margery Fry arranged for Cecil Leeson's part-time salary to be doubled, so that he might devote half his time to the new Magistrates' Association, half to the League. '. . . It is really a great help to have a colleague.' The increasing work of the League, together with work on the U.G.C. report (almost entirely statistical in the earlier years), made life seem 'an endless road of inevitable chores'. She had not been swept into penal reform on a tide of emotion: she had to work on facts. Though prisons had to be visited, she knew well that there was little to be learned from an isolated visit, even by the acutest senses. But the objects of the Howard League were clear. 'Prisons make prisoners:

the Howard League wants to see them making citizens.'[3] Though at first she felt her own inadequacy in smelling out abuses, she believed that many of the prison officers she met were educable. 'I'm sure it's more the system than the people that are wrong often, and I believe showing them what we are after may in the end be quite as important as finding out what they are doing.'

One of her earliest acts in the Penal Reform League had been to get E. R. Ramsay, who had left the prison service to edit the *Prison Officers' Magazine*, on to the executive. But as she came nearer to prison officers she became more aware of the hazards of their occupation. Bred to all the delicate relationships of a cohesive upper-middle-class family, her acute social senses took in the coarseness of prison society.

A grubby week [she wrote in February 1922]. My turn to be Visiting Justice at Holloway. . . . I think it worth while to give much more than the usual half hour to this business and my slow and frequent visits are an obvious nuisance to all concerned. . . . One has a *right* to see everything: but the fact that other people don't look into them so thoroughly makes it seem as if you thought the officials swindlers and brutes. . . . At the same time what the prisoners tell me is certainly often highly coloured in their own interests, and, worst of all, you can in no way protect them from petty, spiteful reprisals for having grumbled.

Three months later, when the Governor of Holloway gave her a kitten, she received it as a symbol of a budding alliance. When two officers from another prison were dismissed for misconduct Margery Fry wrote to the Postmaster-General to try to get jobs for them. But in spite of all her efforts relations between the League and prison officials deteriorated. Ramsay resigned from the Howard League in 1923, writing that 'numerous petty concessions had been made to the prisoners, adding to the worry of the officer's life; whereas the sub-committee appointed by the League to examine the officers' grievances carried little weight'.[4] Margery Fry had at this stage to admit failure in bridging the gap between the reformers and the people working in unreformed conditions without independent representation.

On Margery Fry's first visit to Holloway Prison she found that Ruth's old playmate, Miss Jean Alexander, had got in before her as

[3] Editorial in the *Howard Journal*, 1921.
[4] *Prison Officers' Magazine*, January 1924.

a 'lady visitor'. Whistler's portrait of Miss Cicely Alexander in the Tate Gallery, showing the uninhibited dislike of a child fixed on the tedious painter, indicates perhaps that the young Alexanders took loss of freedom particularly hard: by her own account Miss Jean Alexander took up prison-visiting because she remembered the horror of being shut in a cupboard, 'with the kindest intentions', by brothers playing hide-and-seek. Margery found her at the end of one of the long prison corridors, 'with horrid singing and screaming from time to time coming from the locked cells, with a little handful of girls, dressing dolls and discussing the relative merits of Marie Corelli and Hall Caine'. The light was so poor that after one or two attempts Miss Alexander had to abandon sewing for the cruder arts of raffia. But by 1922 educational work in prisons, started through Dr Hamblin Smith in Birmingham, was accepted, and Margery Fry was the first official Education Adviser to Holloway. She had already sent Marion Richardson to Dr Hamblin Smith in Birmingham: her painting lessons for young prisoners at Winson Green, one warder said, 'had stopped a lot of that sobbing among the boys'.[5] Techniques of teaching the Three R's to reluctant adolescents had to be examined. The older women were taught crafts. A London County Council instructor gave courses in 'artisans' cookery'. A former resident of University House at Birmingham remembers hearing Margery Fry speak about voluntary teaching in prison to a group of women at Maude Royden's Guildhouse ('a poor speech', according to Margery). Through the Howard League a Brabazon Society had been formed to equip prison classes (in the same way as Joan Fry's sewing and basketry had been equipped in the workhouses of Flax Bourton and Guildford). This young teacher received a grant of £2 and from the sale of craftwork produced handed back £5: she claims to have learnt more than she taught.

There were, of course, a good many failures among the classes. At this, and at every stage of her life, Margery Fry was felt to have made some odd choices to set against her brilliant successes in finding paid or unpaid workers. The Frys were accused, and accused each other, of a lack of judgement about people. They suffered from the disadvantage of seeing others always under their own powerful, immediate influence. The clear-headed courage with which people left their presence did not always last long. Yet the Frys were not necessarily mistaken. They may have possessed some exceptional

[5] *Howard Journal*, 1922, p. 16.

power of discerning people which sometimes ran to waste because neither they nor anyone else understood it.

A Scottish lady remembers vividly her one brief meeting with Margery Fry when, as a professor's wife over forty years ago, she was introduced to her on one of her university-prison visits. She recalls her dark, greying hair brushed back, a few strands escaping, not untidily, 'a dress of some soft material with lace at the neck, the colour warm and pleasant, neither garish, nor dull'. Margery Fry listened to her indignant story of how, when she had visited a conscientious objector in prison, the potted hyacinth she had taken him was immediately thrown out by a warder as 'rubbish'. After a pause Margery Fry said, 'I'll tell you something you can do', and set the disgruntled visitor and her friends to sticking coloured pictures on to the calendars which prisoners were allowed to hang in their cells.

'I'll tell you something you can do': it was a touch of puritan didacticism, perhaps; but by this approach to people, which in Margery Fry became habitual, she shared her own joy in making. She knew from her own experience that activity often led to interest, in the end to passionate caring, rather than the other way round.

The Prison Commission Report of 1923, she said in private, was 'a Howard Journal in itself', though it was only after long deliberation that the Howard League ventured to send a message of congratulation to the Home Office. Maurice Waller became Chairman of the Prison Commissioners in 1921 (at the same time as Alexander Paterson joined the Commission). 'The new Chairman . . . thinks me absolutely level-headed and reasonable. There's a useful butter-pat!' Margery wrote home before their first meeting. She found him 'a very good sort', though his apparent gentleness somewhat alarmed her. A month later she was 'full of hope about prison things now. . . . I feel really *wanted* with my advice and information.' On his retirement in 1928 she wrote:

A new breath of criticism, of experiment, of endeavour, has moved over what was a stagnant pool of self-satisfied, unintelligent routine. The prison service has been *thinking* in the last seven years, and the person who has thought hardest of all has been Maurice Waller. His gift for administration is great, so is his grasp of detail, but to our mind his most outstanding quality by far is this, that in an official position he could keep the unofficial mind, the sense of what might be, unblunted by dealing with what is.[6]

6 *Howard Journal*, 1928.

She looks back to the days of Hobhouse's and Brockway's book, to the almost complete isolation of prisons. 'He [Waller] has never looked upon the Prison Service as the private concern of officialdom, he has recognized it as an aspect of the life of the community as a whole.'

In the same week, in 1922, when Margery sat for the first time as a magistrate of the London Juvenile Court, Dr Cyril Burt, then writing *The Young Delinquent*, was her guest at Dalmeny Avenue. Margery later persuaded him to write a pamphlet, *The Psychology of the Young Criminal*, published by the Howard League in 1924. After her second turn in the Juvenile Court she wrote to a friend, 'It impresses me profoundly with the need for psychological advice. Really we are at an *incredibly* crude stage in matters of human nature!' By the autumn she was ready to address a group of women doctors about the need for a 'naughtiness clinic'.

She was, perhaps, a formidable figure from the other side of the magistrates' table, especially to the swaggerers: her features took on some of her father's justiciary aspect; she seemed a tall woman as she sat. There was, she believed, a special art (to be developed, like other arts, by practice) 'in getting a child's story out of it and enabling it to speak freely and making it understand what you mean, and also let me add, in scolding the child where necessary so that the child minds it. . . . You want the young sinner to leave the court in tears sometimes.'[7] She never lost sight of the fact that she was there to deal justly according to the law, that the Juvenile Court was part of the State defence against crime. A good many reformers in the nineteen-twenties would have transferred all children's cases to Chancery jurisdiction, after the American pattern, but Margery Fry saw dangers in slackening the procedure or the laws of evidence, in courts exercising compulsion over a child's destiny. 'I think', she said in evidence to the Departmental Committee on Young Offenders in 1925, 'there is a kind of feeling that a child's matters are small matters, and can be met by kindness and good will, and there is a certain danger of not giving the child his rights if you do not maintain these laws. There is something very splendid in the safeguard to the child in having it tried by the law of the land.'

When the facts were sifted the treatment of the child had still to be decided. As the 'naughty children' stood before her, Margery Fry's immense curiosity was focused on the springs of human

[7] Evidence to the Home Office Committee on Young Offenders, 1925 (unpublished).

behaviour. She was no longer a frustrated educationalist. She talked to children everywhere: from the free, gifted children of her friends who were natural visitants at Dalmeny Avenue to the girls in an industrial school at Bath which she slipped away to when visiting the spa with Lady Fry. She went to Belgium to see the Central Observation School at Moll, to which boys were committed by the courts to live for several months under a liberal régime. She noticed there even 'the menu which is stuck up outside the kitchen in order to give the boys something to talk about during the rest of the day'. In the East End, one close summer day, a prisoner's little daughter told her the games they played in the streets, one for each month of the year.

In the office at Dalmeny Avenue she continued to record facts and figures, to interpret documents to wits less legal than her own. To become, without going through an academic discipline or a professional training, something of an expert in penology gave her only a partial satisfaction. Though scientific method already seemed to her the only means of apprehending truth, she was not resigned to the limitations of the scientist. The essential things seemed always to evade her. At the end of 1921 she wrote to Marjorie Rackstraw, who was working with the Quakers in the Russian famine area, 'I've seen prisons and homes, Borstal institutes galore—I tell myself that after all, the worst treated person in them is in paradise compared with *your* people, but still I hate to think what man has made of man. . . . I don't think I can keep out of direct political work much longer— our "middle-class idealism" begins to disgust me.' So the November election of 1922 found her 'tub-thumping in Finsbury Park, a *horrid* job. . . . Why oh why has one a Quaker conscience? Six blessed electioneering meetings. . . . Of course our candidate [it was Miss Picton-Turberville] didn't get in.' In 1925, when the sound of blasting in a French quarry carried her back to the guns of the Marne, she was still 'feeling ashamed to be working for anything else but peace'. Yet she had found the pacifists impossible to work with. She had marched with them from the Embankment to Hyde Park ('*the* most disagreeable way of spending Saturday afternoon') and invited them to a garden-party at Dalmeny Avenue. 'They seemed such a feeble folk that it couldn't matter what they thought.'

She returned to the example of Roy Calvert, who at twenty-eight was not afraid to specialize, even within the field of penal reform. With Margery Fry's encouragement he gave up a Civil Service post and devoted the remaining years of his life to the one object of abolishing the death penalty. 'He wished', says Mrs Calvert, 'to see a general advance to an enlightened and rational humanity in the treatment of all lawbreakers, and viewing the campaign with the eye of a strategist he saw the Death Penalty as the stranglehold which enabled the forces of reaction to keep their ground.'[8] As early as the summer of 1921, Cecil Leeson and Margery Fry had seen the Lord Chancellor's secretary in the hope of hastening the appointment of a Royal Commission on Capital Punishment. 'He asked me to prepare a memorandum on the American law with regard to murder with proposals which he will submit to the King's Bench Judges!!! Of course I said I'd gladly knock off *that* trifle and am now in a corresponding funk.' While the quiet collection of statistics went on, the grim question was again blown into every eye by the execution of Henry Jacoby, aged eighteen, who had been recommended to mercy. There was more envelope-addressing at Dalmeny Avenue in preparation for a plebiscite of the League on Capital Punishment. Three hundred and forty-six members were shown to be in favour of abolition, twenty-eight were unwilling to pledge the League to any policy, 107 wanted the court to be empowered to substitute a sentence of imprisonment. After this the Howard League was openly for abolition.

Early in 1923, Margery Fry was '*terribly* exercised about the Thompson case. It has completely convinced me that capital punishment is all wrong and must be abolished.' Edith Thompson, condemned with her lover Bywaters for the murder of her husband at Ilford, was awaiting execution in Holloway, a stone's throw from Margery Fry's windows. On 6 January it was known that the appeal for a reprieve had failed and that the execution was fixed for the 9th. *The Times* commented on the 'artificial and unhealthy excitement which had surrounded the trial and the announcement of the verdict'. Again, as in France, Margery spared Lady Fry the grim details, except in so far as she had to justify herself, to show she was about serious business. She did not tell her mother that she had spent some time with Mrs Thompson in the condemned cell, taking her share in passing away those dreadful hours, feeling her way towards this 'flimsy personality',[9] as different from most of the people Margery Fry had met as she was from the popular idea of a

---

[8] Foreword to E. Roy Calvert, *Capital Punishment in the Twentieth Century* (5th edition, 1936).

[9] 'The Most Important Things', broadcast 12 May 1957 in the B.B.C. Home Service.

murderess. On Sunday afternoon, two days before the execution, Margery Fry was touched by the courage of a woman who went into Holloway to sing Negro spirituals to the prisoners: the singer's husband remembers how they were taken home to Dalmeny Avenue to have tea with Roger and Margery Fry and to sing again to the painted virginals.

For a couple of days capital punishment was discussed in *The Times* correspondence, meticulously balanced between pro and con. Then the subject was dropped: but not in the Howard League. *Some Facts regarding Capital Punishment*, which the League published in 1923, was Margery Fry's first publication except for her early poems in the *Nation* and her contributions to the *Howard Journal*. She faced Sir John Anderson, then Permanent Under-Secretary at the Home Office, in a

rather terrifying interview. . . . Not much more than 40, evidently fearfully able, not a person it would be any good to try to get round, altogether rather a splendid type. I don't know how much use it was, nor whether I told him anything he didn't know. He talked about sentimentalists. I said he probably thought I was one, but needn't, and he said, 'No, I was waiting to see what sort you were before I used the word.' When next I had anything on my chest, he would be glad to oblige by letting me get it off.

But, said Margery after another deputation six months later, 'I find I don't now particularly let myself get en- or dis-couraged by this kind of offer.'

The University Grants Committee and the Howard League (so curiously entwined that once she remarked that it was difficult to remember whether students were in for crimes or prisoners in for examinations) were her chief but not her only public preoccupations in the years at Dalmeny Avenue. These were the years of the Burnham Committee on teachers' salaries and she took seriously her membership of the Teachers' Superannuation Committee, partly because she believed there was 'not a soul on it who really knows what an elementary teacher feels like, with Michael Sadler and myself as rather doubtful exceptions'. It was a charmless committee from which she habitually returned feeling that her spine was 'like a set of unstrung beads'. 'They all think me pertinacious and a bore, but I do feel I *must* understand and be convinced about what I'm agreeing to.' She was also spending 'a lot of time at Somerville', having 'laid up some extra work by getting a Committee started about reorganizing the internal administrative work'.

In the autumn of 1923 the members of the Howard League were directed by a pretty little map of Margery Fry's design to its own office in Savoy Street—'A great bore for me . . . but it will make it, what it should be, less my show, and give it more stability in case of my being away or wanting to hand it over.' The office had become 'an almost self-running affair'. Mr Boucher died suddenly in 1924, a few weeks before the International Prison Congress in London towards which he and Margery Fry had been working for over a year. It was a personal loss, for Margery Fry had become a friend of the whole Boucher family ever since she had been asked to tea and had enjoyed the sight of the four children 'taking notes with terrific obviousness of all I said and did'. Bereft of a warm friend and the colleague who would have helped most, she went through the Congress, chairing meetings, managing the bookstall, attending service in the Abbey, lunching in Temple Hall, amused by the splendour of their entertainment, but wondering why 'the help of the unfortunate seemed to demand that *we* should eat and drink handsomely'. After Lady Astor had left a reception at Lancaster House, Margery Fry found herself 'the only woman among 60—and (far more dreadful) the only living thing without stars and medals all over me!' It was this Congress which drafted those minimum rules for international prison administration which were to send Margery Fry far afield in the years to come.

The other occupants of 7 Dalmeny Avenue (there was usually at least one other besides the Fry family and the two maids) had no sensation of living behind the shop when the Howard League occupied the front sitting-room. For some the room was associated less with penal reform than with the sound of the flute which Margery practised at all hours from the day in November 1919 when she began to take 'proper lessons'. In two years she found her way to one of those little amateur orchestras which still cling pertinaciously to life in classrooms all over London. 'After three perfectly lost occasions I found my way a little and found it a *wild* excitement. . . . It really sounded rather lovely when it *did* come in right, amongst all the violins and cellos.' After much discussion over the extravagance she and Roger bought a gramophone. In her fiftieth year she wrote, 'It's odd how music gets to mean more and more to me. I can trace a quite new feeling, when I hear it anywhere about, of pricked ears.'

Her flute went with her on her journeys: in an empty carriage she would run over scales and arpeggios. There were days of painting in the sun with Roger, when, as Virginia Woolf describes in *Roger Fry*, they would set up their easels and sketch with astonishing speed. They stayed in Brittany in 'a rather too Bethlehemy inn', they introduced Marion Richardson to the artists of Provence, they toured Greece with Leonard and Virginia Woolf, by car, not on donkeys as twenty years earlier.

Sundays at Dalmeny Avenue, though unmarked by religious observances, were festive days. At home, everyone wore her best clothes. Sometimes Margery took her girls by tram and train to Epping Forest:

never very far from our kind [she wrote to Agnes in May 1920] and yet somehow we were soaked in air and sun and spring from 11 to 9, and the fact of a great many other people soaking too seemed to give rather a pleasant feeling that the pleasure wasn't a greedy one. It wd. have amazed you to see how many flowers survive that flood of trippers, butcher's broom and bog broom, and that candelabra-ish marsh buttercup: and there were whitethroats by the score out-shouting the children, and a father shrike feeding his baby almost in danger of a cricket-ball, and in the evening the nightingales chose the most walked-in paths to sing, loudly, but really rather badly.

There were always guests when Roger was at home. Once Margery Fry admitted there were disadvantages in living in a picture gallery, when she felt 'rather shattered after a tea-party of nine visitors, mostly not much expected'. Normally she was a brave hostess, believing parties to be 'like soups—if you put in whatever comes along they're all the better'. (She praised Lady Astor's talents in mixing parties.) Though formality and ostentation were scorned, hospitality was lavish by modern standards. It was an unpredictable household, not easily run, even by the efficient and even-tempered Flossie and her sister Mabel. Food was a protest against Mrs Beeton: salads of fruit or vegetables dressed by Roger or Pamela, a cider cup mixed by Margery with sprigs of woodruff from the garden floating in it. Though Flossie was unnerved—and too proud to ask advice—when Lady Fry sent up a brace of pheasants from Somerset—she learned to use the Provençal recipes Roger found for her, including that *boeuf-en-daube* which at this time found its way to Mrs Ramsay's table in *To the Lighthouse*.

The spirit that moved the Omega Workshops cannot be re-created from a range of objects in a museum gallery or from a photograph of an interior 'furnished throughout' for Lady Cunard or the Cadena Café. Margery and Roger Fry set out their houses as they chose, mixing old and new. They painted doors and fireplaces in flowing patterns because it was fun to paint them, not because they wished to impress other people. Margery liked warm colour, but to plan a rigid colour scheme would have seemed to her as vulgarly manipulative as to dye her hair. At eighty years, as at eight, she painted birthday cards for her sisters, laying on with love the orange and purple, the touch of gilt. She and Roger and his friends abhorred drabness, but were not devoted to tidiness and polish. They remained Victorians in their dependence on servants, but they were finding a way towards a culture which did not rest on domestic slavery. Perhaps the Omega Workshops were not as esoteric as some of their modern critics believe. Marion Richardson, at least, went back to the elementary schools from the Frys, invigorated by their understanding and appreciation.

The writers of some of the most significant books of a decade, *The Waste Land, The Economic Consequences of the Peace, Queen Victoria, A Passage to India, To the Lighthouse,* sat at some time on the Omega chairs around the table which Roger had painted, or talked in the garden under Chinese lanterns. They came not as captured lions but as comfortable friends. There were the art dealers, the emphatic German critics, the young painters whose works had to be bought and sometimes hung in the bathroom, the Russian ballet people. By the end of 1920 the house in Dalmeny Avenue had sent out its own book, *Vision and Design,* dedicated by Roger Fry 'to my sister Margery, without whose gentle but persistent pressure this book would never have been made'.

Then in the early summer Roger was gone, to France or Italy. Margery and Pamela would sleep out in the garden. A bunch of old Birmingham students would come for a reunion. The past, on which Margery Fry rarely had time to dwell, returned with her friends: Eleanor Rathbone, already fighting for family allowances, writing *The Disinherited Family*; Dorothy Scott, bringing news of Margery's brilliant school-friend, Gertrude Hildesheim, whom she had seen getting off a bus, an old, grey woman scraping a living by making jewellery; Lucy Kempson; Nelly Bosanquet and her children, including Lucy, at eleven years old taller than her godmother—'I don't know when I've felt so near a young thing—a reckless naughty tongue and a jolly clear head'; Jeanne Lepetit, near and faithful from Hagley Road to the Marne and for the rest of Jeanne's life; Marjorie Rackstraw home at last from her years under the Quaker star of the 'War Vics'.

Then even Pamela was gone, painting in Paris, and Margery was leading for days at a time 'a quiet old maid's life with Flossie and the cats'. 'A party, a thing that hardly ever happens to me,' she wrote after an evening at the Stracheys' in Gordon Square. She could not use an evening dress, she told Lady Fry, for she hardly ever went out, 'almost never, when Roger is away'. A week later she was sitting by Lord Eustace Percy at Lady Astor's house in St James's Square: 'a dinner for lions (a few M.P.'s) and lots of Xtians (strenuous Women Workers)'.

She was living in a world of contrasts, and though left hand and right kept their counsel there was no division in the mind that governed them. From the house where free minds overflowed in shapes and colours, in the sound of flute and virginals, she went down, one Armistice Day, to address the boys' wing of a prison. They had made a model of the Cenotaph in cardboard. One prisoner, a war orphan, laid on it a wreath of poppies. After the two minutes' silence Margery Fry had to speak. She spoke of the value of ordinary people: a bus conductor who was cheerful on a murky afternoon, a neighbourly washerwoman. From the company of Roger's friends, who were fiercely eliminating all the rubbish of the years which seemed to block the way to happiness, she went to the juvenile court where the father of a pale boy, working on a van till nine o'clock six evenings in the week, remarked, "'E's as 'appy as 'e's any call to be.'

She shared with Roger's friends the talk of books and pictures, the memories of people and places, but she would not talk to them about her work. Partly she feared, as always, to seem 'bigotty': but also, among artists of greater gifts than her own, where she had always wanted to be, she now found herself to be a kind of puritan, resisting the ways of the artist as unmistakably as her Quaker forebears. A compulsion which Margery herself felt to be ugly forced her to tell Virginia Woolf at Delphi that her eagles were really vultures. When that beautiful concentration of the writer, more compelling even than Margery's own, was turned on to her anecdotes of people, Margery would fall silent. The artist's licence threatened her own morality.

She remained outside the pattern of personal relationships, in a set in which personal relationships were all-important. Her own experiences of love lay outside the system. She was an old maid. A childlike vulnerability, the price of enduring youth, made use of 'a lot of opportunities for feeling out of it'. To Roger she wrote, when one of his friendships failed him, 'I do hate to think of you having that peculiar left-out feeling. I think I've suffered more from it myself than most people would guess—it's partly a result of that dreadful on-the-spotness we both suffer from, so that only a very good actor can deceive us.'

She was rarely censorious. She believed that an honest devotion to happiness was a cleaner thing than the compulsive well-doing which had distorted the lives of some of her contemporaries. But once, reviewing Clive Bell's essay 'On British Freedom' in the *Howard Journal*, she chastised the limitations of hedonism.

If the only infringements of liberty in the modern State were those which limit people in Mr. Bell's position from seeing Restoration plays on a week-day, or getting their glass of wine at midnight, the attainment of freedom would be comparatively simple. But the problem which the State has to solve in relation to drink and to drugs is not simply its treatment of some poor devil who chooses to drown his misery in them, but of powerful organizations which thrive on producing such poor devils.

No bones were broken. Roger Fry's friends liked her fine impatience. But perhaps, on their side also, there was a lack of ease: like that of Lily Briscoe, the painter, and Carmichael the poet in *To the Lighthouse*, when they saw Mrs Ramsay go off poor-peopling with her basket—

One could not imagine Mrs. Ramsay studying painting, lying reading, a whole morning on the lawn. . . .

It was her instinct to go, an instinct like the swallows for the south, the artichokes for the sun, turning her infallibly to the human race, making her nest in its heart. And this, like all instincts, was a little distressing to people who did not share it. . . . Some notion was in both of them about the ineffectiveness of action, the supremacy of thought. Her going was a reproach to them, gave a different twist to the world, so that they were led to protest, seeing their own prepossessions disappear, and clutch at them vanishing.

Hovering between science and magic like a philosopher of the seventeenth century, always curious about strange skills, Roger Fry discovered a graphologist. He sent up a specimen of his sister's writing, which was thus interpreted:

Immense personal value, great practical ability, extraordinary consciousness of her own and other people's forces. A little too much introspection but corrected by mental quickness and physical activity. Possibility of unhappiness but corrected by balance of mind and sense of humour. Wonderful truth and frankness of expression. Fearless in every sense. Freedom from self-consciousness. Splendid values of every kind—a real personality. But she must be careful to have some real gaiety in her life. It is her protection—necessary to insure her continued strength, usefulness and happiness. She narrowly escaped at one time being a very unhappy person but was cured by ideality and common sense which form the balance so perceptible in her character. She will never change, you will find her just the same when she ought to be an old woman.

Margery was now over fifty and seen most vividly, perhaps, by people of a younger generation. They claimed her for their own time: they knew nothing in her of possibilities evaded or errors corrected, still less of any ambiguity in her present. As she appeared to them, so must she always have been. The pictured doors of 7 Dalmeny Avenue were opened for them. They moved among the coloured furniture, the Chinese bronzes, the pots signed by the craftsman's fingers. They saw on the walls the passionate figures of Rouault, Derain's dark grove, a poppy-field by Seurat, a blue ship by Matisse, a loaf of bread by Marchand which reminded Margery of Buddha in its calm.[10] They felt a strange expansion of their own faculties: they could go out from that place to unlimited adventures. Yet for them also, as for Margery herself at her first coming into Dalmeny Avenue, there was a kind of home-coming: for under all they were aware of a security of love.

[10] Some of these pictures are now in the Courtauld Gallery, Woburn Square, W.C.1.

XI

Principal of Somerville: 1926-1930

AFTER the International Prison Congress of 1925 the country of every delegation, except Spain, was persuaded to fill in for the Howard League a questionnaire on capital punishment. Roy Calvert had by then joined the staff in Savoy Street as secretary for the National Council for the Abolition of the Death Penalty. Margery Fry continued, with no sense of remission, to support the campaign, but was able to give more attention to the other concerns of the Howard League. The image of Jericho, lingering from her childhood Sundays, no longer seemed applicable: walls, though cracked, did not topple. The forces of reform advanced by inches, and advances had to be held by incessant watchfulness.

In November 1925 she gave evidence for the League to the Finlay Committee on Poor People's Defence. In 1923 the Poor Persons' Rules of 1903 were clearly due for revision. The Rev. H. R. L. Sheppard and the Rev. Scott Lidgett led a petition for an official inquiry to be extended to the whole problem of Law and Poverty. A committee was promised by the Lord Chancellor. A year later no action had been taken and a letter in *The Times*, signed by leaders of the Anglican and Free Churches, again raised the issue of justice for the poor. The Finlay Committee was set up in April 1925.

Throughout this period of pressure Margery Fry was working behind the scenes. With Miss Tuckwell of the Magistrates' Association she had drawn from Sir Claude Schuster of the Lord Chancellor's Department the first assurance that Poor Persons' Defence would be examined. Roger Fry found a friend, Mr J. J. Withers, to support the cause in Parliament. Margery Fry again presented the Howard League with a clear-cut objective: to extend legal aid to courts of summary jurisdiction. These courts, she pointed out, had given in one year sentences amounting to 2,725 years of prison: and many of these sentences provided an introduction to prison. She supposed that it was extremely rare for an innocent person to be sentenced, 'but justice dare not be satisfied with an average: though she can never reach perfection, nothing but perfection must content her'.[1]

The opponents of reform argued that there were many prior claims on public money. To this Margery Fry replied that 'justice should certainly not be the privilege of the well-to-do because money is short. If we came fresh to this idea we should be horrified at the very thought, but we have grown up with it and so are used to its cynicism.'[2] Eleanor Rathbone gave evidence to the Committee. So did Margery Fry's new fellow worker, Mrs Rackham, who spoke for the Standing Committee of Industrial Women's Organizations. Cecil Leeson represented the Magistrates' Association. A prison governor and a prison chaplain were also heard.

The Home Office took no action on the Finlay Committee's report. In July 1926 the Howard League began to draft its own Bill and Roger's friend, now Sir John Withers, became its foster-father. R. H. Turton, a member of the Parliamentary Penal Reform Group, twice won first place in the ballot for Private Members' Bills, in 1929 and 1933. It was in this way that the Poor Prisoners' Defence Act of 1930 and the Summary Jurisdiction (Appeals) Act of 1933 became law. The Howard League could take credit for a new system of legal aid for prisoners brought to trial in criminal courts.

Long before this was achieved, however, there had been a change of secretary in the Howard League. In the autumn of 1925 the resignation of Miss Penrose from Somerville College came as 'rather a bombshell'. In her sixty-eighth year the retirement of the great Principal cannot have been unexpected: the shock to Margery Fry was the sudden approach of this destiny which she had seen ahead, through other people's eyes, for over twenty years. She tried to assure her family and herself that her lack of degree put her out of the running, but by Christmas she was 'bothered and harried' by the necessity of a decision. She remembered vividly how after six years the weariness of institutional life had driven her even from University House, which still seemed, after all her university visits, the best communal house she knew. She had been a member of the Somerville College Council since 1904; through her whole adult life she had been active in college affairs. She went back to Somerville as often as to Failand, often enough to lose no affection and to grow no illusions.

[1] Address to the Howard League A.G.M., 1927.   [2] Ibid.

It was the importunity of Mildred Pope, in her 'utter simplicity and great learning, her complete selflessness',[3] which in the end Margery could not withstand. 'Du reste,' wrote Roger Fry to Provence, 'ce n'est que pour la moitié de l'année; car les vacances à Oxford sont gigantesques.' 'The Prison Reform treadmill', he wrote to their mother, 'has got worse and worse of late and more routine-like and mechanical. Indeed for long I've been urging her to find a way out of that.' He was disappointed that after seven years in London Margery was still obscure. He had lived among artists, people who left their signature upon their work. Margery seemed to be wearing her life away on the projects of smaller people. He wanted to see her initiate some personal work. Perhaps in Oxford she would found a science of penal psychology.

In moments of fatigue plenty of expressions of disgust for social reform and social reformers had no doubt passed between this uninhibited pair. But Margery had accepted for herself, as for others, the necessity of drudgery. She was living in London the life of an artist as surely as when she put up her easel beside Roger's in Greece or Provence. As Roger and his friends manipulated paint and clay, Margery overcame the apathy or hostility she met in an inter-view or a public meeting. In fact, she and her brother had similar talents, for he is remembered less as a painter than as a teacher who drew the eyes of less gifted people to repentance and new life. The awakening of an official in the Home Office, the sense of value communicated to a Labour Party worker collecting a subscription, exist as personal memories for hardly more than half a century; but no isotype can trace their effects, their power of survival.

In Dalmeny Avenue, Margery had achieved a family life more complete than any of her unmarried friends had found possible. Now Julian had gone from Cambridge to a ranch in British Colum-bia, Pamela was married and living in Paris. Roger had found at last a fulfilling relationship, a 'marriage without a formula'.[4] The logic of events had to be accepted. Lady Fry was told that, for greater convenience, Roger was moving to a house opposite the Russell Square tube station, where Margery would have her own room to accommodate her frequent visits from Oxford to London. She had already opened her heart to his new partnership. It remained only to make it as acceptable as she could to his unworldly sisters.

[3] From a letter from Margery Fry to Agnes Fry, after the death of Prof. Pope in 1956.
[4] *Roger Fry*, p. 255.

On her thirty-sixth birthday, in her one surviving letter to her brother Portsmouth, she had said to herself and him: 'as one grows older . . . one sees that the limits for each of us are pretty clearly set and that where and when we reach them there will never be any lack of better people to go on working out the great will which I suppose gives us all the meaning we have as individuals or as parts of a greater whole'. Though in twenty years she had come to speak with greater reluctance about the meaning of life, she felt no less dispensable. There were a few anxious weeks while she searched among her acquaintance for a successor at the Howard League. Then, on a visit to Oxford, she heard of Miss Cicely Craven, who had gone from teaching to wartime service in the Ministry of Pensions and the Ministry of Labour, and had then returned to teach history at St Hilda's Hall. When she met Cicely Craven, Margery Fry knew that her search was at an end. It was Miss Craven who brought into the Howard League Albert Lieck, Chief Clerk of Bow Street Magistrates' Court, who in June 1926 began to draft the Bill for Poor People's Defence. Lord Henry Cavendish Bentinck then became President of the League and Margery Fry became chairman. Over the years she descended in status, though not in concern, to vice-chairman and finally to committee member.

One dream now remained before she had to awake, a Rip Van Winkle, in Somerville College. In the years with Roger she had become a European. To her mother (who shared her Southern colouring and love of the sun) she spoke of Provence as 'the cradle of our race', though no grounds were ever discovered for the fantasy. Now she longed to travel beyond Europe. She would visit Julian in British Columbia.

There was a trail of former students, of groups wanting to hear about the Howard League, all the way across Canada. Margery found herself 'under a sky so clear as to seem as if it covered a wider arch than it does at home'. But at Saskatoon she still lacked any sense of 'abroadness'. The Indians were 'disillusioning', the woods suggested 'Corot rather than Fenimore Cooper', the university was 'in almost oppressively good taste'. As to the non-Indian natives, 'their politeness and helpfulness and real courtesy are perfectly delightful', but their parties 'are almost insupportable—tea parties, bridge teas, bridge lunches, bridge suppers every day'. At last she came to Vancouver Island, to the home of Edward and Eleanor West, former fellow workers at Sermaize. With them she saw sixty different wild

birds. She pressed some unfamiliar flowers and posted them to
Agnes. She gave yet another talk on penal reform to a women's club
in Victoria (where a Howard Society still flourishes) and by the end
of August was ready to set out with Edward West, 'for the great
plunge into the back-woods' of British Columbia.

At the end of the railroad, where the crowd waiting on a wooden
platform in the dim light looked like extras in a Western film, they
found Julian. He had brought a car for Edward to drive so that
Margery would not have to travel the whole rough way in his
wagon. The day that followed shone with simple delight. Edward's
stories brought to life the vast landscape which to a stranger would
have been featureless, incomprehensible. Margery saw in him the
dear colleague who had cared in a direct and practical way for the
people and the earth of the Marne valley. He was a mystic at a time
when philanthropy was more approved than mysticism in the Society
of Friends: yet he was one of the few Quakers whom Margery loved
as a personal friend.

Seventy miles from the ranch, where the road ended, they joined
Julian in his wagon. The tree-stumps along the trail were just low
enough for the axle to clear them. Occasional glimpses of telegraph
posts and wires, put up in the gold-rush, were the only human signs.
Birds, chipmunks, squirrels showed themselves unafraid. They
drove for miles beside a lake where Margery's companions pointed
out beavers and otters swimming. When they rested beside a trout-
stream, baby musk-rats ran over her boots. They spent a night as the
guests of a bearded character whom they called 'W. G. Grace', after
the cricketer whose face was as well known to the Late Victorians as
that of the great Queen herself. They fried bacon and bannocks for
supper and sat around the fire listening to tales of horse-thieves.
Margery with difficulty fought down a craving to boast of her own
ex-burglar friends. That night she slept in a tent, on a bed of spruce
boughs.

Julian's ranch, she wrote on her arrival, was 'quite delightful'.
The Indian summer was beginning: next evening Edward took her
out to watch the beavers building. A quiet old horse called John
Brown was provided for her: no one noticed, as he was harnessed, a
tiny sore place beneath the collar. Soon after they had forded the
river, broad and shallow between soft clay banks, John Brown suddenly rose on his hind legs and threw Margery on to a moss-grown
rock. She remembered afterwards thinking in her pain, 'I shall not

have to go to Somerville after all.' Edward left her covered with John Brown's blanket and dosed with Veganin she carried in her pocket. It was dark when he returned with Julian's partner. By lantern-light they made a stretcher and carried her through the knee-deep mud by the river to a dug-out canoe abandoned by some Indians. They laid the stretcher in the canoe and guided it across, up to their armpits in the dark stream. From the nearest telephone, ten miles away, Edward learned that the doctor was detained by a serious case in the hospital another twenty miles to the south. A car could be sent for the patient if they could prepare the road for it.

From miles around the men left their ranches and worked at the road, digging up the stumps which the wagon-axles had been able to pass. In four days a car, a large Buick, driven by a grave Indian, rocked up to the ranch for the first time. Margery was set upright on the front seat, bolstered by cushions. Three weeks later she wrote to Roger from the little hospital at Quesnel:

It's been a very queer experience, a little trip into a Hell which is in true medieval style a blend of horrid pain and grotesque humiliation with some real comedy. At present the pain looms largest—and the decency of people—which is a good reason for not telling you all the yarn till the more comic parts can get their full value. Edward West was wonderful as a nurse, Julian most tender and dear, a woman from 4 miles off simply gave up all her own work and came to look after me, and after nearly a week a doctor got out (he was himself lost for 12 hours on the way) and got me out here. The journey was almost impossible, 14 or 15 hours of car under morphia was so tiring that I wondered feebly whether one did die of fatigue pure and simple—I think I shall get *quite* over it, if ever this sciatic nerve can be got to behave again. Anyhow the air here is lovely and I sit out all day and Eleanor West has come up to be with me and I have retreated into one of those queer lakes of life which seem almost as if there were no way into them and no way out. I *want* to tell you lots of things I'm thinking . . . but though I'm persuaded that I *am* thinking rather brilliantly it all melts when I try to get it into words.

Her flute was beside her and in the evenings when the doors stood open the other patients called for hymn tunes. Disbelief was suspended in this inland sea of experience: for a few weeks the cold brain gave way to the readiness to listen and wonder which softened the austerity of Edward Fry's children. Another Oxonian, who had reported to the Government on tribal settlements, told her marvels of the psychic powers of Indians. The doctor had a story of a patient who worked at a secret gold-mine at 5,000 feet, knowing that when he became unconscious and the camp fire went out his old mare Jane, 'laying her head back, loping nice and steady', would go down to warn the nearest settlement to telephone for the doctor. Edward West rode with a patient recovering from a fall on a hayfork, back to a ranch unvisited for six months, and brought back stories of the wild calves who had never seen a man.

The doctors prophesied that her fatigue and nervousness might last for at least a year. She never, it seems, associated with her injury the miscellaneous aches she suffered from during her years at Oxford. For these she sought the by-ways of medical treatment, from a cure with Roger at Vichy, where 'life was arranged on a system of neatly balanced boredoms', to electrical treatment from 'a nice old bear, shaggy, toothless, dirty but intelligent . . ., currently reported to have used his artificial teeth in making one of his machines'. Few of her friends heard of her accident, or indeed of her Canadian adventures. She threw back her stories into the enchanted lake, but Edward West was there to catch them, and in old age to commit them to a tape-recorder.

In October she was clearing 7 Dalmeny Avenue, with the help of Pamela, who had come over to relieve her aunt 'of the terribly difficult decisions as to the disposal of many moth-eaten dolls and similar treasures'. Flossie was to see her mistress into her house in Oxford and then to return to marry George Riley, sometime member of the Sermaize *équipe*, later Mayor of Islington, handyman, house-decorator, and house-hunter to the Frys and the Bloomsbury remnant. Vanessa Bell claimed the future service of Flossie, and Virginia Woolf of her sister Mabel.

In November 1925 Margery Fry was at Somerville College receiving entrance candidates, one by one, 'in the same room, and I believe in the same chair, that I sat in, and rubbed a hole in nervous agitation through a perfectly new glove whilst Father and you interviewed Miss Maitland about me'. Whatever the outcome, a candidate rarely forgot her interview with Margery Fry. If she was called to the Principal's room at some social hour in the evening, she probably did not realize that the Principal had been kept late at her work. At any time there was something festive in Margery Fry's appearance: a string of fine beads, an embroidered jacket. A cat sitting on the desk would appear to take a wise interest in the conversation. By this time Margery Fry's journeyings had given her some acquaintance with any part of Britain a candidate might come from. She knew how to find out whether a girl had eyes and ears: if other topics failed, she would turn to the great picture above her head, which Uncle Lewis Fry had found in a barn and Roger had identified as a Poussin: she would show how Roger had compared its composition to music. She did not expect a girl to know at that stage exactly what she meant to do with her life. She knew the frustrations which awaited a clever or even an ordinary girl in the nineteen-twenties.

A few weeks before these first interviews she had told a large audience of school-leavers to take their pleasures seriously. They would soon become, not only typists, but librarians, house-decorators, domestic workers in institutions, photographers, hairdressers, gardeners, laboratory assistants. But Margery Fry knew that many were disappointed: she guessed that the hall contained at least twelve girls who felt that their real job was to be Clara Butts, thirty or forty Suzanne Lenglens, at least fifty Mary Pickfords. The trouble was that the world did not want people to do what they most wanted to do. Even the people who were doing the work they most desired to do found that a great deal of it was drudgery. People should realize that this was a general law, not an individual hardship. Acceptance of some drudgery gave significance to leisure: it must be more than recreation for further drudgery. She knew well enough the special problems of women in estimating the claim that other people should make on their time. But in their own time they must do as they liked, resisting 'the pressures to take their pleasures wholesale'. For example, to buy a ready-printed piece of fancy-work and to stitch over another person's pattern in another person's choice of colours was to accept more drudgery and pay someone else for the fun.

Now, to these other schoolgirls who were looking forward to three or four years at Oxford, the new Principal of Somerville presented this unexpected idea of fun. Some of the candidates, she saw at once, were splendid, confident creatures. Most were in some way apprehensive, worried by their responsibility to their schools, to their families, to the world. They left Margery Fry, as people had left her paternal grandmother, prepared to take 'a bright and trustful view'.

Margery Fry did not intend to be seen always behind a desk or presiding at high table. The somewhat meagre quarters provided for the Principal were unsuitable for 'the kind of informal entertainment' which, she told her mother, 'has been almost entirely lacking'.

The idea of the Head of a House (even a women's college) 'living out' did not appeal to the Vice-Chancellor, but when Miss Darbishire offered to vacate Radcliffe House, most conveniently situated in an alley off the Woodstock Road, a compromise was found. A 'rabbit-run' was made from Radcliffe House to the College and most of the students believed the house to be the Principal's official residence, which it has since become.

She invited the students to coffee after dinner, half a dozen at a time, or issued general invitations for listening to records. Roger Fry had taught her to despise cosiness; Radcliffe House was less soaring than the houses of her choice, but in the long, low sitting-room the Omega furnishings, the pictures by Roger Fry and Duncan Grant took on a particular gaiety. It was, one scout was said to have commented, more like a circus than a lady's room. The undergraduates (whom Margery Fry persisted in calling, in her provincial fashion, students) were delighted by the open brick hearth, above which Roger Fry had painted flamboyant patterns. They sat on embroidered cushions thrown on the striped carpet, choosing records from the small library of Bach, Mozart, and Gluck, winding and rewinding the gramophone. The Principal, focusing but not dominating the group, sat relaxed and undemanding in a low chair, her evening dress turned back with an old-fashioned carefulness from her heavy black silk petticoat.

She had cut her hair short: one white lock still shone out against the dark grey. Out of doors she wore a bright red coat for which she had painted large wooden buttons. When, wearing a blue mandarin coat, she played in the Oxford Orchestral Society (then 'a bit of a scrimmage', to which Lettice Fisher had introduced her) the undergraduates gathered round to look at her silver flute, a present from the Howard League. No wonder that Professor Alexander, presenting her for an honorary doctorate at Manchester a few years later, called her a Pied Piper. When she walked into the College the students thought: 'Here comes one of our own sort.' There was that brightness in the air which a later observer compared to a miraculous increase in the wattage of all the electric lamps.

Yet even the undergraduates, especially the veterans of the Third Year, were not sure whether they wanted a Pied Piper as a Principal. Margery Fry rightly surmised that they thought it rather undignified for her to want to know them better. They could not dissociate the image of her office from the 'tall sequestered dignity', as Winifred Holtby described it, of Miss Emily Penrose. In 1889 Miss Penrose, a daughter of the Director of the British School at Athens, had gone up to Somerville at the age of thirty-one, knowing according to her own account a little modern Greek and no Latin. This 'gap in her classical training', as Miss Farnell calls it, did not prevent her from becoming in three years the first woman to take a First in Greats. Immediately afterwards she became Principal of Bedford College. She had been Principal of Somerville for nineteen years.

Patience and circumspection were qualities which Margery Fry had learned: in Miss Penrose they were essential. She had met the University on its own terms. She had insisted that the women of Somerville should go through the melancholy qualifying examinations of the University at a time when such labour seemed pointless. In 1920 the Women's Statute allowed degrees to be granted to those who had qualified. It was gained without heat: in the words of the *Oxford Magazine* it came 'unsolicited, in response to no deputation'. 'It was certainly due mainly to Miss Emily Penrose's statesmanlike vision, unfailing wisdom and powers of leadership', says Miss Farnell, 'that the Oxford women owe their admission to full membership of the University in 1920.'[5]

Before the war ageing Somervillians had already begun to lament the disappearance of the simple devotion to the College which they had known under Miss Maitland. During Miss Penrose's nineteen years the College had become a maturing, self-questioning community. Some of the old institutions had perished, among them that Parliament where Eleanor Rathbone and Margery Fry had made their first speeches. College societies were neglected as the more brilliant and confident women began to live in the University. A few weeks before Margery Fry arrived as Principal a Somervillian, Miss Lucy Sutherland (later Principal of Lady Margaret Hall), had spoken in the Union, supported by Richard Acland and Dingle Foot. She opposed the motion 'That Women's Colleges should be levelled to the ground'. The motion was carried by twenty-five votes, but at least a woman had spoken.

It was the intelligent, confident young women, enjoying the life which she herself would have enjoyed, who appealed to Margery Fry's imagination. It was not altogether clear what she could do for them. Certainly they did not need her to produce their plays. She

[5] *A Somervillian Looks Back*, p. 31.

could polish their rhetoric in a speakers' class, she could encourage
the formation of a University Dance Club. She could help the officials to look beyond their own college, forming intercollegiate clubs
and committees; to look in time beyond their own university, by
affiliation with the National Union of Students, though it is only in
the 'sixties that the participation of Oxford in national student
affairs has become really active.

Academically, her students had other advisers. Most of these
were no longer young. Four of the tutors had been in the College
when Margery Fry left in 1904, three of them already as tutors. She
found them, she told her mother, 'the same band of loyal, first-rate,
intelligent, over-busy people as ever'. She had never lost touch with
them for more than a few months at a time, but while she had been
out in her various worlds, jack of several trades, master of none (in
her own words), they had been winning in the University a respect,
if not a status, for their scholarship. Dedication to truth was a rarity
which Edward Fry's children honoured. Scientific advance affected
Margery Fry with awe: yet she could not accept as the only commendable way of life the strict specialization on which advance
depended. The sacrifices of the scholarly life, of Browning's Gram-
marian, were, she believed, required of very few. Even in the
rigorously selected minority at Somerville there would not be many
original scholars. It began to be suspected by some of the sharp-
witted and not always deeply dedicated young women that the
Principal was not wholly on the side of hard work, that those who got
a Third in Honour Moderations were not necessarily in her eyes, as
in those of the classics tutor, 'lost souls'. Some of the dons reflected
that it had been otherwise in Miss Penrose's time.

Yet there was no laxity. Miss Fry was, as at Birmingham, 'awfully
strict'. The stately arm-in-arm procession to dinner continued,
late-comers could not avoid the awful necessity of bowing to the
high table. Though Margery Fry herself felt no need for the trap-
pings of authority, she bore them with dignity as long as the College
wanted them. She left nobody in doubt that membership of Somerville College was a privilege that carried responsibility.

The Friends' Meeting in Oxford had in thirty years entirely
changed. Arthur Gillett, one of the leading Oxford Quakers, was an
old friend of Margery Fry and a member of Somerville College
Council. But she made no contact with the Friends' Meeting and
though she retained her nominal membership of the Society her

withdrawal was respected. Somerville College was notoriously the home of 'Turks, infidels and heretics': it had never possessed a chapel: and indeed from this issue had arisen the foundation of two women's halls in Oxford instead of the one originally planned. It was after Margery Fry's time that the College received the controversial gift of 'a house of prayer for all nations'. But some kind of informal religious practice had continued in the College from the beginning. Sunday evening prayers, held in the hall before the cold supper known as 'nondescript', were voluntarily attended by members of the College, including the servants, and approximated to the 'readings' of old Quaker families. Margery Fry handed over even this undoctrinal worship to volunteers from the Senior Common Room. Sunday evening prayers became hazardous occasions, testing both for congregation and minister: but through all hesitancies those two principles remained clear which Margery Fry was in the end able to enunciate as 'the purposes which I believe we must, at our highest and most truly human level, take as giving meaning to life': Reverence for Life, Reverence for Truth. 'They have', she said later, 'been embodied to a wider or narrower extent in the ethics of nearly all the great religions of the world, yet the human beings who have lived by them are rare indeed.'[6]

She wanted every student to make some mark in life. This, the theme of her first address to the College, delivered in the ringing tones which disguised her own recurrent uncertainty about her value, was found rather shocking by some of the older women. Though the students no longer wore hats, the idea of what was proper behaviour for the average Oxford woman had changed curiously little since Miss Shaw-Lefèvre's time. Avoidance of 'stage-tricks and vulgarity' could still excuse a tentative and ineffective footing on the scene of life. In 1893 the students of Somerville had appeared to Margery Fry's young arrogance to be, with few exceptions, a dull lot. Sometimes she found them no less dull in 1926: but she knew them to be talented, and she knew that the world needed every talent that could be dug up and used.

She could have eased the lot of some of her students if she had taken them in hand from the very beginning, like the girls at Hagley Road. This was hardly possible. Somerville was growing up too quickly to admit even the shadow of a matriarch. The students said, and sometimes believed, that other women's colleges were inhabited

[6] *What I Believe*, p. 59.

by ladies or girls, Somerville exclusively by women. In some colleges the students were urged to behave discreetly because they were lucky to be in the University. In Somerville also discretion was their tutor, but they believed the University was lucky to have them. The open fire burning daily in each student's room was a symbol of privacy and independence. The regulations imposed by the University were generously interpreted: Miss Fry was not the only member of the Senior Common Room who kept the letter of the law by lending her sitting-room on wintry days to bona-fide engaged couples. She believed that to be ruthless with slackers, to provide students with opportunities of meeting mature people, was a sounder discipline than the raising of artificial barriers between men and women students. She taught her students that worldly wisdom was necessary to avoid frittering away their strength 'in a multitude of insignificant skirmishes with authority. . . . I believe that intelligent young people are more alienated by the confusion of the expedient with the right than by anything else, and if the two issues are presented honestly and separately they can be greatly trusted in all major matters, though in minor ones their taste will not always be impeccable.'[7]

For some students money was the sternest disciplinarian. Public funds were beginning to outbid the small resources which the women's colleges could offer to poor scholars: girls were coming up as commoners with state and county scholarships. Such benefits were not intended to provide luxuries or even maintenance in vacations. Paid vacation work was almost unobtainable. Though the women's colleges watched with tender care over their needy members, it was still hard going for the really poor student. There was little gaiety in the poverty of the 'twenties. Marks and Spencer had not yet achieved their social revolution. Students could be found in the School of Modern Languages who had never had the chance to cross the Channel. Though it was possible to live and write in London on two pounds a week, two pounds a week were uncommonly hard to come by. The frugal pleasures of poor students in the 'twenties strangely resembled those of 1893, except that coffee had replaced cocoa: nor were there any dinner-parties in North Oxford. They still met for tea in one another's rooms, sampled sermons, cycled out to gather Cumnor cowslips. They did not guess that their

[7] Margery Fry, 'Co-education in University Life', in *Advances in Co-education*, ed. L. S. Woods (Sidgwick and Jackson, 1919).

brilliant Principal had once passed the same way, though they knew that her hand was prompt and practical in a financial crisis.

By the late 'twenties it was already extremely difficult for a woman graduate to get a job without further training. Teaching was virtually the only professional training for which a subsistence grant was paid. Many students were thus committed to teaching even before they set foot in Somerville. Rising academic standards had only bound women more tightly to the wheel which carried them from school to college and back to school again. Headmistresses were flooded with applicants for every post they advertised and some of them exploited the situation. Recent graduates were set to try out their undigested scholarship and their lack of teaching technique in junior forms, while sixth-form teaching went as a reward for long service. Young teachers were told what to wear and where to live: they were often treated, in fact, like unmarried daughters in a nineteenth-century family.

At the end of the war Margery Fry had cared more passionately about education than about any other cause. Far on into the 'thirties she was still hoping that the social gap between elementary and secondary teaching would be bridged and that graduates would make their contribution to a unified state system. But she saw that to go on pouring Somerville graduates, regardless of their suitability, into this 'everlasting schoolmarming' was good neither for the graduates nor for the schools nor for Somerville itself. Her apparent distaste for schoolmarming, like her agnosticism, found crude interpreters: there was a certain feeling among the younger members of the College that teaching, like the practice of religion, was an activity for second-class minds.

Margery Fry did not, in fact, care much about the grading of minds. She did not think her graduates should despise non-intellectual jobs. She liked, for instance, to imagine them in trade, honestly distributing good things. Like all her generation at Oxford, she most earnestly wanted her students to marry and bring up families. Though maids from tidy homes in Durham and South Wales were then plentiful, marriage was still considered a full-time career.

Finding that one girl at least had no idea how babies were conceived and born, Margery Fry invited Dr Winifred Cullis to talk to the students. The object of this talk was not the avoidance of scandal, though Margery Fry shared the faith of her progressive contemporaries that uninhibited knowledge would solve most problems:

she hoped rather that the students would be helped to make the best of life, even of the second-best single state which was bound to be the destiny of some. She did not want them to live at the mercy of emotions they did not understand. As always, the students were wary of this solicitude. At the end of the academic year Margery Fry saw herself in the going-down play as the Governess of Pentonville, eyeing her chairman's notes through a silver tea-strainer and informing her charges that they were not solid all through.

The small group of scientists and mathematicians had no tutor in College. Margery Fry gave much of her time to them, lending them books, discussing general affairs, getting them to speak and write. Dr Wrinch, the science tutor shared by the women's colleges, was a married woman: Margery Fry soon became a 'godless godmother' to her daughter. Laboratory work broke the easy pattern of the Oxford day which had been accepted from the beginnings of Somerville Hall. In every sense the science students seemed to look to the future. In 1929 Dorothy Crowfoot, later a Nobel prize-winner, entered Somerville; by her marriage to Thomas Hodgkin, whom she met in Margery Fry's house, she became her kinswoman.

'All goes as usual, tant bien que mal, little worries, little successes, all rather small beer,' Margery wrote to Failand early in 1927. The weeks seemed strangely slow. She went bird-watching with Hilda Lorimer. She bought a white rabbit-skin scarf against the chill of Oxford dining-rooms. A few old friends, such as the Fishers of New College, invited her to dine privately. She could not, of course, be invited to high tables, except in women's colleges. She saw a verse-play by Yeats produced by her old teacher, Constance Masefield, at Boar's Hill. As she slowly paced the wintry garden paths with her old cousins, Robert and Monica Bridges, she heard how he was finishing a long poem called *The Testament of Beauty*.

Lapped round by floods, Oxford that winter became even more introvert than in fair weather. According to Margery's letters home, a storm in a tea-cup was brewing, 'all the horrid stale tea-leaves swilling around violently'. The Union motion against the women's colleges had been the first attack in a campaign of reaction against the acceptance of women in the University. 'I believe really people can't get on here without a row now and then to enliven things, and circulars and meetings and canvassings and votings are meat and drink to them. I *hate* these things.' Two hundred and ten members of Congregation had petitioned the Hebdomadal Council to limit the numbers of women in each college by University Statute. When the colleges offered to limit themselves (having no desire or resources for expansion at this time) their suggestion was rejected because they refused to promise at the same time to vote against the foundation of any new college for women in Oxford.

The proposed Statute was debated in the Sheldonian Theatre on 14 June 1927. The women had chosen the Principal of Somerville to speak for them in support of Mr Cyril Bailey, Fellow of Balliol. It was, she told Lady Fry, 'a very nervous occasion. I was wobbly with fright.' According to *The Times*, 'There was a large attendance of members of Congregation, and a considerable number of visitors in the galleries.' The Sheldonian was packed to the roof, simmering with hostility. Yet there was no incivility in Sir Walter Riddell's opening: he merely demonstrated that the women's colleges were not as other colleges, being created by the University itself, 'and the University must retain the right to vary its attitude to its own creations'. It was assumed without argument both by him and by Dr Hazel of Jesus College that a ratio of one to four was the maximum proportion of women tolerable at Oxford. Dr Hazel thought the ratio was generous. He mistrusted the women's own by-laws, adding somewhat inelegantly that he believed, not in adding another hurdle, but in shutting the stable door.

Margery Fry had once literally marched with the suffragettes, and had more than once defended the fighters for the women's cause against Lady Fry's gibes. But equal citizenship had never, as Eleanor Rathbone had hoped, deeply engaged her interest. By the mid-'twenties she had by-passed the battle. She had always looked for opportunities rather than for status, and it happened that since 1904 she had never in her work suffered a disability, or had to claim a privilege, because of her sex. Women, she told Congregation, did their best work as human beings, not as women. She hinted that women were feared in academic competition. She asked whether anyone supposed that the withdrawal of women from the University would affect the changes which had taken place in a generation in the social relations of men and women. In the interests of university peace, she deplored the prolongation of a 'women's question'.

More than one future member of the University Grants Committee applauded from the gallery and remembered Margery Fry's speech long after more delicate movements of university diplomacy

were forgotten. Yet even by some of the women she was not considered to have spoken wisely. Especially she had held up to ridicule
the silliness in high places which Miss Penrose had taken quietly for
granted. Her speech turned some votes, but the Preamble to the
Limitation Statute was approved by 229 to 164. Margery Fry knew
she had spoken well. Such occasions had always brought her an
accession of friends, new opportunities for action; but in Oxford she
became known as an aggressive feminist, a person to be avoided. Sir
Walter Riddell, however, expressed a wish to be on the Council of
Somerville College, and was appointed as University Representative
in the following year.

Nor did the young men and women avoid her. She had already
spoken at the Union, carrying her motion for penal reform easily—
'a nice audience, ready to lick up every point'. Miss Fry of Somerville was the obvious person to put all at ease as a chaperon to Marie
Stopes, when some men at Christ Church invited her to lecture.
Adrift from the domestic securities of Dalmeny Avenue, the experienced hostess found it 'a nightmare evening'. At dinner, she told
Roger,

the whole Mitre turned its astonished ears to our table. I tried to get a less
obstetrical conversation . . . by talking to her husband of the effect of
childish impressions on one's later tastes and enthusiasms and asked for
his. 'Mine', he declaimed in a ringing voice, 'were all pre-natal. When
my mother was pregnant with me . . . .' The meeting was worse: one lay
don, one canon, one head of the Jesuit Hall, about twenty blushing youths,
an enthusiastic American whose chief object in Europe was to hear Dr.
Stopes and die . . . . So Oxford creeps along.

In Somerville the students now came to see her uninvited, bringing their personal problems and even those of their friends and
relations. Personalities and conflicts seemed more complicated than
in the confident days in Birmingham: 'people are getting cracked or
wicked or worried all the time'. But the advice she gave was, whether
she knew it or not, comparatively unimportant. She was exercising
as a natural gift what others after her would try to learn as a technique: the power to set people at such ease with themselves that they
would begin to work out their own problems.

In 1927 the Association of Senior Members of the College
included an Octavia Hill house-manager and a bookseller who had
'forsaken teaching'. Dorothy Sayers was 'in advertising', a young

sister of Miss Lorimer was buying Oriental carpets—the only woman buying in the Bishopsgate markets—for West End stores. Dorothy Scott Stokes would soon be called to the Bar. These were still the significant exceptions. 'I've begun the annual business of interviewing students for careers,' she wrote early in 1928. 'Most of them would much rather *not* have any, but bread and butter demands it! No, that's rather a libel, but it is much easier to give advice to those who can choose freely. Happily some of them can, and I'm discovering a few new careers to vary the eternal schoolmarming for the others.'

In 1922 a writer in the *Howard Journal*—perhaps Margery Fry herself—had said that the Home Office Committee on Probation was 'sadly astray' in supposing that the service would not attract university people, adding, however, 'those with high Oxford or Cambridge honours are certainly not likely to be attracted': probation officers would more likely be forthcoming from the newer universities, from people whose 'home surroundings had given them early contact with the realities and difficulties of life'. A few Somervillians chose probation as a career in her time, but insist that they were not directed to it by Margery Fry herself. Penal reform was in the air, but there was no pressure to undertake it.

Those who were free to choose a career were the well-to-do: at every turn Margery Fry and her students were faced by the economic disorders of the time, which she rarely mentioned directly. She did what she could to help her students to find their way in a world which offered every kind of frustration. For some it had to be the 'eternal schoolmarming'. Some, after a year or two, found their way to other careers. One became an income-tax inspector. It was not entirely perversity which persuaded young women that inspecting taxes offered more interest than teaching children.

Margery Fry's great days of 'bricks and mortar' were over. It was impossible for the younger members of the College to imagine it without the Hall and Library or to associate the Principal with buildings of such venerable antiquity. The Penrose Building, rectangular, decent, institutional, had been designed by Harold Rogers in Miss Penrose's last years as Principal. It was opened in 1928. Only minor building projects could be initiated in Margery Fry's time. The entrance hall was paved in sea-blue Italian mosaic, the ceiling of a dismal common-room was lowered to make space for three little rooms, furnished by the college carpenter. Roger Fry refurbished the intractable area which then served as a passage as well as a Junior Common Room. When his sister suggested that some students should follow his example by painting their parents' drawing-room fireplaces in gold paint, they reflected how little the Principal knew about their parents and their fireplaces. But they began to look at the rooms they lived in. A going-down student, Miss Cochrane, for many years 'the anonymous donor', gave money for a reading-room. For this project, near to his sister's heart, Roger Fry found an architect, Morley Horder. The first books on the shelves (many of them written by visitors to Dalmeny Avenue), the periodicals on the hexagonal table brought to the students the visual arts, the contemporary writing which had no part in their academic discipline.

There was time at Oxford, as Roger had hoped, for Margery Fry to play with ideas, though not, as he had hoped, any loophole for her to enter its academic life (except for one occasion when, with Dr Moberly, she examined for a Diploma in Theology a student who had chosen Christian penology as her theme). In the paper on 'Having' which she read to the University Psychological Society in 1928, she developed the ideas of property which she afterwards presented to many audiences in many forms. It was Agnes Fry who first communicated to Margery her delight in Samuel Butler's notion of supplementary limbs. In 'Having', Margery tried to distinguish between these 'extensions of the person' (including steam and oil engines as 'detachable stomachs' giving energy from humanly indigestible materials) and those casual accumulations of property, 'six houses or twenty hats', to which the law gave equal sanction. She had asked advice from Mr Hartley Shawcross, then part-time secretary to the Howard League, she had gathered allusions from the Early Fathers to Boswell, from Defoe to William James, as well as from those ephemeral writers on animal behaviour to whom she gave interest and credence. The theme perhaps owed something to discussions with brother and sisters about the economic affirmations of their parents' generation: something also, perhaps, to the two little boys, widows' sons, who had received mysteriously a gift of scooters after being before the magistrates for borrowing rides.

The fun of 'Having', which had gone 'pretty well,' was obliterated by Roger's failure to get the Slade Professorship of Fine Art at Oxford. Even Roger admitted 'a mild shock of surprise' over his rejection. The *New Statesman* was heavily ironic: 'One would have thought that Mr Fry's combined qualities as critic and historian must be well-nigh unique: it is therefore all the more gratifying to know that England is rich enough in art-scholarship to permit Oxford University safely to dispense with his services.' The whisperings of petty politics went on, the 'teacup meteorology' of 'mediocrities entrenched in privilege'. 'The University', Margery Fry wrote to an old colleague who had escaped to a modern university years before, 'is almost non-existent as far as bringing any stimulus or interest into my life goes.'

In 1929 Somerville College was fifty years old. The Principal was invited to write a commemorative article for *The Times*. 'I don't know when I've written a thing which "came" with such great difficulty,' she told Lady Fry. Again, she looked back to Florence Nightingale, into the mind of a woman of genius, bound by the conditions of 1859, to modify her own misgivings about the academic life of 1929. She showed how the argument was taken up by J. S. Mill, 'a more adroit fighter', in *The Subjection of Women*. 'In Mill's essay, the argument for the emancipation of women is founded mainly upon the injury to the community as a whole from the loss of the trained services of able women. Even charity . . . demands the education, the thinking powers, of a skilful administrator.'

On 6 July the University Church of St Mary was packed to the doors for the Jubilee service. Five hundred guests dined in a great marquee in the College garden; and, as one of them found remarkable in such celebrations, everyone, from the Vice-Chancellor to the newest graduate, was served with the same meal. Mrs T. H. Green was there, her last appearance on a public occasion. There were speeches from Professor Gilbert Murray, from the Vice-Chancellor, references to Dame Emily Penrose's D.C.L., congratulations on Miss Rose Graham's D.Litt. 'What would you not give to hear a speech from one of *your* originals?' whispered Margery Fry to the Warden of All Souls as Miss Maude Thompson, a student of 1879, rose to compare herself to the original bus which had been brought out that same year to celebrate the London Omnibus Centenary. The last speaker was Eleanor Rathbone, newly elected M.P. for the Northern Universities.

For every guest who shook hands with the Principal there had been the moment of recognition, of significance: and 'where but in Somerville', asked Lucy Kempson, 'would the hostess of 800 guests have found time at a garden-party to mix the soap bubbles for the

MF—L

grandchildren according to the Only True Recipe?' 'The soup was fairly warm and the ices fairly cool and at least it's *done*,' the hostess wrote to her mother, for after the welcoming and handshaking she felt like that electric eel she had seen with her parents long ago in Naples, 'who had been squeezed by sightseers all day long till there was no shock left in him at all, at all'.

In the long vacation she went to Italy with Roger and Lowes Dickinson. 'In a way the triangle is perfect. Roger gets chess with Goldie and loves his company on the whole and in the abstract. I'm conscious sometimes that the feminine oil-can is useful applied to the wheels of a friendship so old as to partake, inevitably, of some of the rules of extreme familiarity.' It was from this holiday that she brought back those handsome beads which she wore for the rest of her life. They were threaded by her ninety-six-year-old mother and most of them were sold for Joan's allotment scheme in South Wales. The insatiable sightseeing sent her back to Oxford unrefreshed, 'feeling very old and incompetent and rather cynical about it all—wondering whether after all this work and worry the young things turn out more of people than they would without it—I *think* they do, but one ought to be younger than I am to keep sure of it'.

Yet at the beginning of its second half-century Somerville College was renewing its youth: young tutors were being discovered, Morley Horder was planning his brilliant development of the east quadrangle. The students were proud of their Principal, of her popularity in other colleges, of the visitors she brought to the high table, of her links with what were vaguely understood to be affairs of state. She had been present since 1893 at every great occasion in the College. No one who remained or returned there would be unaware of her. Yet by the autumn of 1930 she resisted those who urged her, for the sake of Somerville and the University, to stay longer. She rated her success in these years as Principal no higher than a knack of dealing with the young. Most of those to whom she had come nearest were indeed already privileged, by birth and early experience. On these her influence was immense, and through them its reach is still immeasurable.

She left Somerville College for the third time at the end of Hilary Term, 1931. 'We can only record our gratitude to her', said the Senior Members, 'for having given four years of her life.'

Miss Darbishire's blue damask curtains were rehung at the windows of Radcliffe House, Roger Fry's flamboyant patterns were painted out. The students learned to trust the integrity, the constant, unobtrusive kindness of their new Principal, to know her distinction of mind. Through some of the tutors there was daily contact with greatness. Yet some of the First Year students remembered, with a sense of deprivation, through all their three or four years at Somerville, the uncanny illumination of joy and confidence which had hung about them when, as schoolgirls, they left the Principal's room, one November evening in 1929.

XII

Penal Reform: 1926-1930

'MARGERY is here, like a boy come home for the holidays,' wrote Lady Fry early in 1930. She was then nearly ninety-seven, the Principal of Somerville nearly fifty-six. As long as Lady Fry was there to read and reread her daughter's letters, replacing them in their envelopes and seeing that they were tied, year by year, with pink tape to keep for posterity, Margery would remain 'her child, always her own child'.

All Lady Fry's children were good to her, scrupulously attentive to her wishes: but in Margery she saw herself, the part of herself which she could love. She watched her come in with a pile of new books, or the semicircular leavings of a beetle's breakfast found under a rose bush. Margery would bring out of the morning paper a cavalcade of living people, she would rage because she had never seen a bearded tit, she would make wicked fun of people who ought not properly to be laughed at—missionaries, cousins, her own exalted self.

For the childlike uncertainties revealed in Margery's letters, though she took no great pains to conceal them, were not generally visible. She was by now a public figure, described by journalists, called to mind whenever a list of distinguished women was in question—or indeed a list of people, men or women, needed to underwrite any humane cause. The graphologist's prophecy, that she would be 'always the same', was hidden from her fellow reformers: she was so acceptable that some of the fiercer spirits, in and out of the Howard League, began to fear that one day the radical might be lost in the quasi-official. She was the obvious choice for a deputation, but her charm was almost uncanny.

Though the hollowness within, the pain of homebreaking, lingered through her years at Oxford, there was no outward division between the rich years at Dalmeny Avenue and the remainder of her life. She brought to the University Grants Committee the immediacy of her concern for students. The Report for 1928–9 attacked the system of Board of Education Grants, called for new enterprise on University Appointments Boards. She went up to London 'a-choosing of Prison governors', fitting in here and there a prize-giving speech, but she no longer found it necessary to attend every meeting of the Howard League Committee or to go down to Scotland Yard to try for herself whether a new type of handcuffs would tighten in a struggle. Ex-prisoners, like other people, told her their troubles in detail, but the details of the Howard League administration were handed over to a younger and extremely able woman. Workers for the Howard League after 1926 have no doubt that they belonged to Miss Craven's time. The numbers of those who paid their guinea for penal reform remained small, but the executive of the League continued to hold and attract gifted people.

During most of her period as Principal Margery Fry was serving on the Street Offences Committee. When in 1925 a question concerning payment of prostitutes' fines took her by surprise, her immediate reply was, 'A girl who is morally in danger is still a citizen with liberty to go wrong.'[1] However deeply she desired to find the 'secret spring' of personality, bare justice for an accused person had to be won first. On the Street Offences Committee she took her place, not as a feminist or a moralist or even first and foremost as a penal reformer, but as a keeper of justice.

The Penal Reform League had been asking for the appointment of women police in 1912; the Howard League in the 'twenties was fighting to retain women police (appointed in wartime emergency) as an integral part of the police force. In the earliest days of the Howard League, Margery Fry had gone down to Marlborough Street Police Court, having secured Robert Tatlock as escort, to see how women were treated in the cells. The National Union of Societies for Equal Citizenship (through which Eleanor Rathbone had worked from its earliest days) had in 1919 set down among its six objectives 'an equal standard of sex morals as between men and women, involving a reform of the laws dealing with solicitation and prostitution'. But the leadership in the campaign fell naturally to the Association for Moral and Social Hygiene, an amalgamation of societies founded by Josephine Butler and renamed since 1961 the Josephine Butler Society. It was the A.M.S.H. which in 1923 drafted a Public Places (Order) Bill, generally known as its Street

---

[1] Evidence to the Home Office Committee on Young Offenders, 1925.

Bill. The N.U.S.E.C. circularized all parliamentary candidates in 1924 and a deputation was sent to Sir William Joynson-Hicks soon after he became Home Secretary. Lady Astor sponsored the Bill. It passed its second reading unopposed. It was then dropped because the Home Secretary had given a private assurance that he was considering terms of reference and personnel for an Enquiry. The General Strike and the Home Secretary's illness accounted for inertia in 1926, but it was not until October 1927 that the membership of the committee (a Departmental Committee, not the Select Committee the A.M.S.H. had hoped for) was announced.

The committee seemed to Margery Fry a 'collection of hard-faced reactionaries', though she had a personal liking for the chairman, afterwards Lord Macmillan. Lady Joynson-Hicks, whose appointment had caused a shudder of amusement, was 'evidently very stupid but not too wicked'. Early in the life of the committee fierce publicity was thrown on to their field of inquiry by the Hyde Park scandal. An elderly ex-M.P. and a young woman were accused of misbehaviour in Hyde Park. The case was dismissed, but during the subsequent inquiries into the conduct of the police the woman who had been involved in the case was fetched from her place of work to Scotland Yard and submitted to a humiliating cross-examination lasting five hours. The Home Secretary replied to the protests in the House with a promise of a public inquiry and Margery Fry supposed, like everyone else, that 'Lady Jix' had been taking her papers home to educate her husband. She was, indeed, more favourably disposed to Lady Joynson-Hicks than to the magistrates on the committee and particularly to Hensley Henson, the Bishop of Durham, whose judgements on his fellow creatures dismayed her. Miss Craven attended some of the public sessions and described them in the *Howard Journal* as an 'unedifying sight . . . the atmosphere was that of a debating society rather than that of a council chamber'.

'But', wrote Margery, 'I'm trying to get on to personal terms as comfortable as may be, so that I may have more margin for differing in Cttee.' At the end of their sessions the Chairman found himself probably the first chairman of a governmental committee to receive a pair of slippers embroidered by one of his colleagues, Margery Fry. 'Those who read our Report', wrote Mr Macmillan, 'will exclaim, "How beautiful are the feet in Whitehall of those who bring good tidings".' But the A.M.S.H. did nothing of the kind. It rejected the Report of the Street Offences Committee, though the Howard

League found it better than expected. There was an immediate and spectacular drop in the number of convictions for soliciting, but there was no unity in the forces which might have pressed for legislation. Over the years the numbers of convictions rose again, while bodies like the National Council of Women reiterated their resolutions for the abolition of the term 'common prostitute' and the reform of the solicitation laws. When the Wolfenden Committee was appointed, in 1954, Margery Fry was eighty years old.

The voice of the prodigal's elder sister was not unheard in Somerville. 'She was more interested in prostitutes than in us,' complained one carefully nurtured girl from overseas. In fact, 'street offences' were only the most publicized of Margery Fry's penal concerns in these years. Roy Calvert's book, *Capital Punishment in the Twentieth Century*, sold over 5,000 copies. The subject was discussed in every newspaper and every debating society. When Labour came to power in 1929 it seemed that things might move. The annual meeting of the Howard League was, according to Margery Fry, addressed 'most excellently' by Clynes, the Home Secretary. But a few days later he brushed aside the opportunity of a debate on an abolitionist resolution in favour of the setting-up of a Select Committee on Capital Punishment. The committee was irrevocably split from the beginning: the six Conservatives withdrew while the report was in draft and it came out as the work of the remaining nine members.

Before this committee Roy Calvert carried the main weight of stating the abolitionist case, supported by his international researches. Margery Fry, with Mr D. N. Pritt, gave evidence for the Howard League. She spoke for its members, who opposed the death penalty from various standpoints—religion, ethics, expediency—but were together in the belief that 'there is a great deal of constructive work which could be done if people did not shelter themselves behind the idea that the death penalty was a sufficient deterrent and would secure them from murder'. She had never encouraged or signed public petitions for reprieves, considering such things 'disastrous and unwise . . . attempts to re-try a case by public clamour'. Reform must come through the law. The League had discussed the value of a term of abeyance during which no death sentences should be carried out, such as had preceded the abolition of the death penalty in other countries; it had decided 'that we had better get the whole idea of what we think right expressed and not concern ourselves with half-measures'. Being pressed on this point, she admitted that there might be some value in a period of ten years' abeyance, adding, in that curiously Quaker idiom which came to her in weighty moments, 'I do not know that it is much better than nothing.'

In addition to the memorandum, the committee had received from the Howard League a document written by Margery Fry herself. She had in her time visited three or four women condemned to death. She had seen 'at close quarters what it means in terms of actual human relationships, an intolerable reversal of all the impulses of normal humanity'. These details of mutual consideration between prisoners and prison officials, of the grim quasi-domestic companionships in the condemned cell, she did not wish published. They concerned persons easily identifiable; she had learned them as visiting justice and reproduced them, after some years, from memory: above all, she did not want to see them in the headlines, adding to the morbid exploitation of everything that concerned a hanging.

The Report of the remnant of the Select Committee, published in 1930, recommended abeyance for not more than five years. In 1933 Roy Calvert died at thirty-five, without seeing any legislative results from his labours. Margery Fry was to live to see another campaign. 'It has all been gone over so often before,' she said twenty-six years later, heading off a radio interviewer[2] with a flash of impatience.

She stuck gallantly to the grimmest or, in her own word, the grubbiest sides of her work, but she was most deeply engaged by that care for children which had first drawn her to penal reform. A child was a citizen, with its liberties to be protected, and the State should put no child under restraint, however benevolent, without a legal hearing. But what, in fact, were the liberties of a child compared with the liberties of an adult? What kind of freedom for a child was 'the liberty to go wrong'?

'Whether you can make rescue work a function of the law is, I think, a difficult problem,' she had told the Young Offenders' Committee, using the term 'rescue work' in its narrower sense. The problem of relating to the functioning of the law the prevention of habitual crime was one to which she bent her mind constantly from the day she became a magistrate. All magistrates in the children's court, she believed, should make themselves what she called 'experts' in the treatment available, and its suitability for the offender. Yet

[2] 'Personal Call'.

children could pass through the courts unknown, appearing before different magistrates on successive charges or even on the same charge, if the case were deferred. In the special London truancy courts she had known boys to be sent to industrial schools without even appearing.

In the children's courts she hoped in time to see judiciary and executive powers so working together that there might be a chance, perhaps the last chance if it were missed, to find the secret spring which would open the shut-in personality of the young offender. One of the necessities for such constructive work was an adequate, trained, full-time probation service. Its beginnings, like those of public education, had been fostered by the Church, through the Police Court Mission. The Criminal Justice Act of 1925 made probation a nation-wide service and gave the Home Office power to approve new appointments and to inspect the service. Margery Fry was determined to free probation finally from its denominational ties: she would not be put off by arguments that the 1925 Act had granted the Home Office powers she desired, or that in densely populated areas denominationalism could work effectively. She was not out for persecution. One of her most dearly loved probation candidates, who left her training to marry an Anglican priest, says, 'She was tremendously interested in his life and job, so that I never felt being married to a clergyman of the Church of England was anything in her eyes but the greatest possible opportunity.' It was simply that Margery Fry wanted the best possible candidates. She had talked intimately with many students; she knew that some were being lost to the probation service because they could make no claim to a personal religion and could not imagine themselves working under a committee united by religious convictions. Though probation did not become a wholly public service until the Criminal Justice Act of 1948 the Probation Section of the Home Office was set up before the Second War, in 1936. Again Margery Fry's part in the fight for the probation service becomes anonymous: it was Miss Craven who gave evidence for the Howard League before the Departmental Committee on probation in 1936.

'How your wonderful power of sympathy and interest in all our doings does help us,' Margery wrote on her mother's ninety-fifth birthday. 'I often when I feel I *can't* go on caring about other people's affairs, wonder how you do it!.' As Margery Fry learned more about children, she saw more significantly the 'great and expressive tenderness' which had sustained her own earliest years. This power of interest in other people, oppressive in Lady Fry's narrow domestic circle, had come to Margery as a legacy which she was prepared to spend to the last farthing. The need to know people which had once made her search so assiduously through Miss Lawrence's school or Somerville College for the rare, congenial person now drove her to look for the 'secret spring' in the delinquent, the frivolous, the dull. She knew her own gifts in helping people to discover themselves, but recognized that something beyond 'knack' was needed in constructive work with other people. They must be known more surely, more scientifically, on a scale which would make some mark on the callous ignorance of society about its less successful members. She tried to get medical penology and criminology established as university studies. None of her academic schemes led to any direct result, but she threw out her ideas and kept them alive.

She reproduced for the Young Offenders Committee her recollections of the Observation Centre at Moll, in Belgium, which she had visited three years earlier. Before a young offender was sent for a period of compulsory training he ought to be known, observed 'functioning' with other boys in a free but ordered community. The committee betook itself to Moll and in its Report recommended that three such observation centres should be set up, staffed for medical and psychological observation. It was a bitter disappointment to the Howard League, after the strenuous activity with which it had followed up the Report, when the Children and Young Persons' Act of 1933 made no provision for such centres. Even the unofficial assurance that better facilities for observation would be provided in remand homes faded in the economies of the 'thirties. The 1933 Act, however, gave force of law to the duty of the children's court to 'have regard to the welfare of the child'. On this foundation Margery Fry and her fellow workers continued to build.

One moment Margery Fry's personal contribution shines through a cloud of witnesses: the next, she is anonymous among anonymous colleagues. Miss Alexander recalls that soon after the First War she and Margery Fry sent oranges to Holloway at Christmas. In subsequent years they came as a gift from the Howard League, until in 1928 the prison decided unaccountably that oranges were inadmissible, having 'no educational value'. The same friend recalls Margery's distress on finding that some girls in Holloway Prison were confined in dark punishment cells: soon after her visit the cells fell into disuse. If all the experiences of those concerned with penal reform in the interwar years were pieced together, Margery Fry would probably seem ubiquitous. But her tracks are elusive, and after 1930, except for the chance keepings of her far-flung correspondence, only the high peaks are charted—the foreign travels, the published speeches.

One evening in March 1930 Lady Fry put down a new book on astronomy (apparently James Jeans's *The Universe around Us*), recommending its fresh vision to her companion. A few hours later an attack of cardiac asthma awoke her, and the dying she had dreaded for more than ninety years was quickly over. In her letters to her mother Margery had used the reticence necessary towards a parent who had been distressed to hear of her daughter's occasional smoking at Dalmeny Avenue, but she had perhaps been less reticent than she supposed. Never again would she so blend in her letters the sensuous and the intellectual, the historic and the ephemeral, the 'whiney-piney' and the high courageous. Perhaps, as ageing people will when the last of the old generation goes, she toughened her defences, becoming by some slight change more of a public figure. The communication of fifty-six years was ended, but Margery Fry continued to astonish even acquaintances by her confident openness.

Mariabella Fry had not wished a 'testimony' to be published in the *Friend*. As in life she had concealed her 'unused selves', so in her memoirs she tried to hide her personality in a list of 'things', those she had seen go out of the every-day world and those that appeared in it for the first time in her near-century. So she reveals her extraordinary clarity of sense and memory, her hold of the details of this goodly life. She had indeed a talent for nostalgia—'Better love's yesterday than hope's tomorrow,' she had written in one of those 'copies of verses' which even the shyest of Victorian ladies sometimes circulated among their friends. She had wondered at the first Lucifer matches, replacing the flint and steel with which the servant had lit the nursery fire. She remembered the sound of the flail in Luke Howard's courtyard. She recalled the weight of a carpet-bag which, at seven years old, she was dragging towards her first railway train (for there were no porters), and the voice of a grown-up relative saying, 'Why, it doesn't move faster than a post-chaise.'

Gibb and his horses were dead and for a decade she had been driven by a chauffeur who (according to Stephen Hobhouse) was forbidden to exceed twenty miles an hour. She might have added also to the list of 'things that are' Margery's voice, coming by wireless from London to Failand in 1928. 'I feel less *pain*', Margery wrote to one of her sisters on their mother's death, 'than as if the shape of life was altered and nothing mattered much—as though we could go to the Antarctic or turn Moslem for all any one wld. mind or hinder one. . . . Joan says, "No one to justify oneself to".' In dreams Margery had seen the waters of the Bristol Channel rising over the fields towards Failand. Once she saw them rise up over the ha-ha and the lawn, over the steps and the porch and the chimneys. Then she woke thinking, 'I shall never have to go there again', and dreamt no more of Failand. At the end of 1930 Margery wrote to a friend, 'We all seem at loose ends and uncertain about things. It's extraordinary how all our lives were pegged in place by Mother's— she seemed to *matter* so much more than any of us, that we discover now how completely we all lived by reference to her.'

Isabel had given up her school at Mayortorne. She and Margery found a house deep in the Cotswolds. Morley Horder was taken to see it—'even ruder than usual, but full of ideas'. Margery played enthusiastically with plans. Before she left Somerville the Fellows were invited to Naunton for a house-warming tea-party. But the project was already cold: neither sister was really prepared for a country retirement. In less than two years the house was sold and Isabel, at sixty-three, was opening another farm school near Aylesbury.

There was Agnes, like Ulysses, 'yearning in desire to follow knowledge like a sinking star', with Uncle Joseph's money all unspent except on other people. 'I want to see some more before I settle down to old age finally,' Margery wrote to her. A visit to their nephew in British Columbia would include that prospect of conifers which Agnes had dreamed of. Cousins beckoned from California. There was a friend in New Mexico. Margery chose for the third in the party a friend whom she had met on the Staffordshire Insurance Committee, Mary Michaelis, who even before the First World War had been adventurous enough to drive a car and acquire a week-end cottage. 'M.M.' had become one of the chief exponents in England of M. Coué's auto-suggestive technique, which she is said to have used effectively with stammerers. In the face of M.M.'s enthusiasm Margery had some of the born Quaker's distaste for 'notions': at the same time her curiosity was awakened and she recognized that M. Coué's technique lay somewhere near that scientific study of personality in which she was placing her hope. She knew M.M. for a true companion, level-headed in practical affairs, ready to take more than her share of the chores.

The Chinese lacquer cabinet, after ninety-four years, had a new owner: Joan Fry, Mariabella's eldest surviving daughter. Before Agnes and Margery left they went to see it in Joan's long living-room in the Hampstead Garden Suburb. By the end of April 1931 they were at sea: 'Our cabin's enormous and really luxurious. . . . Poor Agnes, lost at its not being worth while economizing electric light.'

XIII
American and Chinese Travels: 1930-1934

'IT's rather life at half-cock, but that's exactly what I wanted!' Off Mexico, at the end of May 1931, 'the Pacific is as satisfactory as a story book. It is perfectly calm and blue, full of great turtles all swimming south, who cock their heads to look at the ship and pass on.' They were in no hurry to land at San Francisco: a glimpse of Los Angeles, 'the immensity, glaring wealth and general motor-carishness of it all', had already chilled their feet. Such uneasiness soon vanished. Margery wrote to Roger after three weeks in California: 'You'll probably drop my acquaintance after this for I've got to confess to enjoying this country greatly and being not a little charmed by it. It's very beautiful, more beautiful than most people have suggested because most people are—aren't they—stupid lookers.'

Another letter to Roger from Vancouver Island, two months later, told him that *Vision and Design* was a set text in a Canadian university, 'optional, you'll be glad to know'. She urged him to publish his broadcast talks, copiously illustrated for these young students, who, like the girls in Birmingham whom she had taught from the illustrations in the *Burlington Magazine*, had never seen a great painting.

We've jogged along excellently doing very little, seeing many more trees than I like, but I do like seeing Agnes' rapture over them. I believe their soundlessness is a great part of her love for them, she is perfectly at an advantage regarding them, and then all kinds of Father and Failand feelings lend real passion to her love for conifers, surely, to most people, the dullest group of the whole vegetable kingdom. . . . God has repeated himself over them to a really exasperating extent. You *might* well come to California, but in Canada I can't imagine you. It has a provincialism of such pronouncement that I believe it'll be the last place on earth to discard the worship of the Royal family, of the English public school, and of that juggernaut the C.P.R. which hypnotizes its victims into the belief that it is a benevolent and efficient despot, whereas really it stands in the way of all intelligent advance. . . . But you know that I enjoy rowing and bathing and walking and get a great deal of fun out of it all. . . . If you feel painting shadowed by the ghosts of the great Italians I am squirming under those of all the old ladies before me who have messed in water colours. They flicker between me and the paper. But I've had great fun and done some fairly understandable illustrations, some of which you'll think pretty vulgar, I'm afraid.

Her nephew's cabin was now a family home. The two great-aunts shared a room with camp beds, a washstand made from a packing-case, and a bearskin on the floor. Even with only one servant in a house with two young children, Agnes assured her sisters in London, life was not necessarily a round of chores. In the evenings there was time to teach the lady-help to smock, in the September sunshine she sat by the lake, observing that the twelve horses and some cows 'rightly disposed on the largest meadow' made 'a fine show of the old landscape kind'.

For three weeks the sisters lived among virgin forests, Agnes rejoicing in conifers, Margery in animals and birds, both of them enjoying the company of the younger Frys, growing up strong and independent, though, as Agnes said, lacking 'some of the attentions that dear Mab would have required'. But three weeks were enough. After her first visit Margery had warned her Birmingham students not to emigrate to Canada without a return fare. Though she would not be put off a chance to travel by the prospect of physical discomfort, she had no prejudice against civilization: 'we weren't sorry to get to places where water both comes and goes away in pipes (I can't decide which is most important)'. She knew how the ranchers' wives dreaded the long, bitter winters and she looked forward to the days when they would all possess the almost magical washing-machines she had seen in the U.S.A. She never shared Mariabella's fear that when machinery replaced servants middle-class women would lack human problems to exercise their minds and hearts.

In three short paragraphs of the journal Margery swept through a week's travel from Canada to New Mexico, 'from weather of a very English coldness and wetness to a most un-English heat, from dripping pine woods to deserts of cactus and yucca'. They were favoured travellers, on whom strangers dropped such phrases as that of the railwayman who said of a wasteland near the Mexican border, 'It is good for nothing but to hold the world together.' When Margery remarked that it was a pity that the Carriso Canyon was traversed after sunset, the conductor turned out all the lights in the car so that they could peer 'over the dimly lit edge into blackness threaded by a pale ribbon of river far below'.

Margery refused to 'pour adjectives into the Grand Canyon—it can hardly hold those it has already'. She was so afraid to become a bore (remembering perhaps those carriage commentaries of her childhood) that she gladly left the journal to Agnes and M.M. 'My tellings are faint echoes of hers,' said Agnes, explaining that Margery was 'off birding somewhere': or she was preparing a speech for some college which was giving her an honorary degree, or writing up notes on American prisons for the Howard League.

At Santa Fé, among the 'crowds of Mexicans in their vast hats and Indians with long plaits of mingled hair and braid or bright hand-kerchiefs binding their hair into a bob at the back', Margery took over the journal. There the Chief Commissioner for Indian Affairs provided them for three days with a car driven by a Pueblo Indian whose usual job was to take educational supplies to the villages. She was among those tribes and tribal relics which had long ago turned Edward Tylor, her old Oxford friend, from an engineer into an anthropologist. By 1930 a less sensitive tourism had followed the anthropologists and the cult of D. H. Lawrence (who had left New Mexico to die in Europe two years before the three Englishwomen came there). But far more than Margery expected remained. Some of the villages had electric light, some of the educational efforts to keep alive traditions seemed 'rather painfully self-conscious', but there were still schoolgirls weaving, children drawing and colouring elaborate symbolic patterns, apparently untaught.

'I've played hard and enjoyed myself very much indeed,' Margery told her friends: but, added her elder sister, Margery had driven herself hard, 'a habit it's too late to unlearn'. From California to Canada and back to New Mexico she had tried to know the Americans not only in the sunlight of their hospitality, or in those things 'counter, original, spare, strange' which tease a born traveller, but in their dark and vulnerable places. She was particularly interested at this time in the way that prisoners spent their time. In California 'the appearance of great openness' in a women's prison, the marvellous situation on a flowery hill overlooking a bay, even the cretonne frills in the cells, did not hide from her the emptiness of the prisoners' lives. 'I gather that loafing and gossiping are their main resources.' In Nevada, where she entered the state prison in a large party of sightseers, groups of men were huddling into the small patches of shade in the glaring yards. 'They do not look exactly miserable but it is incarceration in its crudest form. The life would perhaps be less irksome, if all went well, than that of a penal servitude prisoner in England, but it is a perfect farce to suppose that anyone could get out of it any kind of training except in crime and idleness. But I should guess that the real breeding of criminals is most efficiently undertaken in the overcrowded County Jails.' She had seen one such, quite near the delightful dwellings of her cousins, where ten women were locked up at 8 p.m. in a crowded dormitory. 'I insisted on seeing the exercise place, which was nothing but the littered-up back-court of a crowded town building. I don't believe any woman ever sees it.' The men, spending their whole time in huge tanks or cages, had neither chapel nor lectures nor exercise. Being asked to speak to local Quakers, 'I ended by saying most of what I thought.' On Vancouver Island there was still a 'stagnation of atmosphere like that of English prisons before teachers were brought in', but the local John Howard Society was beginning to visit and planning after-care.

This European spinster, a member of the leisured classes, who was recommending in a new culture and in different climates her panacea of hard work, won respect because she was not vindictive: she recommended work because she had loathed the taste of idleness and believed that to force it on others was a form of cruelty. So it was with her intolerance of the tasteless 'fancy-work' which in some places prisoners were allowed to make and sell to visitors 'at fancy prices'. She kept, in the face of Roger's pessimism and even of her own anti-sentimentalism, her faith that most human beings would turn to the true and the beautiful if they had a chance. There was no healing power in what was consciously second-rate.

Near the end of her journey her host in New Mexico took her one evening to see a prison just over the Mexican border.

Behind the bars of the court for serious offenders, into which no one offered to take us and I doubt if anyone goes, the unfortunate men beat against the bars for attention. The women do the cooking in a kitchen of spotless black, incredibly filthy. . . . The women looked mad or bad or sad, all of them dishevelled or distressing to see. . . . All we could do was to buy a quantity of cigarettes and see them fairly distributed to the men in the outer court—one of themselves undertaking to get the men in line and give them—whilst the remainder were flung through the bars to

MF—M

the raging crowd of the serious offenders. The whole thing remains a nightmare in my memory.

Margery Fry had known for several years that she must work, through the voluntary society which she had found in 1918 'a sleepy small concern', for all prisoners everywhere. In 1925, while Margery was still secretary of the Howard League, Gertrude Eaton had returned from a meeting with Nansen in Geneva, passionately concerned for the political prisoners detained without trial in Europe, especially in Poland and Bulgaria. But from the beginning of its international work the Howard League was clear that political prisoners must not be considered as a separate group: the League's concern was for all under arrest, for any reason. The development of an international policy was one of the tasks which Cicely Craven had to take over in 1927.

Jointly with the League of Nations Union and the Society of Friends, the Howard League drafted a Schedule of Conditions to be observed in all Civilized Countries in the Treatment of Persons under Arrest or in Captivity on whatever Charge. It was a comprehensive document, spanning many stages of civilization, from the abolition of torture and the provision of elementary physical decencies to such refinements as visits from relatives and from 'societies working solely for the welfare of prisoners'. There was some rivalry between this Schedule and the Standard Minimum Rules drafted by the International Prison Commission after the London conference of 1925. In the eyes of the Howard League the Commission suffered from the limitations of an official body. 'Only the League of Nations', in Gertrude Eaton's words, 'could speak for civilized peoples.'[1]

Constant efforts were made to find a sponsor for the Schedule at Geneva. As G. Lowes Dickinson wrote in the *Howard Journal*, 'No one would hold the baby, greatly as the child was admired.' At last, in 1930, through the good offices of the delegate for Cuba, penal reform appeared on the agenda of the League of Nations Assembly. Both the International Prison Commission and the Howard League were invited to submit evidence. The drafting of the Howard League memorandum was one of the jobs which waited for Margery Fry on her return to Europe. It was also her turn to compose (in a world stricken by the economic collapse of Europe and the Japanese

[1] *Howard Journal*, 1925.

invasion of Manchuria) that Appeal to the Conscience of Civilized Nations which the League had decided to distribute year by year as a kind of broadsheet at Geneva.

The 'citizens and governments of our own and other nations' were exhorted to examine their own practices. 'In particular we urge that financial difficulties and political preoccupations should not be allowed to interfere with efforts for the reclamation of children and young persons who are in danger of entering upon a criminal career.' A final paragraph, in block capitals, told the 'states Members of the League of Nations', according to Margery Fry's lifelong practice, something they could do: 'to hasten the adoption of a Convention setting up an International standard for the treatment of prisoners'.

The trumpet voluntary was not her only music: at the same time she continued to practise the scales and arpeggios of penal reform. When the question of imprisonment for debt arose on the Howard League executive she gave the assurance that she was going into it very thoroughly. In October 1932 she presented the Magistrates' Association with a highly factual address, later printed with the diagrammatic illustrations which, after the patient assembly of figures, were now giving her a creative joy. There is a curious texture in these home-made graphs, reminiscent of needlework patterns. It was indeed about this time that she discovered that graphs embroidered in bright wools on checked glass-cloths were more conveniently stored than crisp paper rolls in an untidy cupboard or a bulging handbag.

In 1931, the year of Margery Fry's visits to American prisons, an authoritative book by L. N. Robinson published in Philadelphia asked the fundamental question, *Should Prisoners Work?* The question of prison employment, the conflict between the deterrent and the reformative purposes of work, was still unresolved. In the eighteenth and nineteenth centuries prisoners in local jails (which they left for liberty, death, or transportation) had plied trades to maintain themselves, not as part of their punishment. In the twentieth century food and clothing were provided, but prisoners were in theory supposed to contribute by work to their own maintenance. Elizabeth Fry had believed that prisoners should work for their own good: 'if we allow them nothing to do they will return to their evil practices'. Though Margery Fry spoke a different language from her great non-ancestor, she held a similar idea of the degenerative effect of idleness. But in 1930 the shadow of the treadmill, retained until 1898 as a deterrent long after it became obsolete as a source of productive power, still hung over the question of work in prisons.

Work was to Margery Fry the exercise of the faculties, as distinct from drudgery, the practice of endurance. She believed that work could be found suitable to stretch the faculties of most people. Long before the first occupational centre was opened she was seeing the possibilities of simple manual work for the mentally subnormal. She was, however, as the school-leavers of 1926 had discovered, a realist in insisting that society would only buy the skill it wanted. If she herself had been faced with the horrid choice, she would rather have worked in the old-fashioned, easy-going prison laundry she described in 1934 than in the rush and rattle and heat of a modern steam laundry, but it was idle to suppose that the prisoners were making a serious contribution to their own maintenance or acquiring any qualification for working in a commercial laundry on their discharge. 'Men and women with their arms in gray soap-suds pound and scrub the dirty clothes, slushing the water over the uneven floor in a leisurely fashion. A row of flat irons on the gas stoves is all the equipment for ironing, the steamy hours go by drearily and heavily. . . . The laundry struggles through the prison work but rarely takes on anything further.'[2]

She did not expect men in prison to work for anything but 'the normal inducement—the expectation of some direct profit'. In 1928 Margery's old friend Champion Russell had corresponded with Alexander Paterson about the introduction of a wage system in prison. The Howard League raised £250 for an experimental scheme in Wakefield Prison. A second scheme was introduced in Nottingham. In 1932 the report of the Committee on Persistent Offenders recommended that the question of employing prisoners should be thoroughly examined. In the following year the Home Office Committee, to which Margery Fry had been appointed, stated boldly that suitable employment was 'the most important factor in the physical and moral regeneration of the prisoner'.

The times were bad for prison employment. Far from contributing to the national wealth, prisoners seemed to be filching jobs from law-abiding people, for most of those in prison would not have had a chance in the free labour market. Trades such as mat-making were needed for sheltered workshops for handicapped people. The

[2] *Howard Journal*, 1934.

economy programme of 1931 reduced prison staffs: more officers were needed to supervise labour than to guard men locked in cells. By the end of the year, from the eight hours of associated labour recommended in the Prison Rules and the six and a half hours actually achieved, the hours had sunk below five. 'Men sit and sew by hand beside idle machines,' Margery Fry reported in 1934. 'The dismal and unremunerative occupation of picking oakum has increased.'[3] She had said of Maurice Waller, a few years earlier, 'he has kept the unofficial mind, the sense of what might be, unblunted by dealing with what is'. This was her ideal, and however hurt and thwarted she might be by the daily catastrophes of the interwar years, she carried her aspirations timelessly. Yet she preferred to express them in concrete terms. 'I have household gloves for government departments in my mind,' she wrote to Champion Russell. Though she was never one to fly on every pretext to the editor's letter-box, *The Times* in 1936 (on Coronation Day, as it happened) published a long letter from her recommending large-scale drainage schemes as suitable work for prisoners.

The house which Margery and Isabel had bought in the Cotswolds was sold early in 1932. They made a great bonfire of their letters to each other. Then, as one of the last acts of her tidying-up, Margery wrote to resign her membership of the Society of Friends. She hired Flossie's George, then out of a job, to find her a home in London. He did his work well: 48 Clarendon Road, on the wrong side of Holland Park Avenue, was not the small labour-saving house with a cookshop round the corner which Margery had promised herself for her old age, but it remains unmistakably a Fry house. In the little front garden Margery contrived a streamlet: from the French window at the back an iron staircase leads to her small garden, where she grew camellias and morning glories. The garden opens into one of those communal grass plots, squares in reverse, which grace some of the older London suburbs. The house stood even in 1932 'absolutely on the borderline of slum and respectability'. The bottom end of the street provided 'a ready outlet for surplus buns and ice-cream'. For the parties began again: the former students of Birmingham and Somerville, the Howard League and the civil servants, even the prison officers.

I wish you'd been there the other night [she wrote to Champion Russell].

[3] *Howard Journal*, 1934.

It really was a wonderful display of the lion and the lamb doing the happy family business. One uninvited Home Office official telephoned in the middle to ask if he could come and then filled in the intervals of my shaking hands with the guests with problems of indecency upon which even I didn't feel enabled to guide the Department. They stayed late, they ate lots and they asked to come again. Holloway Prison stayed to the end and took off the 'floral decorations' to grace the gaol.

St Ursula remained her adopted patron saint, for there was always at least one young girl living with her: perhaps the daughter of a Somervillian at the other end of the earth, perhaps a musician needing a home where practice was tolerated.

Rioting broke out in Dartmoor Prison. The Children's Act, in spite of its generally progressive tone, extended the use of birching. The Lausanne Conference on Reparations, the World Economic Conference, the Disarmament Conference failed one after another. Penal reform seemed at that time one of the least promising causes. Margery Fry stuck to it the more assiduously, the more profoundly convinced of its relevance to the health of nations. Yet, though she followed a clear course in penal matters, she could not avoid the dilemma which obsessed her friends: their horror of aggression in Europe and Asia, their repugnance to any preparations for war. In 1933, when Germany withdrew from the Disarmament Conference and gave notice of withdrawal from the League, she joined one of the deputations which urged Ramsay Macdonald to use Britain's whole weight to bring about disarmament. 'A terribly pathetic occasion: he seemed blind and broken and rather peevish.' She put in a word about the exportation of arms and the Prime Minister she had found so congenial in their former meetings snapped at her like a terrier.

She lectured in Athens and in Darlington (calling on Helen Fry at York and seeing that she was provided with woolwork). She went to the Isle of Man on an educational commission requested by the Tynewald. She rejoiced that Isabel was going to work at the Caldecot Community, that Roger was lecturing weekly at the new Courtauld Institute, that a *Times* appeal had brought Joan over £600 for South Wales. And in the spring of 1933, soon after the burning of the Reichstag, she rejoiced (in spite of the agonies of despair in the world) over 'the luckiest thing that had ever happened' to her. The Universities China Mission, endowed from the indemnity paid by the Chinese after the Boxer Rebellion of 1900, had invited her to make a lecture tour of Chinese universities. 'It's taken the world a long time to discover you,' wrote Roger, 'but there's no doubt about it now.'

One of the privileges of wealth which Margery loved to exercise, and which she did her best to introduce to her more frugal sisters, was to provide herself with a travelling companion. Travel in such company was a munificence which a friend was able to accept as in part exchange for services rendered. A friend was needed to fortify Margery against the apprehensiveness which Mariabella had so conscientiously built into her adventurous offspring. Again the choice fell on the well-tried Mary Michaelis, whose qualifications to talk on hygiene were another recommendation.

The Japanese had invaded Manchuria only six months earlier, soon after Mao had set up the Chinese Soviet Republic in Kiangsi and Fukien. Chiang Kai-Shek's government was in Nanking, playing for time with the Japanese while he tried to root out the Communists. Canton and other cities were held by 'independent governments', under various groups of war-lords. 'I wish fearfully I knew more about it and how wise or how quixotic you are being,' Roger wrote. Margery decided that if she were in real danger she would not have been invited and that where there were other middle-aged English-women in China she had no excuse to hold back.

S.M.F. and M.M. opened another journal. They sailed for Canada, where Margery was to take part in the Pacific Relations Conference at Banff in the summer of 1933. Margery got through some of the hateful hours on the liner by embroidering a map of the Chinese provinces on glass-cloths. (Finding this aid to learning insufficient, she later made a jigsaw puzzle.) 'It's extremely difficult to gauge the use—if any—of these Conferences,' she told the University House Association at Birmingham. Privately she told Roger that she had 'got on rather unexpectedly well' and after her set speeches had been asked to chair some round-table sessions: 'a very tough business as there were no resolutions and you'd just got to make some 30 people of all nations discuss, keep them near the point and yet not get the talk too rigid . . .'. She and M.M. 'imposed themselves shamelessly' on two of the delegates returning to China. The four travellers shared a table on the boat, and hearing the two sages wrangling over the difference between 'hot-boiled' and 'hard-boiled' Margery made a useful assessment of the linguistic difficulties ahead.

Roger and Margery had both inhaled deeply the fragrance of the ancestral Chinese cabinet. They had lived among the Chinese objects

Roger had collected. The translations made by Roger's friend Arthur
Waley had become their poetry more than that of any English school.
An eighth-century Chinese poem, 'On Finding a Painting of Buddha
on the Wall of his Prison Cell', had even appeared in one of the
earlier issues of the *Howard Journal*. Roger and his circle saw in
Chinese culture an acceptance of human life, its pleasures, its pains,
its place in the universe, 'a happy disinterestedness . . . a gravity
never altogether untouched by humour . . . the reward of not having
fallen into the habit of human arrogance'.[4]

So, just as Margery had seen 'all kinds of Father feelings' in
Agnes's pleasure in the tedious Canadian conifers, so now all kinds
of Roger feelings prepared her for the Chinese scene: the plains seen
from the train on the first night out of Nanking seemed the flats of
Somerset, 'willow-sprinkled country, with slow-running ditches and
narrow dykes between'.

Never did anyone want another to share impressions as I want you here
[she wrote to him in October, from a town near Peking]. There are tracts
of time when we patiently visit institutions and social experiments and
homes for prostitutes or writhe under Americans and English of the least
sympathetic sort, when it would be unbearable that you should be by but
there are lots of others when I feel as if I could almost force you to see
through my eyes the things that would so delight you. . . . The country
is the absolute opposite of America, every scrap of it is so lived into and
human labour has enriched it so—almost every stone is a scrap of carving,
the commonest little village houses have extraordinary style, lovely
proportions and the most tactful enrichment of their simplicity by little
borderings of bricks and tiles at the eaves and gable ends, and gateways
with carving everywhere—the beauty of the *minor* architecture no one
had prepared me for.
. . . But [she adds] This country is rather bewildering to one's values—
In some ways the missionaries seem so horribly out of place, but on the
other hand the greater part of the work we have seen (rather super-mish.
than mish.) is so much the only thing done for endless suffering and
sickness that one is obliged to admire.

'The beds', she admitted later, 'are like tombstones and the
pillows are stony griefs.' In her wakeful hours she worried about her
lectures. 'The Chinese politeness is absolutely invulnerable. It's unthinkable that they should give one the criticism that one's longing
to get. The one thing I *am* learning is to bow and bow and then when

[4] Roger Fry, *Transformations* (Chatto and Windus, 1926), p. 80.

all seems over to turn round and begin again.' M.M. gives the other side of the picture in a glimpse of S.M.F. at a university function in Nanking, 'ravissante, semi-academic, semi-reverend-clerical, altogether fitting'. At a dinner given by returned students from Oxford and Cambridge, where S.M.F. gave a 'brilliant after-dinner speech on England seen from China', the Chinese wives turned up in force to look at her.

A younger Somervillian, Innes Jackson, who wrote of her travels in China a few years later, found in the character of the cultivated Chinese male 'something gentle and womanlike, though not effeminate . . . that gives him patience and restraint'.[5] It was a familiar quality to Margery. She was at home with the Chinese, and in this vast country, humbling to one who had grown up in England in her time and class where every enterprise was underhung by a safety-net of social and cultural connexions, new intimacies began to flourish.

There was much to offend her in the old China. She and M.M. insisted on walking when the pointed shoulders of the rickshaw-man began to strain uphill. Sedan-chairs were worse: 'hot with shame', she felt she was being carried in her own funeral. The condition of the townspeople was 'pitiable'. In Shanghai, 'the vilest place I've ever been in'—where the impasse between the International Settlement and the Chinese had resulted in anarchy—they saw in a silk factory and a foundry the miseries of child labour, 'wretched little girls standing shaking with fatigue stirring cocoons in boiling water, their heads and faces sodden with steam, small boys handling red hot metal in a wretched roofed-in space between two buildings, the only place they have to live and sleep and work (probably to die) in'. The Settlement prison, a 'hygienic horror of cement and bars', held 6,000 people on ten acres of land in the middle of the city, including a 'reformatory' for boys of twelve upwards. This was not the only prison Margery Fry managed to visit, for in a smaller establishment of a hundred prisoners, where she learned that meat was served only twice a year, she offered to pay for pork for a stew. She was presented with a bill for three and ninepence, and to ease her conscience added sweet biscuits for everyone.

New China was drab, even ugly. It took 500 days of skilled work, she learned, to carve one horn of a traditional roof: the beauty she admired was dependent on an immense gap between rich and poor.

[5] E. M. I. Jackson, *China Only Yesterday* (Faber and Faber, 1938).

In Nanking she found twelve girls and 500 boys dressed exactly alike, living under a spartan military discipline in the Central Political Institute, preparing for civil service in rural districts. S.M.F. found a lecture to these people 'very alarming. . . . At the word of command the 500 rose as one man and sat down again. . . . At the end they applauded, also at the word of command.' But they listened, and clearly followed—'They gave an impression of eagerness, even of a rage for work': and the women's dean, adds Margery, was 'very friendly'. Out in the villages near Peking, Margery found her sympathy with the new national movements more spontaneous. At Ting Hsien, a decaying town within seven miles of walls a thousand years old, under a lovely pagoda which went on glowing after sunset, they became 'Fry' and 'Mick' to the Yen family, who with a hundred helpers ran a Mass Movement Centre.

Margery was collecting a store of 'missionary pictures' and curios, 'stirred up by recollections of missionary meetings in Failand schoolroom when the things on the table made up for all the mish-mish talk *and* Greenland's Icy Mountains'. She knew beyond any compulsion of gratitude or compassion that she wanted to speak and work for China. Yet it would not be the strangeness and beauty of China which would be the substance of her talks in crowded halls and small, chilly, unpublicized meetings all over Britain: it was the precarious renewal of Chinese national life which held her imagination. The new Chinese, going about practical neighbourly tasks in drab clothes, were as wonderful to her now as the builders of Peking.

S.M.F. and M.M. did not hurry home from China. As usual, Margery played down their endurance. 'We are not feeling boastful about the journey I am now to describe [to Angkor and Saigon]. After talking big about making our way across the Malay Peninsula we succumbed to the advice of those who urged a car. . . . It is true that our charming driver, as he established us for lunch, waved a showman's hand round the landscape and said "Ici serpents, ici tigres", but we saw no beast so rapacious as the hotel manager who charged 12% for changing our good money.' Around Angkor the mixture of trees and ruins reminded her of the Piranesi engravings. She enjoyed at Angkor Thom a bas-relief of 'very vigorous elephants and all sorts of daily doings', was bored by the triumphs of Vishnu. She was impressed, not deeply moved, by the Angkor Wat, 'a sort of religious Versailles'.

So they came to Siam, to a little railway station on the frontier, 'oddly like a piece of Canada'. In Bangkok there was a royal welcome from Princess Noy, one of Margery Fry's Somerville students, who gave them a western-built house to themselves. Next door lived the princess's six-month old daughter, quick to smile on her godmother-elect. Margery had been warned that sponsorship in Oriental countries carried serious responsibilities. She protested that at sixty she was too old to be any kind of mother to a creature of six months: but she could not disappoint her princess, or resist the little Siamese Margery. In one particular, however, she was firm with her old student. When it was discovered that the persons who appeared to be laying the carpet were really making obeisance to the English visitor, Margery promptly obtained a royal ordinance that neither she nor M.M. was to be 'crawled at or to'.

M.M. and S.M.F. left Saigon on the third day of 1934: the year that Dolfuss was murdered, Hindenburg died, and Hitler became supreme in Germany. 'I return to Europe with great reluctance, except for my special dears,' Margery wrote to her sisters. Yet old memories came to the surface, wound about with the legends of her race, as she sailed past Crete and on to meet Roger at Marseilles.

In China she had found, besides the antique beauty she had expected, a phoenix vitality which remained not only in her memories and her mementoes but in friendships that would go with her for the rest of her life. It had been, she said, looking back on her sixties, a 'formative experience'. She may well have remembered in China the words of Spinoza which Roger had read two years before at Goldie Lowes Dickinson's cremation: 'A free man thinks of death least of all things; and his wisdom is a meditation not of death but of life.'

So, when Roger died in September a few days after a fall in his room at Bernard Street, these seemed again, as he would have said, 'the right words'. After she had heard them again she went to Cornwall. 'I seem to have been able,' she told Isabel, 'walking on these utterly lonely moors, to get to something of the way I know he always wanted me to take sorrow, not to ask for exemption from the ordinary laws, not to see one's own trouble written large upon the universe.'

'Physically and mentally, a dusty world,' she wrote a few weeks later. 'We are beginning the work of listing and dating Roger's pictures.' Soon she was preparing his papers for Virginia Woolf, whom he had wanted as his biographer. He had been planning a history of the world's art. Only three years earlier he had written to her: 'How disgracefully short life is in comparison with one's own education—I feel I'm just beginning to be able to feel things with some sort of nicety and objectivity of apprehension and now I know my miserable body will soon begin to creak and groan. But after all the point is one can feel better and better and understand a little more what the world's like.' His creakings and groanings had often been audible: Margery had listened to them sympathetically, at the same time taking it for granted (for Frys and Hodgkins lived to great ages) that he would be there even when she herself was old. But the doctors said that his body had, in fact, been worn out.

Work poured in: meetings for international penal reform, for China. The B.B.C. had discovered her. Only across one channel a stone fell. Early in 1935, when her advice was asked about a portrait-painter, she said, 'I am helpless without Roger: I know nothing of the younger men.' She continued to enjoy the art of her own genera-tion, and the art that was timeless. 'The Chinese show is lovely, not all of it of course, but a great deal,' she wrote in 1935. She was content to know that young men and women were working in the arts, sometimes to buy a picture from one of them, to give them her full attention if they asked her for it, but their movements passed her by. There were no novelists for her younger than E. M. Forster and Virginia Woolf. The London fog settled gradually on the pictures, on the pagodas painted on her doors for fun, on the Arnold Dolmetsch virginals, even on the Chinese vases: but almost imperceptibly when she was there, for visitors to Clarendon Road found her presence no less bright than it had ever been.

XIV

For all Prisoners: 1934-1939

It seems to me [Margery wrote to Isabel in 1935] that on the one side stands absolute pacifism (and I still incline to thinking that's the ultimately right position) on the other the question of what course is the nearest right for a nation which after all is still armed. So that I seem to be driven to saying (in imagination) to the government, 'I think the upholding of the League of Nations by force if need be is *your* right action, but I wouldn't stir a finger to help you with it',—and *that* seems a fairly untenable position, doesn't it? And the difficulty of knowing what to think adds a sort of anger to one's misery about it all.

SHE had faced a similar dilemma in 1900, as an obscure academic librarian, a traditional Quaker. When the terrible question returned in 1914 she had found a reasonable personal solution, again in the context of family tradition. In 1935 she had resigned from the Society of Friends. She was a woman in authority, broadcasting to thousands as well as consulted by young men and women who believed she held, and would share, some of the secrets of happiness and goodness.

In the interwar years she exchanged her thoughts with Isabel rather than with the other sisters who, in various blends of fanaticism, common sense, and saintliness, maintained their testimony for peace. Yet though she no longer rested on family tradition she was not alone. The poets were calling on everyone to be involved in the political struggles of the time, and all Margery's friends, even her pacifist sisters, were to some degree involved in the misery and the anger. In their most wretched hours the Fry sisters offered one another the solace of honest communication.

A year after Roger had died Margery went back to Provence alone. She saw herself as a solitary, half-comic little spinster battling her way with her umbrella past the dogs in the dark kitchen of the Maurons' house. She continued Roger's task of 'amanuensis-dictionary' to Charles Mauron, who was translating *The Seven*

Pillars of Wisdom. On her return she spoke at University House in Birmingham about the price of maturity, the increased capacity for pain in lives widened by knowledge and by contacts with other people. Looking at her old students, now middle-aged, she hoped they were 'not haunted but graced by the thought of friends never to be seen again'.

In the autumn of 1935 Margery Fry took over the Howard League bureau at Geneva from Gertrude Eaton. It was opened each year during the session of the League of Nations Assembly, so that Gertrude Eaton and her colleagues could, in Gordon Rose's words, 'corner, badger and coax the delegations of the member nations into taking some sort of interest in penal problems'.[1] The great hope shared by the Howard League and the International Prison Commission was that a substantial number of governments would bind themselves by a Convention to keep the Minimum Standard Rules. In 1934 the Assembly got as far as recommending them. In preparation for the following year Margery Fry began to collect, through her ever-expanding network of European contacts, instances of violation of the Rules.

Before she got out of the train at Geneva, in September 1935, she saw an Indian woman of her acquaintance waving from another train. A Californian cousin had left a card at her hotel. 'It is going to be one of those awful places', Margery surmised, 'where more know Tom Fool than T.F. knows.' She had herself drawn up the statement for use at Geneva.

The Howard League interests itself in the treatment of all persons under constraint, accused or convicted of crimes or offences, and of those who are detained by the State as a preventive measure. It is equally interested in such persons whatever their race, and whether their offences or alleged offences are political or otherwise. The League does not, in general, occupy itself in methods of trial as well as of treatment. It expressly holds that no places of detention should be exempt from the operation of certain minimum standards in the treatment of prisoners.

With Miss Margaret Franklin she obtained an interview with the secretary and the assistant secretary of the 5th (the Humanitarian) Committee of the League of Nations. 'We came away to feel more than ever as if we were walking blindfold amongst a bed of sea-urchins.' The Convention, it seemed clear, was a long way off. The

[1] *The Struggle for Penal Reform*, p. 319.

office was unexciting: two Greeks dropped in and asked for information, a journalist said he wanted to write an article on the Howard
League, 'but all he proved to want was a good, well-washed-down
lunch with a maddeningly long opportunity for reminiscences afterwards'. Ladies promoting other good causes sent invitations to
propagandist tea-parties.

The Assembly opened on 9 September 1935. Three days later
Sir Samuel Hoare hobbled to the tribune (he had been flown out to
Geneva on his back) to pledge his Government's support for the
League of Nations Covenant in the face of Italian aggression. It was,
according to A. J. P. Taylor, 'the most ringing assertion in favour of
collective security ever made by a British statesman'.[2] Sir Samuel
Hoare (then Lord Templewood) recalled later how he had looked
from the sophisticated ranks of delegates on the floor of the Assembly
to the galleries, where sat 'the grim-looking crowd of the hot-
gospellers of Geneva'.[3] From her place among the hot-gospellers,
Margery scanned him with the ruthlessness which she habitually
turned upon the eminent. The speaker knew that his cool precision
had irritated the Commons, but he believed that it moved the
Assembly by its contrast with the florid rhetoric of foreigners. 'Something of the Preparatory School H.M. in the delivery (and even
matter),' was Margery Fry's judgement. 'A maddening tom-tom
beat on the table, a de haut en bas tone, a certainty that everyone
else recognized the complete moral superiority of England as much
as we do ourselves—a real disingenuous failure to recognize that
after all we *have* egotistic as well as altruistic interests in the
Abyssinian dispute—seemed to me to prevent its being a *great*
speech.' Laval's speech was 'rather more warmly delivered, one yet
realized that every sentence was calculated'. Those who followed
were 'each so full of nobleness that there was (to me at least, who
love to see bubbles burst) a relief in Litvinoff's remorseless list of the
things the League had *not* done. . . . But I do carry away the sense
of more reality than I'd expected from the Assembly.'

'Our own affairs naturally seem rather absurdly non-typical and
rather intrusive in this atmosphere.' The International Penal Congress was held that year at Berlin. The Howard League had decided
against sending a representative when Cicely Craven had heard that
their chairman, Mr D. N. Pritt, would be denied admission to

[2] A. J. P. Taylor, *Origins of the Second World War* (Hamish Hamilton, 1961), p. 19.
[3] Lord Templewood, *Nine Troubled Years* (Collins, 1954), p. 169.

Germany. But some of the delegates, snubbed in Berlin, came on in hope to Geneva. Alexander Paterson assured Margery he would not leave while there was a chance of a hearing for penal affairs. She herself had interviews with delegates from eighteen countries. 'Some people are quite friendly—those who think their own affairs are in order, I think.' 'I've no desire to be here longer than need be,' she wrote to Isabel on 18 September, but she was occupied, one way or another, 'redrafting resolutions, speaking to meetings where audiences are almost comically lacking (but Quakers organized a good one), interviewing unwilling delegates and arranging interviews with others, no less unwilling, but more skilful, who somehow don't turn up'.

On 25 September the Assembly passed a resolution condemning practices contrary to the Standard Minimum Rules. 'How far *that* will affect governments who rely on cruelty I am very doubtful': but she sent Miss Craven a telegram of congratulation. A week later the tide of violence and despair seemed to be already washing over her small constructions, as Mussolini invaded Abyssinia with the panoply of modern warfare, including poison gas.

Margery Fry told her London Committee that all things considered penal affairs had gone better at Geneva than expected: by the next session a Convention might be in sight. She began work on *The Prison Population of the World*. During the year her international advisers warned her that many conventions were still unratified: it would be better to drop the idea for the time. She returned to Geneva in September 1936 to address more envelopes: 'no ambitious programme, only to get our stuff into as many hands as possible and perhaps some vague unostentatious resolution through the "humanitarian commission" '. 'Our stuff' included her own three-page survey, *The Prison Population of the World*. It was, she knew, seriously limited. She had no figures for Russia and the German figures, high as they were among European countries, took no account of concentration camps. Yet the survey was impressive enough to call for more publicity, more inquiry.

Wretched weather deepened her depression in the middle of a continent where oppression, torture, secret execution were daily increasing. Only the less guilty personages were approachable. 'I cling to a radiator, suck the newspapers dry, and wait for a message as to when I can go to see the Yugo-Slav foreign minister to tell him how badly their prisoners are treated—an exhilarating prospect! I got a

5. Principal of Somerville, 1926–1930
Portrait by Roger Fry

6. Visiting a prison at Plovdiv, Bulgaria, 1937

good snubbing from Princess Starhemberg for similar interference yesterday, and I must say I'm not surprised.' At last the message came. 'I stupidly battled all along the Lake front in the teeth of a gale [the Fry sisters remembered only intermittently the existence of cabs], and arrived all battered to find that the man who went up in the lift with me was the Minister, so that I'd no time to collect my hair, my breath or my wits or mop my streaming eyes.' He was moreover 'the usual kind of elegant gentleman who has never been near a prison. . . . My evidence really was too shaky, though I'm afraid there's a strong probability that it is true.' Thus shaking off her regrets in a letter to Isabel, she was ready to arm the Home Office official and the Rumanian rapporteur for the debate in the Humanitarian Committee. Both speakers did well: the Committee recommended a resolution, passed by the Assembly two days later, instructing the I.P.P.C. to inquire further about the world's prison population.

The Howard League next published *For All Prisoners.* The cover bore one of Margery Fry's own graphs, edged with her characteristic chequered border. Contrasting penal methods were shown side by side: Great Britain had its juvenile courts and probation system, but retained hanging and flogging. Belgium had observation centres for young offenders and the death penalty had fallen into disuse, but long sentences of solitary confinement were still imposed.

She wrote home as she waited for the 1937 Assembly to open in its new building, 'really fine, very modern, very elegant, with marble panels and varied woods and deep soft carpet (but a fierce English voice behind says, as badly ventilated as the House of Lords). Well, it seems a terrible irony if all this is only the tomb of a great ideal. I think that now they are inclined to find the once despised "social questions" useful as floats to a raft sadly leaking.'

She had been one of the Aga Khan's 2,000 guests at his 'very swanky presidential party', where she had sat in a fat leather-clad seat and listened to an excellent concert conducted by Ansermet. But on the whole, she felt, she was operating at a very humble level. She had known diplomatic hospitality as the daughter of a plenipotentiary and found 'the usual almost exclusively serious-minded female tea-parties v. boring'. One or two new acquaintances cheered her as she went about her daily employment of 'button-holing unwilling victims'. An Englishwoman, Miss Irene Ward, held firmly that 'if a subject was important irregularities in raising it mustn't count'.

MF—N

Weary of political dilettantes who knew all about penal affairs on paper, she was grateful to a young Corsican lawyer who remembered that they were discussing people in prison: 'Si on veut mener une vie digne il ne faut pas les oublier.'

She was aiming at a full-scale debate in the Humanitarian Committee in 1938. In 1937 the difficulty was to find a proposer. The French and English, 'frozen in general caution and better-notness', could be screwed up to the point of supporting but not of proposing. At last a Chinese friend approached her: 'I've had no time to read your stuff: is there anything you want done?' The army of the Kuomintang was being mowed down by the Japanese around Shanghai. Margery believed that her friend had been crying all night, 'but he was neat and Oxfordy as usual. Three minutes outside put him in possession of the situation. Neat little speech proposing, was backed up well in debate.' Penal affairs were on the agenda for the following year.

The Howard League's offering to the Assembly in 1937 was a twenty-page pamphlet tabulating official information from every continent about the custody of prisoners before trial. But the question, 'What is the procedure in cases where the arrested person is not brought before any judicial authority?' had 'frequently been misunderstood and very little information of value has been gained on this point'. The concentration camps were still undocumented. Yet the legal secretary of the Humanitarian Committee said publicly that the Howard League was achieving more than many governments. Margery Fry heard this with mixed feelings. Jealousy was easily aroused by the prestige of a voluntary society.

A few months earlier Eleanor Rathbone had returned from a tour of the Balkans with the Duchess of Atholl. She confirmed Margery Fry's worst suspicions about the penal systems of eastern Europe, and at the same time urged that these countries, menaced by lavish German propaganda, were kindly disposed towards visitors from Britain. Margery was afraid of eastern Europe: in a sense China was far nearer. But she had to see for herself. Her colleague was Mrs Rackham, a founder-member of the Magistrates' Association. They went as a Howard League mission, but in order to avoid a national label they invited a distinguished Swedish psychiatrist and criminologist, Dr Olaf Kinberg, to join them. Margery Fry met Professor and Mrs Kinberg for the first time in a Bucharest hotel. 'It was love on both sides from the first moment,' says Mrs Kinberg.

Apart from her visit to the Belgian observation centre, this was Margery Fry's first journey abroad specifically to see penal institutions. It was 'from the national angle, a curiously interfering thing to visit foreign countries, ask to see their prisons, accept their hospitality and help, and then proceed to analyse and criticize their Penal Systems'.[4] But she was not, she told herself, going as a national: penal affairs concerned humanity. In Bulgaria, after some trapesing, they got a 'bear-leader' from the Hungarian Minister of Justice. They were practised viewers of institutions, noticing, as they exchanged polite remarks with their hosts and their guide,

the rows of suspiciously clean towels, carpets precariously balanced on stairways, little mountains of filth in corners still showing the sweep of the brush, coloured paper pinned and tucked round ineradicable dirt and muddles (the newly-opened quires still littering the store-room), parades of plants in unlikely places, surgery or cobbler's shop, flower pots whose freshly turned earth showed their occupants to be newly moved in, prisoners hastily pushed aside and doors shut, dripping passages smelling too freshly of soap, naïve enthusiasm of a sick woman over a radiator warm for the first time.

To this sharpness of vision the Kinbergs added not only the Professor's scientific experience but also the gift of tongues: the Frys had a working knowledge of two or three European languages, but the Kinbergs could leap from one to another without reference, it seemed, to their native Swedish. They had also that gay irreverence which put Margery at her ease. Her own pleasure in strange places, her quick delight in the sight of an unfamiliar bird, gave her three companions from time to time a feeling of holiday on this grim autumnal journey. A photograph taken outside a Bulgarian prison shows her between the stalwart Kinbergs. Behind and above her crowd the fierce peaked caps and epaulettes of the guards. She clutches a stiff bouquet, she is small and thin in her easy-fitting tweed suit, but the smile is the same as that of the mid-Victorian child.

They saw no political prisoners or prisons. Sometimes their requests were ignored, sometimes refused. 'It is a fair conclusion', commented Margery Fry, 'that what is not shown is at least not better than what is.' In every system she found something to praise, something to recommend to other governments. At Vac in Hungary

[4] *Howard Journal*, 1938.

the prison hospital was better than any in Great Britain. They found in the same country a highly developed prison industrial system (though they wondered why the prisoners' earnings were so often spent on bread in the canteen). A tiny home for delinquent children run frugally by the Save the Children Fund in makeshift premises was 'a very good thing of its kind': the lockers made from Quaker milk-boxes had a familiar look. In Rumania, Margery Fry was astonished by the social enterprise shown by women still denied the vote, the 'poor women's lawyer', the boarding-out scheme run for difficult or abandoned children by a woman landowner: on whose estate, after seeing 'rather too many rows of drooping children in large institutions', Margery Fry watched the troops of children going home from school, natives indistinguishable from fosterlings. Buildings varied from 'excellent to unspeakable. None of them for sheer unaesthetic gloom, for sunless courts and forbidding aspect, can beat an English prison.' After a series of Hogarthian interiors, she checked in herself, however, a tendency to applaud the mere absence of squalor. 'Sometimes the places most obviously inadequate and most frankly shown gave a better psychological impression than others,— cruelty and cleanliness are not incompatible.' Women's prisons were sometimes run by nuns. In a private letter Margery described the whiteness as 'almost painful. It seemed like putting people for several years into a refrigerator in the hope of freezing the wickedness out. Two woodpeckers playing mad games in a little bosky courtyard seemed more alive than the whole of the rest of the place.' But in her report to the Howard League she gave such institutions their due in time and place. 'With standards as they are we hesitate to wish for a change. Where one hot-blooded rebel would suffer, the old and feeble and the docile are probably happier than they would be under other supervision.'

'Well, has it been worth while?' Margery Fry asked herself on the way to Sofia, where they were to spend 'the usual interminable hours over coffee-tables talking to people more or less remotely connected with our job'. 'Getting into touch with people, official and unofficial, is our principal gain.' There was, for instance, the Bulgarian judge who received them stiffly, but later came back with great modesty and frankness for another talk. But in the end, especially as she recalled the troops of wretched little boys shut up in vast institutions which no woman normally entered, Margery Fry's generalization, against all efforts to be non-insular, rose from the heart. 'England

and the North Sea countries and perhaps France really do *feel* a little —does anyone else?'

In England, at the centre of the tiny group of people who visited prisons or paid their guinea for penal reform, an outsider had pushed back the frontiers of Margery's own unconcern. In 1930 Mr Clifton Roberts, who had been in the Colonial Legal Service in Africa, had spoken to the Committee of the Howard League about the need for penal reform in some of the Crown Colonies. Immediately the League formed a Colonial Sub-committee which went quietly to work. In a little over a year its objective seemed in sight: Lord Passfield, as Colonial Secretary, accepted the idea of a standing advisory committee to deal with general principles of penal administration. It was 1936, however, before the Colonial Office, persuaded especially by Alexander Paterson, set up such a committee. Margery Fry became a member and continued to serve on it, through its various changes of name and function, for the rest of her life.

In the same year as the formation of the Colonial Advisory Committee, the report of the Departmental Committee on Social Services in Courts of Summary Jurisdiction laid the foundations of the modern probation service. On this committee the Howard League was represented by Miss Madeleine Symons. As Margery Fry had once said, there was never any lack of good people. She watched with interest this able magistrate who would perhaps be the one to take over her own 'special things'. For herself there was the Committee on Justices' Clerks in 1938.

'But what was life really like?' she asked herself when she began to write her annual letter to University House. She kept no diaries, she had no regular job. She suspected that a recording angel, if she believed in one, would tell 'a livelier story than a mere record of meetings and committees—"Pipes went wrong . . . wished the plumber to . . . . Forgot to go to see . . . meant to forget, at the bottom of my heart. . . . Spent far too much on a hat".' She had spent less time than usual in the Children's Courts, a good deal of time over the Association for Intellectual Liberty and the China Campaign Committee. The B.B.C. was 'immensely interesting'.

She became a Governor in 1938: one of those 'persons of judgement and experience and independence' who advise the B.B.C. on matters of policy. Her experience of broadcasting went back ten years to the days when the new Corporation had just won its freedom to broadcast controversial matter. For a whole hour, from half past nine to half past ten one Monday evening in 1928, Miss Margery Fry, J.P., and Captain Arthur Evans, M.P., had debated capital punishment. The artificiality of the proceedings had exasperated her: she became shrill. It was not an evening she cared to look back on. But in 1933 she was given another chance. On Sunday afternoons she broadcast talks on 'Pioneers of a Humaner World'—Mary Godwin, Florence Nightingale, Robert Owen, Lord Shaftesbury, Sir Samuel Romilly, Lord Lister. Margery Fry liked, with every justification, the sound of her own voice. She enjoyed filling penny notebooks with details of great lives: not only for their achievements, but because as Mariabella Fry's daughter she had immense curiosity about the way people lived. She was unsentimental, in the Strachey tradition: where would Florence Nightingale's immense devotion to the relief of human suffering have got us, without her 'undoubted love of power, her delight in being where the strings were pulled, her skill in wangling, the recklessness of her amusing tongue'? Nor did Margery Fry intend that her unseen audience, once awake, should sink back into well-fed stupor: what could she say of Shaftesbury's ultimate success, 'here in London, where 3,000 people are still living from 5 to 11 in a room, and only last year evidence was given in Parliament that children of 14 may still be found in this country working 80, 90, 100 hours a week'?

From the first days when the listener moved the cat's whisker delicately over the crystal until the sound, small in volume but un-distorted, met him in the privacy of earphones, to the early television set sent her as a perquisite of office, the sheer human ingenuity of mass communications delighted her. She was not one of those who feared they would smooth away the endearing oddities of local dialect and custom, making everyone alike. She had too much faith in nature's' infinite variety. 'We must look in the future', said Margery, 'for the formation of an educated society whose diversity shall be found, not in the superficial distinctions of class but in the precious variety of fully developed human beings.'[5] Early in the nineteen-thirties a daily help, a woman of intelligence, told Miss Fry she had been listening to a scientist talking about his beliefs. 'What does he believe?' asked Margery. 'Much the same as you and me.' Margery imagined the downcast eyes, the murmured 'I don't under-stand such things' which only thirty years earlier would have met the question.

[5] 'Breaking down the Barriers', *B.B.C. Quarterly*, Spring 1957.

She urged her former Birmingham students to give the B.B.C. the benefit of their suggestions. The Crawford Report on Broadcasting of 1926 had already hinted at the dangers of giving the public what it asked for. Within rather narrow limits Margery Fry trusted popular taste: that is, taste reflected in the letters of articulate people, not in the results of scientific listener research which the B.B.C. was soon to develop. She overestimated the popular appetite for constructive talk: but it was real talk she wanted broadcast, 'the jousting should not always be so gentle in the mock combats, and in fact the combats should more often be genuine'. She also may have overestimated the stimulating power of a dialogue of ideas that was merely overheard. But although she was a great talker, she was even more remarkable as a listener: listening, like the practice of all skills, gave her immense pleasure as well as some misery, and it was a pleasure she wanted to share. She had no sense, it seems, of belonging to a vanishing culture, no idea, for instance, that the Biblical allusions which she and Roger sprinkled over their letters would become to a second and third generation of agnostics a dead language: the intelligentsia was as stable to her as to the University Settlers of the 'nineties, but she believed the boundaries of the intelligentsia could be stretched almost to vanishing-point. Its exclusiveness was no part of its charm. Perhaps no one ever described the comfort of belonging to an intelligentsia more warmly than Margery Fry, in an article written for the *B.B.C. Quarterly* after twenty years of broadcasting:

In the past this freemasonry of thought, while it was not shared by all the wealthy nor denied to some people extremely short of material riches, has been on the whole confined to what are usually called the educated classes. For many of them, it has been far less the result of the formal education they received than of the habit of mixing among people who are themselves experts in their particular job—hearing the doctor talk of medicine and the banker of economics . . . the kind of general information which is all that most people can claim is not so much knowledge of things as knowledge about knowledge, a sort of mental map of what there is to be known and perhaps of where it could be learnt, together with a shadowy outline of the frontiers of human ignorance. It is rather more than that, a dim sense that even the knowledge we have, our collective picture of the world we live in, is subject to constant revision, is differently interpreted from decade to decade, contains much that is still opinion. . . . This sort of vague culture, easily enough described as superficial, is, of course, not the mark of the real *savant*, but it does form the basis of a great deal of the intercourse of those who claim to be 'educated people'. It forms a common ground of things taken for granted which makes for easy intercourse, for conversations in which there need be no condescension of superior, or self-consciousness about inferior, knowledge. There may be a little bluffing on one side or the other—a few easy admissions of ignorant gaps, but the mental overlap is enough for free movement of common thought.[6]

'We none of us pretend nowadays not to be political animals,' she told University House in 1938, excusing her activities outside penal reform. Political activity to the Fry family meant the pursuit of humanitarian causes, including the prevention of war, the preservation and sometimes the extension of traditional liberties. From time to time the sisterhood would fear that one of their number was being used by more devious persons. Perhaps this, as well as an intolerance of publicity and a liking to be handy when strings were pulled, was why Margery Fry preferred a small group where she could know everyone to a widely publicized movement. She committed herself to a small society calling itself 'For Intellectual Liberty'. It held one big meeting and survived only for a year or two.

A woman who was interviewed by Margery Fry at Clarendon Road as a possible secretary for the Association for Intellectual Liberty remembered her twenty-five years later

as being remarkably quiet and controlled,—contemplative and unhurried. . . . I wanted very much to become a university lecturer. . . . I told her this and my impression was that she was disappointed. I have thought since that perhaps she didn't share my illusions about the academic life and in later years I found myself thinking again of that interview. She made me feel that she was interested not only in the Association but in my own good. She had a grave and thoughtful way of looking at one and left one with a dim perception of issues much larger than one had suspected.

Contemplative and unhurried as Margery Fry appeared, she was at this time spending herself for the China Campaign as if she served no other cause. The China Campaign Committee began modestly with a meeting and a clothing collection at Whitfield's Tabernacle in Tottenham Court Road, but it had from the beginning its imaginative touches: a meeting was held at the dock gates when the first consignment of medical supplies went off to China. Work for the Campaign

[6] *B.B.C. Quarterly*, Spring 1957.

was based for Margery Fry on her personal friendship with Chinese men and women. She travelled up and down, showing her 'missionary pictures' and talking about resurgent China, sometimes in provincial towns where few had heard of Somerville College or listened to her broadcast talks, and where no penal reform group provided an audience. One foggy Sunday afternoon she spoke to a meeting organized by a not particularly flourishing group of women Co-operators. The hall was too large, the chairman too deaf: Miss Fry was good to have come so far, but as to what she'd said, the chairman couldn't express an opinion. 'Nonsense! She spoke beautifully!' pronounced a stern pedagogic voice from the back row, where an elderly Somervillian had lined up the staff of the local girls' high school.

Hope rose among penal reformers in 1938: 'Pentonville is going', announced a headline in the autumn *Howard Journal*. Sir Samuel Hoare was Home Secretary. He had a personal and even hereditary interest in penal affairs. Like Margery he was of Quaker stock, and unlike her he counted Elizabeth Fry among his ancestors. From his point of view he and Margery Fry had enough in common to form a working partnership. Later she told him she had two ambitions: to see a bearded tit and to see the death penalty abolished.

The death penalty was not mentioned in the Criminal Justice Bill, promised in the King's Speech in October 1938. Sir Samuel Hoare differed from the Howard League. Though he leaned towards the abolitionist position he feared that this emotionally charged controversy might turn debate against the Bill and imperil other reforms which were possible and overdue. The Bill foreshadowed the end of prison for young people: it was to be abolished immediately for those under sixteen and could be ended for those under twenty-one by an Order in Council. Though the Howard League disagreed with the Home Secretary on several points, Miss Craven wrote in the *Howard Journal* with her usual moderation, 'he has a sympathetic press, a House of Commons which is urging him to drastic action and prison officials who, judging by the reports they issue, are anxious for radical change'.

In Geneva, on 19 September 1938, Margery Fry heard of the Anglo-French proposals which Benes had been asked to accept: the immediate cession to Germany of all districts with a German population of over fifty per cent. 'It's all simply awful,' her letter to Isabel began that night. 'It's all like a funeral of all one cares for,—and it

may be absurd, but one has a sense of personal shame into the
bargain which is overwhelming.' The Chinese were 'gentle but
bitter: one said over and over "All is not lost" but it seemed the
comfort you give to children, not believing it yourself'. Even shame
was adulterated: 'life', she had written a few days earlier, 'is lived on
a hideous see-saw of shame and fear of war'. When Chamberlain
returned to London on 1 October, offering 'peace in our time',
Margery, like other people, found herself looking for justifications
for her tremor of relief: rumour at Geneva said that the Germans
had intended to shoot 3,000 political prisoners at the outbreak of
war. Everyone, even in that pre-nuclear age, had expected the
'Blitzkrieg' to break in a cataclysm: finding themselves still alive,
people like Margery Fry had to use what peace remained as best they
could. Shamed and dishonoured as she felt after Munich, she had
more to do than lay ashes on her head.

The debate in the Humanitarian Committee, during this most
wretched session of 1938, was the best discussion of penal affairs ever
heard at Geneva. Attention was now focused on prisoners held without trial. No figures were available for Germany, the U.S.S.R., or
Japan, but even so the fate of 200,000 people was under consideration. For Margery Fry the holding of this debate was in some sense
a personal triumph: she knew that she was now recognized as an
international leader in penal reform.

Isabel scolded her for lingering in France after Geneva: Margery
had left an appalling gap in the family circle when war had seemed
inevitable. Now she dreaded returning to see her own battling
emotions reflected in Isabel or to face Ruth's militant pacifism—
'You know Geneva hasn't been at all a picnic,' she wrote to Isabel,
'and frankly I'm very tired as well as very discouraged and old. It's
not as if I were good at politics—I'm *not*. I feel the awful difficulties
too much.'

At Clarendon Road that autumn of 1938 her resident guests were
Czech Jews as well as Chinese. In November she visited Agnes in
Somerset. 'The world is not quite shut out, but it is dimmer there.'
Agnes had uprooted herself from Failand and removed her books,
her pictures, her embroideries and scientific specimens to Brent Knoll.
There she entertained schoolchildren, hiding Easter eggs for fifty in
her garden as at Failand she had hidden them for two. She sent down
boxes of embroideries or paid for art shows for the stricken valleys
of Wales: her possessions, it was said, were always on the move.

Soon, even among the credulous, Neville Chamberlain's 'peace in our time' became as irrelevant as a Christmas garland after Boxing Day. By the New Year of 1939 it was already asked not whether, but when, war would come. Yet the Howard League held a Conference on the Criminal Justice Bill in preparation for its Third Reading. Margery's days were more crowded than ever with speeches, broadcasts, committees, parties. There was more fun of a formal kind—a ballet, a concert, a theatre—than at any other time in her life.

On 26 January 1939 she lost another anchorage. The Labour Party Executive expelled Stafford Cripps after the circulation of his memorandum calling on members of the party to unite with those 'of all parties or of none' in a Popular Front to expel the National Government. Next day, at a meeting of university women in Manchester, Margery Fry said she had resigned from the Labour Party. 'So now you'll be a Liberal?' someone asked. 'I have never been a Liberal and I can't imagine that I ever shall be,' Margery replied. 'I have always belonged to the Labour Party.'

The date of Hitler's attack was being prognosticated as commonly as in peacetime people surmise the date of an election. At the end of January one of Margery's friends in Whitehall told her it would not after all be 1 March, but some time in September. Puffs of optimism still rose from the Government. On 10 March Chamberlain told a press conference that Europe was settling down to a period of tranquillity. Sir Samuel Hoare denounced the 'jitterbugs' who feared war. But the Criminal Justice Bill never had its Third Reading. Attempts to rush it through the committee stage by dropping any mention of corporal punishment had failed. By April the Bill was ready, but the Home Office was overwhelmed by arrangements for Air Raid Precautions and other paraphernalia of defence. Gas masks and air-raid shelters were ready for issue. For once there was no scarcity of work for prisoners. The Bill was dropped.

Five days after Sir Samuel Hoare's 'jitterbug' speech German troops moved unresisted into Czechoslovakia. A week later the Fry twins were seventy. Margery had two sisterly greetings to send, each, as always, unique in its tenderness. To Isabel she wrote, 'I must have a moment's truce with miseries to tell you how I love you, and count on you and hope that we may somehow jog along together, till better times come.' As a birthday present she sent wool and cotton for embroidery—'No silks, observe—you can make things to sell for China if that will ease your conscience.'

The Howard League had acquired a brilliant ally in Dr Radzinowitz, who had been sent in 1938 by the Polish Ministry of Justice to examine penal affairs in Britain. In June he met representatives of other international penal organizations at Geneva to decide the minimum rules for untried persons which were to be laid before the League of Nations. He took with him Margery Fry's own draft.

Before the September session at Geneva, which she noted in her diary with a query, there was time for her first visit to Scandinavia as the guest of the Kinbergs. (She had already, as the alarms of March grew fainter, visited the Maurons and Jeanne.) She found the Baltic warm enough to swim in. She slept in a little wooden hut by the sea. She discovered sailing and listened to the Kinbergs playing Mozart. The unconventional household, the mixture of art and penal reform, had a familiar feeling. Moreover, though she was not the first of Mariabella's children to fly (Ruth had beaten her) she had made her first flight in this, her sixty-sixth year.

But I must say the plane looked horribly small and fragile when I saw it— about 30 ft. long, inside too low for me to stand up in, like a tiny motor coach with places for 8 people, 4 a side, but it can't take 8 if there are heavy mails. But as I had it all to myself the whole way this ? didn't arise. It is, as A.R.F. says, amazingly un-alarming. In a way that seemed to me the most miraculous thing, that living millennia upon the earth we find in the air so natural an element. We came down at Hamburg where 1/6 bought 1 cup of indifferent coffee, and at Copenhagen where I strolled about the ground and watched the crowd outside as if I'd been a Whipsnade beast. At intervals the three charming young men who flew the plane came along to tell me where we were or what we were doing, when to wake up and blow my nose to prevent earache, so I'd no time to be dull.

At Stockholm she inadvertently kept her friends waiting while the pilot showed her 'all the gadgets in the cockpit'.

XV
The Second War: 1939-1945

At eleven o'clock on the night before her early departure to Sweden, Margery Fry had received at Clarendon Road a message from the Chinese Embassy. The Japanese had demanded that the British authorities in the Concession at Tientsin should hand over to the District Court four Chinese suspected (as it seemed to the Embassy, on flimsy evidence) of murdering a Chinese who had collaborated with the invader. The District Court was in the hands of the Japanese army and its puppets. Margery Fry was asked to do something to save these four lives. It was a Saturday night in August: everyone she rang seemed out of town. At last, however, Norman Bentwich replied. Two minutes before midnight she was dictating a night letter to Lord Halifax, the Foreign Secretary, informing him that she and Norman Bentwich were applying for a writ of habeas corpus on behalf of the four Chinese.

Her action returned to her with startling clarity over the radio as she set out from Saltsjöbäden on Sunday with eight Kinbergs for a three-day cruise in their little yacht. On Monday the *Manchester Guardian* had a leader on the affair; Lord Listowel, as President of the China Campaign Committee, added his name to the application. The British Court in Tientsin rejected it on the grounds that the applicants were unknown to the prisoners. The application was then brought before Mr Justice Cassels in London. It was again rejected, the applicants to pay costs. Counsel for the Foreign Office found the application absurd 'though he did not wish to cause pain to people of good-will and humanitarian feelings'. On 26 August a letter from the Foreign Office to the Chinese Embassy pointed out that it was the regular proceeding for Chinese suspects from the British concession of Tientsin to be handed over to the District Court. This letter appeared in *The Times* on the same day as photographs of gas masks being distributed and stained glass being taken down in Canterbury Cathedral. Readers of *The Times* heard no more of the affair, but the four lives were, in fact, saved, perhaps through the enormous publicity and considerable delay caused by Margery Fry's midnight action.

Britain had been at war for a week before Margery got back to London. She did not see the blackout curtains hung, or the city schoolchildren, with their gas masks in cardboard cases, being led from house to house through the countryside—two of them to Agnes's welcoming door. Her sense of displacement and uselessness on her return was therefore the more extreme. She was in the war, but she had no touch of idealism about it. There were no portraits of admirals or generals hanging on the Fry walls, not so much as an empty scabbard or a brass button in their attics. She saw only the loss of hopes and slowly-won achievements as the boys marched out of Lowdham Grange and the unfinished Borstal was turned into a prison, as Pentonville and Holloway, emptied under the immediate threat of bombing, were filled again with internees.

The operation of moving 750,000 schoolchildren from the big cities had been carried out smoothly. As the days passed and the big cities were not wiped out, the children began to drift back, the discontents of rural hosts and urban guests began to cry aloud. In Cambridge a large group of concerned people saw a chance to examine some of the questions which evacuation had opened. 'I think', wrote Margery to Agnes, 'the evacuated children are such an illumination of social conditions and also such an experiment for the future of children who have to be away from home that some worthwhile stuff may come out.'

The Howard League office had been cleared, the more valuable books and documents dispersed, the current papers taken to Miss Craven's house in Welwyn. In answer to Dr Susan Isaacs's invitation to take an advisory post in the evacuation survey, Margery Fry moved to an hotel in Cambridge. She and Miss S. Clement Brown became joint honorary secretaries to the Research Committee.

'There are rather too many lions for the Xtians, i.e. psychologists, students, workers for the children,' she told Isabel. She was looking for something more immediately practical than research. She was no longer of an age and status to haul mattresses from lorries, as in 1915, but she had some idea of fostering a group of children too naughty or unhappy to settle in their billets. She would care for them in her own way as Isabel, in spite of age and illness, had cared for her little group of refugees at Church Farm. Margery soon found that an amateur approach was impossible to these fosterlings for whom the State had taken responsibility. 'The derelicts' home is indefinitely put off—got into a maze of inter-authority committees and conferences—if it happens it'll be something too official and big for me—I *don't* want to be a "matron".' So she told Isabel, but others saw that she was accepting frankly that the domestic day-to-day care of a group of disturbed, not very bright children was outside her capacity.

I think a few weeks can be put in not unusefully in scotching the wild talk of complete failure of the [evacuation] scheme [she wrote to Isabel early in November], laying down some principles if it *has* to go on, and deducing something as to use of boarding-out for difficults if ever this unbeginning war ends. It's a comfort even to play at work and of course it's far less lonely than London. The Chinese are inviting me to meet them. . . . But *practically* I'm doing almost O eating my head off and my purse out in a too-comfortable hotel. . . . I have a lot of writing to get through, gradually, some reading of prison documents I *must* do and my Clarke Hall lecture to finish—but I feel a cumberer of the ground all the same.

A few days later she heard that the Clarke Hall lecture, which she was to have delivered that month in the hall of Gray's Inn, was cancelled.

At the beginning of the survey[1] everyone shared the chores. Margery Fry had been all her life a nimble and willing folder, sticker, and addresser, but this time her rheumatic hands fumbled at the card index. All her work until then had been for people taken out of their own homes and placed, however temporarily, in an institutional setting. 'I'm *quite* clear now', she had said in France in 1915, when she had to find out the needs of refugee families, 'that I'm really unsuited for social work. I feel so much the impertinence of coming into people's lives.' The Cambridge inquiry was intimate and domestic. Though the dispersal of the children had been a government operation, they were now living in ordinary families: foster-mothers had to be questioned about the children in their care. Moreover, they had to be approached through a questionnaire. Margery Fry, who had always come like an artist fresh to every human contact, found it almost impossible to keep the rules. She had been impatient with the Cadburys of an older generation because she had seen that social justice could not depend on a chance proximity to wealth. That it could not depend either on chance

[1] Susan Isaacs (ed.), *The Cambridge Evacuation Survey* (1941).

proximity to an amateur of genius was a possibility which she in her generation found hard to imagine.

'I'm quite liking seeing people here,' she wrote to Dorothy Scott, 'but feel so numb it's hard to believe one's alive or real.' The loss of normal activity, the reversal of twenty years' work seemed to stop her blood. Her keen ears were listening all the time to the throb of misery in Europe and China, waiting for the thunder to break nearer at hand. For the first time in her life she was known, even beyond letters to her sisters and close friends, to be bored and cross. Christmas seemed in prospect even more tiresome than in Margery's girlhood, when the young Quaker had never come to terms with the festival but had hung about on its edge 'like a mermaid'. 'One must avoid the fictitious gaiety of hotels and such at all costs.' But the usual number of friends, made and kept over fifty years, received their appropriate presents.

She was asked early in 1940 to visit France to see if anything could be done for intellectual refugees. She was embarrassed by Isabel's elation at the news:

I don't for a moment think I can inspect, or alter, the conditions in the camps, specially the Spanish ones. . . . It may seem horrible to limit our efforts but I believe I'm right simply to go for the 'intellectuals'—not because humanly they matter more, but because they both have more effect on international feeling and hold more of the keys of the future than the rank and file. . . . I am in *terror* that the whole journey will turn into a wild goose chase. I *don't* feel inclined to take any Communist stuff *quite* at its face value—I *quite* expect it's partly true. . . . But I *know* an old thing like me can't do a big crusade.

From Paris she wrote that Jeanne and the Maurons had been glad to see her. She had enjoyed delivering people's gifts to various refugee groups, and

like an idiot I fell in love with the water colours of one of the painters and am bringing some to England to see if I can get an exhibition for him. He and his wife are terribly hard up and it seems awful for such lovely work to go unseen. But I foresee ennuis in abundance over it. I doubt if I've done much good about the refugees—a little perhaps. I feel once more a useless parasite on society, for what I can do is about done. Tant pis.

In May the German troops poured into Holland and Belgium. In June France fell. Pamela's Rumanian-born husband watched

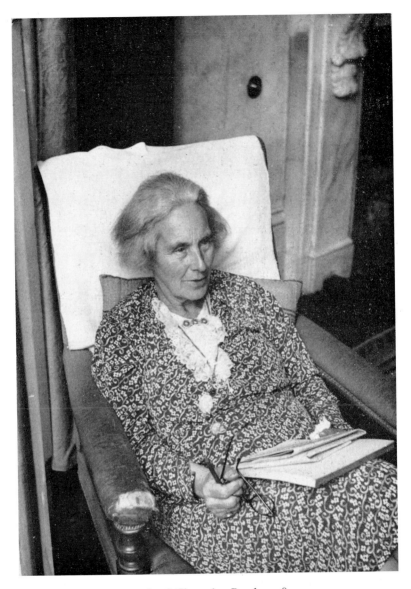

7. At 48 Clarendon Road, 1948

8. With her great-great-nephews Andrew Cole and Stephen Taber, 1950

from a great distance a camouflaged liner move down the Mersey, taking Pamela and their three half-Jewish children to Canada. Margery tried to get in touch with Jeanne through Americans, Swedes, Chinese. 'One sits powerless to do anything and afraid of embarrassing the people who *are* trying to act by amateurish questions and offers of useless help.'

The Germans were on the other side of the Channel. The Clarke Hall lecture, announced once more for June, was finally abandoned to the printers. A French professor of mathematics was installed for an indefinite period at 48 Clarendon Road. Margery began to be anxious about Roger's papers, still in the house in Mecklenburgh Square, Bloomsbury, where Virginia Woolf had lately finished writing his biography. She had lectures about China to give in Birmingham and Staffordshire. Then she was 'at leisure to be bombed'.

Part of her leisure she used to visit women interned in Holloway. There she was horrified to hear talk of the dark cell which had gone out of use twenty years earlier. She found it was not the original punishment cell but a rather more humane version with double doors which was being found useful as a 'cooler' for prison hysteria. She suggested rational occupation as a more effective treatment: could not internees make things for their own people, refugees, or prisoners of war? She convinced the greengrocer at the corner of Clarendon Road of the human rights of internees: he got hold of a few cases of oranges to send into Pentonville and the Cadburys offered to pay for more. She kept up her visits to provincial prisons more zealously than ever. She watched hopefully the work of Dr Radzinowitz and Dr Hermann Mannheim, the beginnings of a science of criminology in Britain.

There was plenty to keep her in London, even in August. While the Battle of Britain was in mid-fight less than forty miles away, Margery was drying her hair and writing letters in the front window at Clarendon Road. London in August, she told Isabel, was 'tired and stale, much more autumnal than the country, a region of petrol smells and sparrows, and white cabbage butterflies. But my dear little willow-wrens come to flirt about the fountain and each time I see one it gives me an absurd little stab of pleasure.' She had just come from lunch at the Chinese Embassy, where she had sat as hostess opposite the Ambassador, 'in a company of ghost-statesmen: old Lord Cecil, deaf and bent and standing for so many dead and dying hopes'. The next day there was to be a delegation to Mr Butler about the closing of the Burma Road. Pentonville was being thinned out: two hundred internees had left that week. She hoped to get some concerts for those who remained. She had been teaching little Frank, child of her current refugee guests, to play animal-grab in the re-inforced basement she used an air-raid shelter.

A week later the raids on London began in earnest, fire-bombs followed by high explosive. The temporary parlourmaid, a little creature whom Margery had feared looked too puny for her duties, had gone home to Barking for her half-day. She was back before the night was over, having walked twelve miles through deserted fire-lit streets, and 'wouldn't have missed it for anything'. A night's sleep in a proper bed seemed a far dream. One night when the raids began early she had to stay in a house on Highgate Hill with Kingsley Martin, Dorothy Woodman, and the Chinese Ambassador. She was perhaps half a mile from the nursery where sixty years before she had tried not to scream when the Volunteers drummed their way up the Grove. She spent one night playing animal-grab with a little homeless boy she had brought home from the Children's Court. On another, when a former Somervillian shared the shelter, Margery brought out from under her rugs a small red book and began to read in ringing tones: 'It is a truth universally acknowledged, that a single man in possession of a good fortune must be in want of a wife.'

For Londoners the journey from home to work and back again was no longer a journey between certainties. 'Somehow my life seems more scrappy and disconnected than I can cope with,' Margery wrote to Champion Russell. 'Nothing done—and yet no time for doing the little nothings that I might do. I must say I wish I could "go to it" at one definite matter. However here's the ump-teenth air-raid and I can't get on with telephone dealings or walk up to the bank.'

'But, oh my dear,' she told Russell (for Roger was dead, and the sisterhood must not know she was afraid), 'I'm *not* a good example on these beastly nights. . . . The A.A. guns are some of 'em v. near and shake the house. Then some sort of screaming incendiaries whistle by,—*I* thought they were time bombs, but each seems to be followed by a fire, then come the engines—then it's quiet for seven minutes and you think you might sleep—then comes that horrible plane booming and it all begins again . . . These are my little war-worries, too small to tell to any but the most understanding of friends.'

Yet set down on paper things fell into order. Isabel was ill, but Margery had found a nursing-home near Malvern. Two more of de Gaulle's men had moved into Clarendon Road, one 'Jesuit-raised, but now free-thinking—very thoughtful, but curiously ignorant of what has been thought'. Mrs Stubbs and the little maid could manage very well by themselves for short spells—'China wants some attention—I'm to address the T.U. leaders on it on Thursday'. In the second week of September 1940 the Memorandum on the Probation of offenders, prepared by the Colonial Advisory Committee, was sent out from the Colonial Office to its territories.

Ruth's house was totally destroyed in October, but Ruth was safe in the country. Then, as Joan Mary Fry and her companion sat in the reinforced passage of her house one night a near-by explosion tore off the roof. The Chinese lacquer cabinet was unharmed in the place where it had stood since its removal to the sweet security of the Garden Suburb ten years earlier. But Romeo the kitten had escaped and until he was found Joan could not go to Clarendon Road. When she arrived there Margery was humbled by the old lady's courage and lack of bitterness.

Then Isabel had to be fetched home from the Malvern nursing-home to Church Farm. There Margery made her base. As 48 Clarendon Road might not last through the winter and Church Farm was cold, she took plenty of blankets. A great deal of time was spent in trains and buses as she went up and down to meetings in London. As she walked through Tavistock Square to 'a rather melancholy little meeting of the Magistrates' Association Emergency or Keep-Alive-Committee' she 'hated to see the house where Leonard and Virginia Woolf lived till a year or so ago a mass of tumbled bricks with a bath hanging out vertically by its pipes'.

Virginia Woolf's *Roger Fry*, published in July, was already in its third edition. 'I believe Roger has come at the right moment for many people,' she had written to Margery in August, when the raids still harrassed rather than obsessed the lives of Londoners. Margery had sent Virginia Woolf her own small book, the ill-fated Clarke Hall lecture called *The Ancestral Child*. Virginia Woolf wrote back, crowded among the books and tables and Omega chairs sent down to Sussex from Bloomsbury:

What a fraud you are! You say you're not a writer and then out you come with all the fascinating ideas and theories as thick as trout in a stream and as clear as crystal. I read it with the greatest interest, what's more rare with the sense that you've only indicated and must go on to develop. I'm sure you're on the track of something hidden and important. Please write a whole book about 'having'—and our ancestral selves. I've dimly guessed at so many, but haven't your facts or insights. . . . When shall we meet tongue to tongue and argue it all?

But Margery was not a fraud. At this time even letter-writing caused her physical pain. Public writing set weights in her pen: only the idea of speech lightened them. She saw herself addressing the distinguished gathering in one of the Inns of Court as

a life-long dilettante, jack of several trades, master of none. . . . Neither archbishop, judge, cabinet minister or administrator, neither doctor, lawyer, psychologist or sociologist, I have no territory of my own to defend, so that I can at least freely play the vagabond, and in the course of my remarks I shall be frequently found on enclosed premises, quite obviously with a view to committing depredations on other people's learning.

Professor Olaf Kinberg's theories on the growth of moral sense fortified those ideas of 'having' which had grown in her mind for some fifteen years. But chiefly she touched her readers by her own vision of the boys who came before her in the Chelsea Juvenile Court, 'gangs of little urchins going off to see what sport the King's Road offers on a Saturday afternoon', people who emotionally still roamed the primeval forest: citizens more amenable to the rule of Sparta, where children learned to fend for themselves and being discovered in theft was the sole guilt, than to the Metropolitan Police Regulations and the Common Law. Or they were like that spook which haunted an old library: 'he walks along the level of an older floor, and the modern boards seem to cut his legs at the shins. . . . For most people there is only misery ahead in a constant warfare with the actual world. . . . But we must not lose our sense that our system is not part of the nature of things, that it is frequently itself the defaulter.'

So through a grove of metaphors she would lead her hearers to the clearing, the practical issue. They must persuade the state educational system when peace came to provide emotional outlets, tastes of 'wild life', so that children could mature without losing their initiative and independence: and she dragged in by its heels (a way in which she never scrupled to handle a good cause) a plea for 'skilled diagnosis, tender handling' for young offenders who were not merely immature, but warped.

Meanwhile, for urchins as well as magistrates, new ways of life were establishing themselves in London. Food rationing made outlawry unviable, but any boy was free to sleep away from home. 'London is really rather ghastly,' Margery admitted, 'so many children still there, the tubes invaded by middle day by families and their bedding,—and alas the refugees with O to do arrive v. early and are not loved for keeping out the natives.' Because Isabel needed her she backed out of a prospective tour of London to preach evacuation. 'There's no solution (for a woman anyhow) of the old problem of what is due to family and what to the larger world.' She had persuaded Pamela to leave: now, as well as the sisterhood, she had her niece's husband on her conscience. Affection grew between them as she visited the lonely house in Essex or he made himself useful at Clarendon Road, sounding an occasional disciplinary note to the Free Frenchmen housed there. She had to visit Agnes in Somerset. 'Of course the flesh (mine!) is only too willing to seize on any excuse not to stay in London.' Agnes was grandmothering two schoolboy evacuees from Poplar. (Was she perhaps the foster-mother in *The Ancestral Child* whose children put on their top-coats at dusk and explained that they were going out 'lifting'?) Again Margery was humbled by her sister's tender generosity to these not very responsive children. She believed that her own tolerance, immense as it seemed in her own world, would not have run so deep.

At the end of 1940 Margery watched, from a cousin's balcony at Epping, the glow of that second Great Fire of London, when Guildhall, eight city churches, the publishers' warehouses around St Paul's, were all ablaze, and the cathedral dome, veiled by smoke for days, seemed a miraculous symbol of survival. 'The fluidity of the future has almost reached gaseousness,' she told Isabel. 'I really don't seem able to arrive at that virtue the parents valued so highly of "sticking to plans".' The pages of her engagement diary, once crossed and recrossed by half-legible entries, were now blank except for an occasional 'Meeting?' But somehow the meetings were held.

She had to hand on to others the visits to internees, when late in 1940 she was appointed to the Government Committee on Non-enemy Interned Aliens (people charged under the much-discussed '18 B'). Her friends were glad to see her there, but she hated the job. 'I've been so ashamed of idleness I couldn't refuse, but the papers

I've been pursuing, the known reactionariness of the chairman . . ., the utter impossibility of applying any of the ordinary machinery of justice, all make me dread the meeting. But one can but try!' Dread turned to

discomfort—almost misery. It's nothing to do with *justice*. It's what we've always decried in other countries, keeping people shut up, without trial, on suspicions you never reveal to them, so that they don't really know what charges they should answer. *But,* they have mostly come in without proper papers, deportation is impossible, *trial,* or even the form of enquiry into their past lives, are impossible where you can't call witnesses, where often their countries are over-run and their police-forces disorganized or abolished. To tell the sources of suspicion would often mean the revelation of secret sources of knowledge wh. are vital (or are said to be so) to our own secret service. And, there are, I think, definitely secret agents sent over in the guise of anti-Nazis. . . . I realize more and more the vital importance of all the formalities of trial, when I see how haphazard any decisions made without them are. But even granted that we are *not* trying these people, are, in fact, only used to oblige the security people to make out a prima facie case for internment, I still feel it could be better done than we are doing it. . . . There are times when I feel I can't go on—but then I have to admit that I see no chance of substituting a fair trial for this most unsatisfactory procedure, and if so, what right have I to throw the dirty work on someone else?[2]

Some colleagues appeared to regard her as a nuisance, others as positively dangerous, but she saw no solution except to stick it, and to bring on to the committee one of the best-informed people she knew, Albert Lieck, the police-court clerk whom Cicely Craven had found for the Howard League. His dry encyclopedic mind did not seem to Margery to apprehend the whole truth, but his legal omniscience had an international reputation. When he died a few months later Margery wondered whether she had helped to kill him, but concluded that he had enjoyed having work to do.

For herself, as for prisoners, Margery sought 'rational occupation' as a remedy for misery. In the same letter in which she discussed the Aliens Committee she threw out to Champion Russell the suggestion of an 'ABC for Juvenile Magistrates': 'it would be such fun to do it together'. Her suggestion for a title was 'Early Worms for Young Beaks'. Though the little book came out soberly entitled *A Notebook for the Children's Courts* in the bleak days of 1942 there is fun in it.

[2] Letter to Champion Russell.

' "I saw these lads going towards High St." will be better grasped than "I observed the accused proceeding in the direction of the main thoroughfare".' There is an eye for detail, for good manners— 'Neither witnesses nor accused nor Bench should have strong light in their eyes.' 'It is better to go to a private room than to have a whispered conversation in public.' And again, freshly worded, there is the insistence on justice. 'The view that a child's welfare may best be served by a finding of guilt leading to treatment and care is no excuse for a decision which has not been strictly justified by the evidence given. . . . Particularly where the parents are ill-conditioned and truculent, and the child obviously an ill-licked cub, it is hard to remember that it is not general unsatisfactoriness but the commission of a particular act forbidden by the law that has to be proved, and that it must be made clear to the children and to their parents that this is so.' A former probation officer who reviewed the *Notebook* in the *Howard Journal* recalled 'those days in Court when everyone breathed a sigh of relief as Margery Fry created from a tangle of emotional and legal difficulties a clear and hopeful pattern of action'.

The Colonial Advisory Committee met throughout the war, 'not regularly, but usefully'. It was worth while meeting, Margery maintained, if only to assure far-flung prison governors that their reports were being read with attention by a few people in England. In some ways, in spite of the enormous complications of the local and colonial systems of justice, penal reform had a fair field in the colonies. There was no legacy of Victorian Pentonvilles. In many countries prison labour could be used for public works without the impediments of a highly organized industrial system. People like Margery Fry were determined that this landscape should not be scarred by the growth of large penal institutions. Young people especially must be kept out of prison. Local systems of restitution—as, for instance, the payment of small debts by ordinary labour—should be preserved. Probation systems must be established as soon as manpower could be provided. During the short period when Malcolm Macdonald was Secretary for the Colonies plans for a complete probation service, which had been developing slowly for ten years, gathered speed. Through the months of the 'unbeginning war' Margery Fry and her colleagues were preparing the Memorandum which went out from Westminster during the autumn bombardment. She became a member of a Subcommittee on Juvenile Delinquency chaired by Alexander Paterson.

As a result of its report the Advisory Committee was reorganized as the Colonial Social Welfare Advisory Committee. Though she had helped to bring this committee into being, Margery Fry made it clear that her place would be on the sub-committee for penal affairs. Her eye was on the ball: she had no taste for a general humanitarian knock-up, for indeed she had no taste for penal reform unless she played to win. It was a pursuit which lasted the rest of her life. Sometimes a prompt phrase would set the committee laughing, sometimes she would sustain a passion of indignation for weeks on end. Always she read every word of every document.

'There is certainly no apathy about the country, people demand meetings and conferences and plans,' Margery wrote to Agnes in 1942. In the spring of 1941 the raids on Britain died away as Hitler turned towards the east. Many who had survived the bombardment were thirsting for something more than the grubby day-to-day struggle to carry on physically. The interest in political and social institutions, kindled in the days of the Popular Front, the Penguin Specials, and the Left Book Club, was not yet spent. There was even a demand, as among the French women in the First War, for 'un peu de poésie dans la vie'. Margery Fry must have rejoiced to find herself in 1941 one of the first members of the Council for the Encouragement of Music and the Arts, the war-familiar CEMA, forerunner of the Arts Council.

She was talking more than ever. The B.B.C. found her an excellent chairman of the realistic, controversial kind of discussion she had wanted broadcast. She took part in the earliest series of 'Any Questions?' Early in 1942 she lunched at the Café Royal as a member of the team for which the name 'Brains Trust' had just been invented. She had become one of the elect who are asked to talk about themselves. 'No philosopher but ready if wanted,' she once telegraphed to Broadcasting House. But penal affairs and China, she told University House, were still her main interests, the friendships of Chinese men and women one of her greatest personal joys. 'I am increasingly sure that before this century ends China will be making her full contribution—as she has never done yet,—to the thought and philosophy of the civilized world.'[3]

Penal affairs in Britain were at a standstill, but Cicely Craven and Margery Fry formed an international committee, drawing on the exiles then in England, to consider post-war plans. More than one

[3] Letter to the University House Association, 1941.

group of the kind seemed to be forming: the Howard League wanted theirs to by-pass the question of war guilt and to consider the problems that would arise if the Allies had for some time to police Axis or liberated territories.

On 1 April 1942 Margery wrote to Agnes: 'This is a letter I hate to write because I know it's going to hurt you. Yesterday a bombshell fell in the shape of an invitation to me to go to the U.S.A. to speak and confer about penal questions. I'm getting to think I shall have to go. The only excuses I can make are "my sisters would be anxious", "I'm rather afraid of being drowned or overtired" and somehow in the circumstances of today neither seems to sound very convincing. Truly what I mind most about it is that it means adding a new anxiety to the sisterhood.' She also dreaded loneliness. This time there could be no travelling companion. She was even afraid of finding nothing to say. 'I wish the whole thing were a little more definite, a little less just "a good thing to promote good feeling in general"!'

Before the end of April 1942 she had gone, crossing the infested Atlantic by deviations unimaginable to the four sisters at home. Three of Mariabella's surviving children were now in their seventies. They had never before been so long without Margery. She was away for a year, and they could speak with her only through delayed and censored letters. She landed at Halifax on a Wednesday morning. On Thursday evening she addressed a social welfare conference at New Orleans: 'my last lap was in a police car which had the privilege of crashing past the traffic lights'.

The year seems to have gone by at a similar pace. She divided her time between penal affairs and 'goodwill in general'. Her notebooks, evidently written at speed, have a Dickensian raciness. There had certainly been advances since 1931: in a school for boy convicts she found 'a carefully picked staff, including a very good footballer. Directors of everything (almost B.B.C.—one was a Director of Home Life).' In one prison 'the men eat in a grand dining-hall, all very collegiate, cafeteria serving, menu *sounds* marvellous. They have the free run of a good deal of the building, gymnasium, a splendid library. All sorts of plans and schemes for individual treatment, and discussions of their adjustments quite à la Balliol. The percentage of non-reconvictions is good, but no better than with our unselected first offenders—is it perhaps all too artificial for real character-training?' Even in the most humane prisons, she wondered whether they

need be so vast. But there was much which, with modifications, she
wanted to transplant—the Ford Boys' Republic at Detroit, the pre-
trial settlement of children's cases in Washington. 'Here a paternalism is accepted against which, I think, our people would kick. But
I'm converted to the view that it's well to put domestic and Chil-
drens' Courts together.' She noticed the Federal institution for drug
addicts, the prison in New York State for young men of educational
ability. She gave particular attention to the newly instituted Youth
Convention Authority in California, which had been given wide
powers of treatment for young people over the age for the Juvenile
Court and below the age of twenty-three.

As in England, she visited universities as well as prisons. 'I confess that I am green with envy of the spacious buildings and landscapes of their universities. Some of the buildings are lovely, some
hideous, but there is an amplitude in planning for the needs of
education which rather puts us to shame.'

'I'm very well,' she told Agnes after six weeks, 'talk a lot, people
like it—what if anything it *does* I don't know. The war seems further,
if you understand me, less black but more sense of guilt.' As the year
went on Margery was ashamed to find her sense of guilt weakening:
it became nicer, rather than more unsettling, to be warm, well fed,
to sleep quietly in a real bed. She tried to remember what England
had been like. Over and over she told audiences about Agnes's boys
from Poplar.

Again Agnes did her war-work: again Margery kept Agnes's
letters. These marginal notes on wartime feared no censor: the
bicycles that had taken the place of cars, 'old ladies and babies pedalling along like mad', the beauty of night in the blackout: 'I must go
to bed and I think Venus will light me.' Again, as in another war, she
told the small events in her neighbours' lives, important enough
when measured by the scale of individual worth which the Frys
carried with them. 'I think my heart, if ever I had one, is now nearly
a stone and responds only to pinpricks—small recognizable woes of
humanity,' Agnes wrote after the fall of Singapore.

In California, Margery picked out the story of the fall of Tobruk
from a sponsored radio programme: ten years later the advertising
slogans still stuck in her memory like burrs. In the colours of the
southern summer she felt she was living 'in one of those horrid
children's pictures with black backgrounds'. In the autumn she
made her way to Canada at last, and saw, she declared, the same old

shabby kingfisher by the lake which had been there nine years earlier. Mackenzie King invited her to tea in Montreal: 'two hours in the company of the most discussed man in Canada, and came away with almost no impression at all, but of a kindly old man apparently occupied entirely by his shrubberies, his sham ruins, his donkey and his dog'.

She was 'all right but rather tired', in consequence worried about 48 Clarendon Road, exasperated more than usual by being taken for Elizabeth Fry. She sent off her Christmas presents in good time. Agnes was a little startled to find that her parcel contained boots for the second year in succession ('You pour out boots as the sun pours out light'), but the boots were stuffed with treasures rare in England —hairpins, elastic bands, sticky paper, reels of cotton. Winter set in, the bitterest for fifty years—'twigs the thickness of a grass stem carrying ice as big as my finger, much destruction among trees, much dislocation of traffic: wonderful beauty'. Hitler's troops, beaten by the Russian winter, were giving themselves up among the ruins of Stalingrad.

By the end of March 1943 the ivy at Brent Knoll was in bloom as never before—'Great globes of gold flowers in crowds on the bushes'. In April, living from moment to moment in dread of extinction, Margery Fry again crossed the Atlantic without incident. As usual, she feared returning to a jobless world: would, she wondered, her sharp eyes be good at plane-spotting? As usual, she found occupation at various levels. 'China things are stirring, and not always easy.' The United Chinese Aid Fund had been launched with splendid patronage and publicity. At the end of a column in *The Times* the China Campaign Committee was named in small print in a list of supporting organizations. The new organization handed over its gifts to Madame Chiang Kai-Shek. The China Campaign Committee, as far as Margery Fry was concerned, had avoided political bias. It was committed to helping a hospital in Communist territory. The Campaign became a magnet for the British Communists, fiercely opposed to the new Fund. 'The new United China Aid Fund', Margery told Agnes, 'is of a very different colour from our old Campaign, yet we make part of it and *must* cooperate.' This even-handed justice brought upon her a request to succour some victimized ex-members of the British Union of Fascists. She sent them to the National Council for Civil Liberties.

That summer de Gaulle's men were seen more rarely at 48

Clarendon Road. 'I have had much insight into a strange, dangerous, immensely brave world of underground activity.' Their lives would in all probability be short, and Margery must make them as happy as she could. One married a wife of three weeks' acquaintance: a home was waiting for her upstairs.

During Margery's absence the International Committee of the Howard League had been held together by Miss Craven and Miss Reekie, who took over the secretary's chores while Miss Craven was working at Barnett House in Oxford. There was particular concern about the state of European prisons when the war ended: it seemed certain there would be a flood of political prisoners, Quislings and collaborators of every degree. Without foresight all standards of penal administration might collapse. This question proved impossible to discuss: it was inconceivable to some members of the committee that loyal citizens should criticize their own governments. But the committee still held: Margery Fry and her colleagues found something it could do. Long and profitable discussions opened about the treatment of young offenders, leading to the publication of the international symposium, *Lawless Youth*, in 1947.

As Mussolini's forces collapsed and the Germans were held in the east, Margery Fry was working ahead for the time when peace would bring in the deferred Criminal Justice Bill. At the end of 1943 her article in *Agenda* (a journal of reconstruction, published by the London School of Economics) surveyed 'The Future Treatment of the Adult Offender'. It was later reissued as a pamphlet by Victor Gollancz.

There is grave danger that we shall go on in the future as we have done in the past, climbing a little way up the slippery pole of reform, like the snail in the children's puzzle, whenever public demands, an energetic Home Secretary, or exceptionally enlightened officials at the head of affairs afford the needful impetus, slithering back under the weight of apathy and routine when it is withdrawn. . . . The puzzle snail reaches the pole-top at last: but our goal, a system where equal and enlightened justice shall limit crime to the utmost with the least possible loss of lawful liberty, is a long way off, and to reach it by the climb-and-slip method will take too many years.

In her discussion of the courts she now began to point the morals of the increasing number of motoring offences. People of a class which had previously seen the courts only from the Bench were now appearing as defendants. She remarked also, in suggesting that education could play an important part in the prevention of crime, that a lack of shame prevailed among dangerous drivers. The most fundamental change she suggested was that for all young offenders, and for other groups, the courts should merely determine guilt and fix a maximum period of treatment; that the method of treatment should be determined by a separate authority.

She reiterated the things she had always fought for. Some were still to be won, others which had been gained in form were still neglected in practice: legal aid, child guidance, the provision of a variety of institutions, better conditions for prison officers, the encouragement of psychiatrists to take up prison service, the abolition of capital and corporal punishment, the provision of paid labour and of after-care. Any reform, she said again, was in danger of failure if it had to be carried out in Victorian prison buildings. 'The old bottles would not, unfortunately, burst with the new wine; they would simply turn it to vinegar.'

In 1943, Margery Fry, at sixty-nine, learned to make coffee and porridge, to boil potatoes, and even to bottle plums. The single-minded cunning then needed to get and keep a servant was not in her nature. She was never sure whether it was more important to have an efficient servant or to give a home to someone who lacked it. Besides, though she was often absent, her guests were always present. She had accustomed them to being treated with tolerance. When the mistress was at home she expected to be waited on with old-fashioned thoroughness. She had, moreover, a curious blindness about the inconvenience of her house, where worn-out saucepans were not replaced, even when they were obtainable, and every cup of tea had to be carried upstairs. Lady Fry had perhaps taught her daughters too little about what really went on beyond the baize door: all the sisters, in their different ways, were at the mercy of the domestic predicament.

Her seventieth birthday passed. As magistrates were scarce, she continued her magistracy for three more months, 'in a general sense of futility and uncertainty, as to whether we were doing more good than harm, the probation officers dead tired and only the wicked showing any green bay leaves'. At the end of June 1944 she sat on the Bench for the last time. Yet the B.B.C. saw her not as a falling but as a rising star. She was booked for Brains Trusts for a year ahead. 'If I were just a friend, or a cousin say,' wrote Agnes, 'I should be awed by such grandeur, but being a loved sister I may feel proud as Punch.'

In June 1944, a week after D-Day, Hitler's latest miracle weapons hit London and were immediately named by cockneys the doodle-bugs. They came by day, when families were separated. People looked back nostalgically to the wailing sirens, the snug shelter-life. At the Colonial Office or the University Grants Committee it was the duty of the chairman to give warning, for the benefit of any provincials present, that if the humming of a flying-bomb stopped they must dive under the table. Margery boasted to her friends that she was generally the last down. Once she was by far the last to reappear. She explained that she had become entangled in her string of beads.

The launching-grounds were captured—the flying-bombs stopped. A wronged Chinese wife—'a regular Conrad story'—was sent for refuge to Clarendon Road. Margery had to get police pro-tection against the outraged husband. Then the Chinese wife and the *poilus* left: only the young wife of one of the Frenchmen re-mained, quietly creating her little slum upstairs. Margery took in a bombed-out couple, with a wailing baby. They helped in the house, but made it smell.

New rockets came over from Holland, dropping from an immense height without warning. 'I've always felt slightly aggrieved', Margery wrote to Champion Russell, 'on behalf of the discreet birds who are described as "of skulking habits". I feel worse now, as this is exactly how I should be classified at present, . . . keeping as much as possible in the basement, out of reach of flying glass. There's an ignoble picture for you!' But this terror, an even more costly weapon for its inventors than the earlier missiles, soon passed.

Cicely Craven had sent out a questionnaire on Juvenile Delin-quency while Margery had worked at her essay on the Adult Offender. At Christmas 1944 the Howard League executive dis-cussed Miss Craven's report. There was much controversy, even in that select body, about the nature of the authority which it was hoped would finally take the Children's Court out of the system of criminal jurisdiction.

The year 1944 had not been unproductive. To Margery it had seemed the vilest of the whole war. But early in 1945 her French professor returned, covered with gold braid as a naval officer. Friends reappeared from China. Margery's great-nieces came home grown up from Canada. In February letters arrived from France. Margery could talk again to Jeanne Lepetit and Jacqueline Merle and the Maurons, piecing together the tale of their steadfastness. This time, when the war in Europe ended, Margery was not at odds with the general mood. There was no wild rejoicing: there were too many ruins, too many prisoners. The war in the East continued. Margery had her own quiet personal causes for celebration. Astonishingly the sisterhood had survived. Many more Colonial territories had a probation service than at the beginning of the war. There was no special mark for VE-Day in the calendar of the Howard League. The committee had already decided to buy a new duplicator. The old one had done them much service in twenty years, and more would be needed in the peace for which they had been preparing so long.

XVI

'What Life Has Taught Me': 1945-1955

BELSEN and Auschwitz were uncovered: the dark hinterland of 'The Accused' was being explored. New voices were asking for an international charter for prisoners. Margery Fry had already noticed the occasional ignorance of thinking people about what had already been thought: but she knew that such ignorance could precipitate action. She did not want time to be wasted: what had been won in the tedious vigils at Geneva during the 'thirties must not be lost. 'At least', she wrote to *The Times*,[1] 'the fact that the right treatment of prisoners has an international aspect has been publicly admitted. Unanimity as to what ought to be prohibited has been, and may be again, reached by a number of independent states.'

Her letter led to a press conference. Gilbert Murray presided and Margery Fry's colleague was M. Delierneux, Director of the Belgian Ministry of Justice. They did not linger over past horrors: M. Delierneux stated that at that moment there were 50,000 persons under arrest in Belgium, a country which had prison accommodation for 4,000. Margery Fry asked the press to urge that penal affairs should be given a permanent committee in the 'new world organization' (still nameless).

In 1946, after seven years' delay, she represented Britain in the International Penal and Penitentiary Congress. In the following year she submitted a memorandum on Human Rights at the invitation of U.N.E.S.C.O. Attempts were made to elbow the I.P.P.C. out of the United Nations because it admitted a representative from Spain, but it survived as a leading member of the United Nations Standing Committee on Penal Affairs. The Howard League agreed, on Margery Fry's suggestion, to submit an annual memorandum according to its prewar practice in the League of Nations. She had already promised a memorandum on capital and corporal punishment.

By the end of the war Margery Fry was older than Gertrude

[1] 19 May 1945.

Eaton had been when she handed over the Geneva Bureau. The international work of the Howard League was still her job, but Mrs Robinson (Madeleine Symons) went with her to Geneva in 1948 when the United Nations first considered penal affairs. In 1949 she took an important part in conferences in Paris and Utrecht, in 1950 at Lake Success. International work brought its rewards in friendships. Distinguished Europeans and Americans were delighted to find in this reforming English spinster 'a woman still'. Penal institutions were open to her for comparison—though it was a long time, she complained, before the Home Office would recognize that any country but Britain had advanced from the nineteenth century. When her conferences were ended in Paris she could 'share as it were Jeanne's invalidism, taking little potters at Rennes'. She had golden visits to Provence from which she would return with gipsy colouring to the grey office in Westminster. But in the main this nursing of international relations was physically exhausting, at first profoundly discouraging, usually boring.

At home others had arisen to take care of many of her concerns. After the Second World War, at an age when most people began to feel the discomforts of chronic nostalgia, Margery Fry was at ease with the times. In spite of the menaces of the atomic age, she knew where she was going and that she was moving with the tide. Again war had shown the defects in the national system of education, again an Education Act had been passed before the end of the war, giving education a full Ministry and providing in principle secondary education for all. In 1947 the school-leaving age was raised to fifteen. Early school-leaving, she had said, entailed a loss of capacity to the community which would be measured only when a genuinely universal system of education had been reached. In 1948, when *Times* correspondents feared that subsidized school milk and meals would undermine parental responsibility and filial respect, she joined her signature to those of Barbara Wootton, Eileen Younghusband, and Madeleine Robinson under an ironic description of boys and girls at private schools sitting down to their dinners 'with a sense of gratitude and filial duty engendered by the knowledge that a cheque had changed hands'.

There were inevitable limits to her radicalism. It had been tiresome, rather than shocking or surprising, when more or less distinguished parents rang her up at Oxford to ask her to 'have a look at their daughters'. 'Influence' was a part of the world she had grown up in, though as she grew older she grew increasingly suspicious of both influence and patronage. She came from a social class as incorruptible as any the world has ever known, a class which would unhesitatingly prefer a first-class candidate of unknown origin to a second-class candidate from its own number. It was in the lower ranges that talent became harder to recognize, hidden by awkward manners and an unfamiliar basis of experience. When privileges are few they must be bought or inherited or competed for in a fierce examination system. This last, with all its consequences, the Frys were brought up to detest: better to see the spoils shared by the known schools, the known families. If Margery Fry had given her life, as she had once hoped, to public education, she would have wanted a widening of opportunities, so that human beings, in infinite variety, should enter the adult world with their powers discovered and on the way to development.

Her ideal was still the common school. 'A real democracy must be based on an education uniting, not separating people in the impressionable years of childhood, yet it must be such that the most intelligent parents can accept it for their children.'[2] She assumed that 'the most intelligent parents' were at liberty to choose their children's education. It is unlikely that she imagined the children she knew best passing under the yoke of the eleven-plus. The moment when these 'most intelligent parents' would accept the common school was, and is, deferred. At what point could they abandon for their children privileges which had meant much to themselves? The new National Health Service was accepted at every social level because patients were attended by the doctors they already knew. State education was not widely known: the upper-middle class were more conscious of its failures than its successes. A few of Margery Fry's friends gave their children a baptism of democracy in the lower classes of a state primary school, but after she left Somerville she very rarely met anyone who attended a state secondary school. By 1944, for over twenty years, she had encountered public education mainly through the children who came before the courts.

Natural inclination would have led her to work for the education of ordinary children. Instead she had to feel for the exceptional, the university student and the delinquent: for she could not work without integrity of feeling as well as thought. In colonial affairs she not

[2] *What Life Has Taught Me*, p. 52.

only had to feel and think for unattractive people (the half-forgotten prisoners, the old lags became her care as others emerged to take up the cause of young offenders), she had to imagine strange tropical cultures which by the nineteen-forties she knew she would never see. 'Those boys in Fiji might have been in the next street,' said a colleague. Yet she did not suffer from the pathological long-sight of Dickens's Mrs Jellyby. When on Monday morning the same colleague apologized for having scrutinized less carefully than Margery the documents which had arrived on Saturday, she said only, 'These Africans are my boys: you have three of your own at home.'

Contrary to expectations based on the figures of the First War, offences of a more serious kind, especially sexual offences and crimes of violence, had continued to rise since the 'thirties. Prisons were overcrowded, employment in prison at a standstill. The percentage of indictments among boys of fourteen to seventeen more than doubled between 1938 and 1959. The reformers had to go on patiently looking for the causes of crime in the face of a clamour for toughness of treatment. There was a backlog of work. 'The war has put the prison clock back almost to 1922,' the Howard League Report had opened in 1943. But its first conference after the war looked forward. Ideas had been maturing for six years: the work put into the Criminal Justice Bill went back much farther. Margery Fry's concerns were all at once coming to the boil. She had to speak for China. She had to put in more hours than ever before with the University Grants Committee. For two years before her resignation from the U.G.C. in 1948 she was on a Sub-committee on Social Studies. She told her old students in 1948 that she could no longer do the stairs on her 'visitations', but she told her colleagues (who in this instance disagreed with her) that in university affairs the days of the amateur were over.

The discussion about possible changes in the children's courts, opened at the Howard League by Cicely Craven just before the end of the war, continued unresolved. Margery Fry accepted in principle that children under fourteen were not criminals. She also knew that in most cases the facts were not in serious dispute and the proper treatment of a child showing delinquent tendencies was really the issue. But she was reluctant to throw over the insight and experience built up over the years at the Home Office. She was still more reluc-tant to hand over to a 'Welfare Council' the power to remove children from their families. She reiterated that justice must be shown to be done, that a child removed from his family must understand that he had received this judgement through a specific and proved course of conduct: and, moreover, that the judgement could be appealed against.

She was planning a physical withdrawal from concerns which engaged her mind and heart as deeply as ever. Written records show only the part of the load which she still felt she must carry personally. Surviving fellow workers remember how, although she raised her voice less often, they always felt her to be there. A few wondered whether she was quiet because she was losing grip: to others it seemed that a general humility flowed like George Fox's 'ocean of light and love' over the old springs of arrogance and impatience which still spurted when pompousness or lack of consideration hit her in moments of fatigue. About this time she wrote in one of her notebooks a sentence of R. L. Stevenson, 'One person I have to make good, myself: but my duty to my neighbour is much more nearly expressed by saying that I have to make him happy if I may.' She had seen happiness destroyed by war and the persecutions that came before and after it. She had also seen the greatness of ordinary people. She was surrounded by able and well-concerned men and women of a generation, two generations younger than her own. She had been favoured in her sisters, wise in her friendships. The love she had given came back, as one of her friends had hoped, 'like sunlight from a brick wall', bringing her fresh resources of sympathy and patience.

Again it was Madeleine Robinson who went in with Cicely Craven to give evidence for the Howard League to the Home Office Committee set up in 1945 to consider the care of children 'who from loss of parents or from any cause whatever are deprived of a normal home life with their own parents and relatives' (Curtis Committee). The death of Denis O'Neill, a child cruelly neglected while boarded out in a remote farm by a local authority, had brought an outcry leading to an official inquiry while the committee was still sitting. The exceptional cases of bad institutional treatment, quoted in the Curtis Report to demonstrate the dangerous loopholes in the existing system, filled the headlines. Margery Fry was called on to write and broadcast, to move people to action in the children's cause before emotion had evaporated. But neither the Report nor its terms of reference had satisfied her. She and others wanted to know more of the pressures which break up families, which may break a child in a home which appears to be normal.

At Cambridge in the early months of the war she had met Dr John Bowlby, then working for the London Child Guidance Clinic. By the end of the war she was communicating up and down the country her excitement about his study of *Forty-Four Juvenile Thieves*. When in 1950 she read his report on *Maternal Love and Mental Health*, published under the auspices of the World Health Organization, she telephoned Dr Bowlby to insist that it should be published in a popular version. He asked her whether she would do it. Within a fortnight Dr Bowlby received a draft of the opening chapters. The book was published in three months. The Pelican edition of *Child Care and the Growth of Love* came out in Margery Fry's eightieth year. Ten years later it was still selling at 15,000 copies a year. Margery Fry's share of the royalties, which she had been at first reluctant to accept, went to the Howard League and among other projects financed an inquiry into the background of people convicted for cruelty to children.

Meanwhile Margery's own full-length book, 'which had hung round her neck for years and years', slipped inconspicuously into the world. *Arms of the Law*, published in 1951, was dedicated to the memory of Maurice Waller. The middle section, an essay on 'Fear as a Deterrent' reproduced from the first Eleanor Rathbone Memorial Lecture, was sandwiched between a section on current penal affairs and an historical review of theories of punishment, thriftily compiled from her well-stuffed commonplace books. She believed that everything of importance she had ever uttered had gone into this book, but perhaps for the general reader the aphorisms were too tightly packed. For the student there was too much of the White Knight (whose touch Virginia Woolf had already noticed in Roger Fry) in the way Margery Fry had thrown the book together in the margins of her life. For she was nowhere near the summing-up, the end of the quest.

She did not feel it necessary to be present when the Committee of the Howard League went through the Criminal Justice Bill, clause by clause, but she had been on the sub-committee which prepared for meetings. She had no faith in the suspension of the death penalty, which seemed a possibility. She wanted to press for abolition, according to the original line of Howard League propaganda, that the death penalty barred all reform. She believed that many of the men and women most competent to deal with offenders could not enter a prison service which might call on them to take part in the ritual of execution. She had tried to argue statistically against the use of fear as a deterrent: now the findings of psychologists seemed to explain the figures, to reinforce her theory that the people most likely to commit crimes of violence were least likely to look ahead to the consequences for themselves.

In an article in the *Observer* in November 1947 Lord Templewood declared himself a convert to the abolition of the death penalty. But Mr Chuter Ede, the Home Secretary, announced that although he was in favour of abolition in the long run this was not the moment for it. 'I'm very much afraid we are going to be defeated,' Margery Fry wrote to Professor Kinberg in January 1948. 'A tremendous rise in crime—(no need to explain to *you* the economic and psychological reasons for this, one could have predicted it with certainty)—has made people jumpy and vindictive.' She was lecturing everywhere on the Bill, 'but the leaven works very slowly'.

The question of the death penalty had been omitted from the original Bill, but the debate in April raged around it. Mr Sidney Silverman's amendment proposing a five-year suspension of the death penalty was carried by 245 votes to 222. The sisters read in their newspapers of the wild enthusiasm in the House. 'Very dear of you to write about C.P.,' Margery wrote to Isabel, 'it's a relief but not final yet, as the Lords may put it back again. The thing that gives me more satisfaction is that none of the Law Officers voted for retention.' To 'Majölle' (Maja and Olaf Kinberg) she wrote:

The death penalty is by no means settled yet. The House of Lords will probably reject the amendment and send it back to the Commons. The Commons will almost certainly reaffirm it, and send the amended Bill back to the Lords. The Lords can't then *alter* the Bill, but they *can* reject the whole Bill, and if they are feeling truculent they may do so. You see, I'm afraid recent brutal attacks on policemen have turned public opinion and the Lords could argue that *they* were representing the real will of the people. This might be rather a good move in the constitutional struggle for the drastic reform of the Lords now going on. So the question may turn into a big constitutional issue.

The death-penalty clause was, as she expected, defeated in the Lords. A new government clause, distinguishing degrees of murder, was rejected even by Lord Templewood, who had pledged his support for abolition. To avoid the total loss of the Bill the Commons had to abandon any reference to the death penalty. It must have seemed to Margery Fry that the cause was lost for her time. The National Council for the Abolition of the Death Penalty was wound up, its membership and small assets transferred to the Howard League. Frank Dawtry, who had organized the 1948 campaign, became secretary to the National Association of Probation Officers.

Yet there was enough in the Criminal Justice Bill to warrant a celebration. The prison age limit was raised, with the general enactment that no person under twenty-one was to be sent to prison unless the court could find no practical alternative. The Act looked forward to a time when alternatives would be so numerous that imprisonment for people under twenty-one could be ended by an Order in Council. It recognized at last the part of 'duly qualified medical practitioners' in diagnosing mental disorder and helping to prescribe treatment for offenders. It recognized some of the prisoner's 'privileges' as part of his rehabilitation, not merely as rewards for good conduct. There was a great reformer, Sir Lionel Fox, at the head of the Prison Commission. The makeshifts of wartime had helped to show that for some prisoners an open system was practicable.

So George Benson and Kingsley Martin decided to celebrate by arranging a dinner for Margery Fry at the House of Commons. Her instant response to the idea was that she would like to hear nice things said about her while she was still alive. It was a good company: the Home Secretary and one of his predecessors, the Secretary for the Colonies, Civil Servants from the Home Office, the Chairman of the Prison Commission, the Principal and two former Principals of Somerville College; the China Campaigners, the criminologists, and the penal reformers, the framers of policy and the addressers of envelopes (sometimes the same people), Marjorie Rackstraw whose friendship went back to Birmingham days, Professor Pope who remembered Margery in Victorian Oxford, Miss Jean Alexander who had been afraid of Margery's jackdaw at Bayswater and the dark cupboard under the stairs at Aubrey House, but had braved the roaring of the guns in France and the dim corridors of Holloway Prison. Nice things were said: Margery was compared to a redstart, that elegantly colourful little creature said by Collins's Field Guide to be characterized by 'confiding behaviour towards man and jaunty attitudes'. She was given another enchanting bird in terracotta of the Han period. Yet all the warmth and lustre of the occasion, the knowledge that penal reform was moving around her and beyond her, could not wholly conceal a signal to retire, to grow old.

On New Year's Day, 1946, Eleanor Rathbone had died without warning, in mid-campaign for starving Europe. Perhaps this was for Margery the day of 'the solemn realization which comes when we cease to say, or think, "If I should die" and say instead "When I die" '.[3] She represented Somerville College at the memorial service for Eleanor Rathbone at St Margaret's, Westminster. It seemed a strange place to remember Eleanor Rathbone, an agnostic cradled in Unitarianism.

This seems an occasion for getting something off my chest [Margery wrote to Dr Janet Vaughan]. Eleanor's death brings vividly home to her generation that our own deaths are, in the nature of things, not to be so very long delayed.

I'm a little worried by the way in which, as soon as people are dead, orthodoxy sets in about them. I am myself a reluctant, but so far a fairly complete agnostic: there is nothing I could affirm as my belief about the existence of God or the future life, except so far as a tendency to disbelieve in both could be called a belief. I should *like* to hold both doctrines, but liking always seems to me rather a warning than an argument. The College would probably want to do something to get my friends together in my memory and I do think it good that this should be done. But I hope when the time comes you will see that it isn't a service—music can say better than words the feelings about which all statements are rash, and if some reading is wanted please let it avoid the dogmatic!

Lucy Kempson, once Librarian of Somerville College, later research historian at the War Office and Tutor at Bedford College, still signing herself 'Cherub' to her contemporaries, was in her own tidy and cheerful way preparing for death.

I was turning out some old letters the other day. . . . Anyhow, there was a letter from you written from Failand the year after we went down so utterly miserable at the sense of what is now called frustration—that you were and apparently always would be a mere idle lump of flesh with no more elating prospect than to go to Switzerland with the parents, selected sister and 'the *most* tract-distributing uncle'. It brought back so vividly what indeed I'd quite forgotten—the utter sense of hopelessness of those long, hot, empty summer days—and the conviction that nothing ever *would* happen. That was the price we paid for the 'Security' in which we grew up.

Lucy Kempson tore up the thick, yellowing pages and left them for

[3] *The Single Woman*, p. 35.

the bonfire—not knowing that her own reply still lay forgotten in a box at Clarendon Road—'Oh Margery, the future does lie so nakedly before us. . . .'[4]

The year 1945 was a watershed. From 1914 history had its own grim but intelligible logic. Those minds which were still active in 1945 and had inhabited the unfamiliar country beyond 1914 were worth investigation. Margery Fry was asked more than once to contribute to a symposium of her contemporaries—'What Life Has Taught Me'—'As I See It'—'What I Believe'. She thought she had already said all she had to say: but some things she was glad to repeat to a wider audience. She wanted to talk about the place of voluntary work in the new 'welfare state'. She was glad to see trained professional people taking over more and more of the work which had once been done by amateurs. But she believed there would always be a need for voluntary work, for voluntary societies like the Howard League. 'Even where laws are passed they are apt to fail in their full effect unless there is a group of citizens, ready to give time, money and work to their support.'[5] When the League, after a quarter of a century, was reconsidering its functions, she urged that the office of watchdog must be given due importance.

Prison education had virtually ended in 1939 except for the correspondence courses organized by Mrs McNeille, one of Margery Fry's former Birmingham students. (These, initiated as a stop-gap, proved of lasting worth for men who really wanted to study a chosen subject, not merely to get an evening out of the cell.) Margery Fry was on the committee, which reported on possible developments in prison education. It was agreed that the old voluntary system had had its day—'the intellectually under-nourished prisoner was offered, not a diet prescribed by experts for his condition, but an assortment of dishes that happened to be on the menu at the moment'. As a result of the Report evening institutes under local education authorities were eventually set up in prisons. But Margery Fry pleaded that some voluntary teachers should still be admitted, under professional supervision. She believed that some people should still enter prisons as ordinary citizens, working for love. Perhaps there was a distinction, already outdated, in her mind between vocation and profession. But one aspect of voluntary work, to

---

[4] See p. 48.
[5] From a typescript called 'Voluntary Service'. This was the theme of numerous talks and broadcasts given by Margery Fry after 1945.

Margery Fry 'the key-card in the game of patience', still remains. She insisted that in the welfare state the voice of the consumer must be heard. In the nature of things he might be too young or too old, too sick or muddled or frightened to speak audibly or coherently. There must be unofficial people to speak for him.

Margery Fry made a word, 'thenadaysers', for people who when they begin 'Nowadays . . .' always proceeded to a condemnation—'yet to declare from one's own youth precepts for the young is so universal a fault of age that one cannot hope to avoid it'.[6] She felt pretty certain, for instance, that 'scrupulosity' like her father's was becoming rarer. The formal teaching she had received seemed in retrospect negligible beside what she had learnt from her father, or from Roger, who had taught her to recognize as a characteristic of life its individuality, the difference between one and another of a species. She was aware, in herself and in society, of the mystery of man's revolt against his mortal nature, his demand for 'an ever wider range of satisfaction in living'. She opened her mind to this mystery, lest the orthodoxy of unbelief should become as arid as that of belief.

Her articles of faith, in Schweitzer's words, 'reverence for life, reverence for truth', in Blake's 'Mercy, pity, peace and love', were, like any other beliefs, reached emotionally, through the influences of childhood. She knew that if the pressures, the personal admirations had been different she might well have conformed to a religious discipline. 'Even as I write I see my own view of life as springing from a liberal Quaker tradition of essentially nineteenth century form.' 'It is the intolerance, not the variety of speculation which brings tragedy upon the world.' She had no way of proving that life was not 'a negligible freak in a senseless universe', but she knew experimentally that 'to life we belong, and our wisdom as living beings is to enter in the fullest degree into our heritage'.[7]

Materially, the heritage was meagre in the early postwar years. Bread was rationed in 1946 and shopping coupons did not go completely until 1953. The Fry sisters were among those who rose to the challenge of rationing like poets to the sonnet form: yet always with the most scrupulous honesty. When Margery found that her table-cloths had disappeared during one of her absences, she boiled out the lettering from flour-bags and decorated them with drawn-thread embroidery. In long evenings of conversation she reseated her

---

[6] *What Life Has Taught Me*, p. 54.   [7] *What I Believe*, pp. 61, 63, 66.

mother's drawing-room chairs with fine beadwork in a convolvulus design which she had drawn after consultation with the Victoria and Albert Museum. So, while the young set up house with orange-crates and aluminium teapots, imagining that they would never want to burden themselves with fine objects, the old preserved some of the minor graces of civilization. The grim winter of 1947 tried their endurance. 'Beloved Fellow-Hermit,' Agnes addressed Margery when the snow lay frozen outside their draughty, overlarge houses where there was fuel for only one small fire. It was long after Easter when the thaw set in.

Margery's seventy-fifth birthday fell in 1949, the same year as the tercentenary of Charles I's execution. She repeated with wonder that she had been alive for a quarter of the time since that event. 'Seventy-five years', wrote Isabel, 'since you arrived in this world to my dismay, and seventy-three years at least of happiness, friendship and understanding.' Now Isabel wished for her 'a little while in which you could amuse yourself with prints and flute and coloured wool and travel, and for us to sit and talk without too oppressive a sense of all that might be done to make this world a happier place to live in. The only bit of advice I can offer is that you shouldn't waste too much energy on seeing that every stray Tom, Dick and Harry has their bread buttered on both sides.'

But even the issue of capital punishment was reopened. The appointment of a Royal Commission in 1949 took the abolitionists by surprise. As the National Council for the Abolition of the Death Penalty no longer existed, responsibility fell on the Howard League. Again Margery Fry prepared her personal memorandum, again she worked behind the scenes, especially in getting over representatives of countries which had already abolished the death penalty. The Commission produced, according to Gordon Rose, 'a model inquiry, comprehensive, searching and sensible'.[8] During its course the chairman, Sir Ernest Gowers, that master of plain words, was converted to abolition. But by its terms of reference the Commission could not recommend abolition, only discuss the limitation of the penalty to certain crimes and suggest alternatives.

The Howard League would in no circumstances consider limiting the penalty to certain degrees of murder. When the Commission suggested a course so unacceptable as leaving the decision between life and death to jury discretion, it was, in fact, drawing attention

[8] *The Struggle for Penal Reform*, p. 218.

to the conclusion that a choice must be made between retention and abolition.

One innovation in the Royal Commission inquiry was the evidence given by Dr Hill and Dr Taylor about the findings of the electro-encephalograph. Margery Fry had already met Dr Grey Walter at the Burden Neurological Institute and had considered the possibility that some organical disturbance of the brain (open to diagnosis by mechanical means though not by the usual criteria of insanity) might predispose certain persons to violence. A few years earlier she had crossed swords with a contributor to *Lawless Youth* who she believed had made too much of biological tendencies to delinquency, too little of the effect of environment. She knew that material security had given her a great deal of happiness, and even some goodness. Though penal reform could not wait, she felt a kind of presumption in looking farther for the causes of crime while people had to live in wretched surroundings, in constant economic frustration and anxiety. On the other hand, there were clearly some people on whom material benefits and the most understanding efforts of social workers had no effect. 'The presence in a prison, or still more in a Borstal institution or an approved school, of a person who is physically incapable of responding to such influences is at once a definite hindrance to the working of the place and a waste and discouragement of the efforts of those in control.'[9]

'She felt', says Dr Grey Walter, 'that there was something to be said for the "black sheep" as well as the "ewe lamb" hypothesis.' The 'black sheep' hypothesis was uncongenial: though she had abandoned the claim to see 'that of God in every man',[10] her actions were governed by a sense of the sacredness of personality. She held no clue as to how to handle people who, while innocent of any criminal action, might be shown by the inexorable pointer of a machine to be potential murderers. 'The imperfections of our instruments demand constant vigilance against abuse . . . This implies the maintenance of law, of courts before which the right of interference with the lawbreakers must be proved as vigorously as ever.'[11] But if science was able to throw light on human personality its findings, however distasteful, must be assimilated.

Professor Kinberg encouraged her to take the electro-encephalograph seriously, even though the English doctors were on the whole 'very snooty'. And, of course, the machines delighted her. When an

[9] *Arms of the Law*, p. 67.   [10] George Fox in 1656.   [11] *Arms of the Law*, p. 70.

old lady without scientific training shows the interest of a twelve-year-old boy in a piece of mechanism she can easily be accused of credulity. But Margery Fry had her answer. 'I think the whole human being is such an unknown thing that we've got to attack our ignorance from every possible side.'[12] She believed that the discoveries of the twentieth century about the human mind would in the end prove even more significant than those of the nuclear physicists. Whether she took Grey Walter or Kinberg or Bowlby as her guide, her conclusions were practical. 'You've got to learn to love as you've got to learn to do other things, and if you don't learn at the right time, you may never quite get your relations with human beings right. But in the meantime, I don't think we can stop trying to get our prisons better until the world's perfect, or until all mothers are able to look after all children.'[13]

In 1950 she presented her report at the twelfth and last conference of the I.P.P.C. The United Nations Organization was taking over responsibility for international penal affairs. In the same year Cicely Craven was succeeded at the Howard League by Hugh Klare, who had among his many qualifications a European outlook. When the British Council asked her to direct a course on juvenile delinquency she got her overseas students to tell about their own countries. She also joined in their fun; in their company she visited Windsor for the first time in her life. Her simple good manners, her lack of condescension and complacency made her an ideal speaker for overseas students. No foreign accent or imperfect idiom could prevent her from hitting the centre of a question.

Her own household became irrevocably international. Margery told 'Majölle' in 1949, 'The gloomy fact is that we of the dying middle-class generation in England, struggling to avoid the solution of "going into a home" (and homes enough don't exist), are living on the mercy of foreigners. Joan's housemate is a naturalized German, Isabel and Ruth have Estonians and Poles, Agnes is trying for Latvians and I for Swedes. What a queer record this would have seemed 50 years ago!' The change was not easy for a generation nurtured in insularity, however conscientious later in its internationalism. After an experience with a Central European who 'never purred', Margery accepted Mrs Kinsberg's offer to provide her with a succession of cheerful Swedes, whom Margery employed in pairs. She was still St Ursula to a procession of English maidens,

12 'Personal Call.'   13 'Personal Call.'

and to Noy, the Siamese princess who at fifteen, after her mother's death, was brought over to her English godmother to be educated. For these girls Margery kept Christmas as never before. She made decorations for the Christmas tree, she invited other overseas students to share the fun. 'Xmas purchases and parcels fill the mind,' she wrote to Agnes, 'and in their curious way worry the conscience. Do I, or don't I, admire the people who refuse to fritter away time and money and thought? I can't tell: only I think without this strange ceremony I should lose touch with many people of the not-quite-so-close (to speak like a milliner's catalogue) whom it wd. be a pity to drift from entirely, and then so many of our friends are harder up than we that some largesse seems allowed.'

There was trouble in a girls' institution: someone must visit, 'preferably Miss Fry'. She must get in her say about a social worker for Holloway at the Howard League Committee, then leave early (it is to be hoped, in a taxi) to meet Dag Hammarskjold at a party. She must go down with Mrs Creech Jones to see the Mayflower Home at Plymouth, the home set up by the Salvation Army to train mothers accused of neglect (an experiment shortly to be followed at the Elizabeth Fry Memorial Home near York). They went on to visit Dartmoor Prison. Florence Barrow had her to open flats for single women in Birmingham, Ruth Fry had her to talk to the Pedestrians' Association.

Her Somervillians gave her a seventy-seventh birthday party at the House of Commons. At seventy-nine she rewarded herself for her work on *Child Care and the Growth of Love* with a visit to Canada. Since 1926 the changes were enormous. This time she flew over the Rockies, 'like a fossil sea, their snow caps like foams on the waves'. She wrote to Agnes of 'dogwood, lupins, tiny tiger-lilies and deep pink wild roses, yellow pine and Douglas firs as well as lots of *green* trees which pleased me more. . . . I conscientiously visited prisons and met penologists but of that I needn't bother to write.' She returned in a Bedlam of eight hundred passengers, but found peace to read Grey Walter's *Living Brain* and to explain, with diagrams, the ship's radar apparatus.

From Canada, Margery brought back the game 'Scrabble', which spread in widening circles of her contemporaries. She invented new rules for solitary players or for those who found the original game too easy. She sent out ingenious and decorative markers as birthday cards. The pamphlets she had written, the speeches she had made, had gone often enough into the wastepaper basket, in at one ear, out at the other, but she was certain she had been able to give some H.H.H. (Hours of Human Happiness). Once she had given Phoebe Sheavyn a box of oilpaints and spent a day painting with her. In her sixties and seventies Phoebe had been exhibiting and selling her paintings, an autumn harvest of flower pieces and sunlit landscapes.

On her eightieth birthday there was another dinner. Again Lord Templewood spoke: this time he said he was certain that capital punishment would be abolished in her time. As she left she told a friend it was her last dinner-party, there would henceforth only be tea-parties for old women. But, in the phrase she used through life to reassure people she felt she had tormented by her personal anxieties, she knew it would be all right, really. She was constantly adding names of new friends to her address-book. She kept for their children a drawer full of prison-made felt creatures, of tales of Orlando the Marmalade Cat. Young people still told her about their love affairs and refused to believe her when she said she could not advise from experience. She was no longer surprised when men became her friends. More than one old man, at an age when even those honours which old men look to have seemed to be falling from him, had come upon the miracle of being in love with a brilliant girl of his own generation. It was no longer true, as Margery had told an insistent young questioner fifteen years earlier, that no one had actually asked her to marry him: but it had seemed wise to leave things as they were, not to break into another family or out of the sisterhood.

One hot day, as her hands lay in her lap, she saw that the veins stood out like those of her father and mother. She knew then that she was really old. Later rising, afternoon dozing were shortening her day. She had, like other old ladies, her little time-consuming rituals, the daily crossword puzzle (strangely nostalgic: the slang was of her own youth, the literary allusions to the Bible or Dickens). She played games with Miranda, her own marmalade cat. But she still had the pulling of strings, the remorseless arguments, the devising of strategy to take effect in a world she would not see. At the end of a working day she could still feel grateful for life as the bus came up with its lights reflected on the wet London pavement.

It occurred to her that old age had nearly always been described from outside, by younger people. For most of human history old people had been a tiny minority. Now, she learned almost daily from the newspapers, they were becoming so numerous that they were a 'problem'. They were no longer listened to: they were planned for.

She knew that from her place of vantage she must speak for the voiceless old people. She told the Pedestrians' Association that old age was intermittent: at eighteen she had sometimes felt eighty, at eighty she sometimes forgot she was not eighteen. This natural phenomenon explained some of the apparently silly actions of old people on the roads. After she had opened the Brook House flats in Birmingham in 1951 she was amazed by the number of letters she received from women of her own age: she had shown them their own longings, not to get slovenly, not to be eccentric, not to close their hearts.

The B.B.C., planning a series on human relations in 'Women's Hour', rather oddly asked her to talk on marriage. She had certainly shown some understanding of the theme in her twenties when she had comforted a married friend by remarking that marriage, like the best sort of almond pudding, needed a certain roughness to give it flavour. But as a spinster of eighty she said she preferred to speak on 'The Single Woman'. It was a tough talk. When the *Radio Times* alleged that Miss Fry maintained that a single woman could be a complete and happy person, she was furious. For what she had really maintained was that the single woman had 'to make out her life without the natural ties of a human being'. 'Yet it cannot be denied that there are attractive people who don't marry, and even the un-attractive have their claims to be considered.' In one brief and deceptively simple talk she ranged from 'our Miss Smith' in the City, who knows all about everything, and where the papers about the Uruguayan order of last month will be found, to the 'monotonous courage of years spent in caring for relations sick or old for whose happiness and comfort many women barter their own lives, gladly enough perhaps when love prompts, often at the mere call of duty'. With melancholy running deeply under the sparkle of wit, for she herself was well set on 'the wearying downhill journey' of old age, she spoke of ways in which the single woman might aspire to keep 'a mind open to the outside world and the possession of a heart at leisure from itself'. Again letters poured in. Some regretted her lack of religious consolation, others felt it a poor thing that the great Miss Fry should have to find satisfaction in such sensuous pleasures as 'warmth in sunlight or fire or even in a hot bottle . . . the ripe juiciness of a plum'. Most had found relief in her understanding of their condition.

In her eighty-first year the International Association of Gerontology was looking for a speaker to open its Congress. After three or four refusals from other people, Professor Tunbridge came to Margery Fry. She said she had no qualifications to speak, except as a gerontological specimen. She would speak very personally. She called her talk 'Old Age Looks at Itself'. She was in splendid voice. From the first sentences, when she played with numbers in the Fry fashion, adding up her parents' ages to 188 and her own and her sisters' ages to 417, she held the great audience in Church House. Her theme was the continuity of personality, the fact that 'old people' are people indeed, only incidentally old. 'To the administrator an individual may be just "that old woman, I think her name is Jones", but to herself she is *the* Katie Jones who won a prize for scripture and had the smallest waist in the class—with a thousand other distinctive features—who just happens to be old.' She claimed for old people the great human right to make choices in their lives. It seemed that as Margery Fry looked back, searching for the essence of personality which survives from infancy to old age, she cast off the ephemeral writings which had perforce exercised her mind in her adult life. She went back for her quotations to the great books which she had perhaps met in the long, vacant days at Failand —Homer, Euripides, Aeschylus, Shakespeare, Montaigne; to whom she added, in the translations of Roger's friend Arthur Waley, the Chinese poet Po-Chii, who seemed to her 'to have added a third dimension to our literature'. These shed a light over her own prose, the most beautiful she ever spoke, as she drew to 'the inevitable end which each must face for himself, whether in the bright light of faith, or the dimmer equanimity of reason', quoting again that Chinese poet of 1,100 years ago:

> When this superintendence of trifling affairs is done
> I lie back on my pillows and sleep with my face to the South.

But Margery Fry was wide awake. The sense of creative fulfilment, the beauty of her own speech, the warmth and enthusiasm of its reception, had exorcised for the time the terror of its theme, old age and death. She remained throughout the conference. Her table was gay at every meal. She was borne off to a performance of *Rosenkavalier* at Covent Garden. The gerontologists felt that night that they had been entertaining a wonderful child.

MF—Q

XVII
Victims of Violence: 1955-1958

'HAS not the injured individual rather slipped out of the mind of the criminal court?' Margery Fry had asked in *Arms of the Law*. Though the main business of her life was to seek humane treatment for criminals, she never forgot that lawbreakers hurt and destroy. She saw the objections of the 'man in the street' before he raised them: she was in general less sentimental than he, because she wanted not vengeance but justice.

One dark night in the late 1940s, as she went through an alley behind Holland Park station, now respectably overlooked by police flats, a man seized her handbag. 'He pulled and I pulled and "pull baker, pull devil" and devil pulled hardest and I was pulled right over.' As she fell she realized with some satisfaction that though the bag was gone she still grasped the handle. She got up in a rage, hailed a passing car, and went in pursuit. The empty bag was found in the road, but not the thief. She knew now what it felt like to be criminally attacked. She also knew that even if her injuries had been worse than fright and a bruised finger, even if she had been a poor woman dependent on her health for her livelihood, the law could do nothing for her unless she could produce the thief and get damages from him. 'I think more and more of the other side,' she told a friend in America. Long before this incident she had known through Agnes of a girl in Somerset who had spent her life in a wheelchair after being raped by soldiers early in the Second War.

The victims of violence were few, but not therefore to be forgotten. In April 1953 Margery Fry brought to the committee of the Howard League the outline of her plan for compensation. Often she had been set on fire by a wandering spark from another mind: this, in her eightieth year, was, it seemed, the first major scheme she had initiated. Yet she herself would not claim originality: she had, she said later, received the idea as a legacy from an old friend. She was almost certainly referring to a letter from Champion Russell, when he was visiting his son in Uganda in 1935. He told her of the tribal system whereby the chief collected from a murderer and his family the means to support the wife and children of his victim.

In tribal societies, whether in Africa or in Anglo-Saxon England, compensation could be reckoned a family responsibility. This was impossible in the modern fragmented society. 'The wages of sin are often rather small,' said Margery.[1] Her words are still broadly true in spite of the technological advances in crime since she uttered them. An offender is rare who can pay compensation in proportion to the injury he inflicts. Even if the victim was awarded damages in a civil action he was often no better off: Margery Fry's favourite example was that of a man blinded as a result of an assault by two men in 1951. He was awarded £11,500 damages, which his attackers were to pay at five shillings a week each. When they left prison they had still four centuries to go before the debt would be paid.

Though Margery Fry held that payment of compensation (allowed within narrow limits by the Probation Act of 1907 and the Criminal Justice Act of 1948) was part of the proper treatment of the offender, it was clear that any adequate compensation must come out of public funds. She suggested an analogy to the Industrial Injuries Scheme. She did not claim the compensation scheme as her own idea, but she soon knew it would have to be her own cause. The people in the Howard League did not catch fire. They had a great deal on their hands: the complex Criminal Justice Act was only five years old, the report of the Royal Commission on Capital Punishment was shortly expected. They saw at once, as the Home Office Working Party saw six years later, that the scheme bristled with difficulties. To Margery's own mind one of the worst was that two ministries would be involved, the Home Office and the Ministry of National Insurance. Legal minds wondered whether the State would be invited to involve itself in guilt. Though they were used to Margery's perennial youth, some may have wondered how far a woman of eighty would be able to take her negotiations. It seemed also that she was interpreting 'violence' in no narrow sense: she had mentioned the victims of heartless fraud. Not everyone could grasp the connexion, so clear to Margery's own mind, between the objects of the League and the philosophy of her scheme: to her it was part of the transition from wild vengeance to a constructive penology.

[1] 'Ought the State to Compensate Victims of Violence?' (discussion with Mr R. O'Sullivan broadcast November 1956).

She understood the objections, but she was disappointed. However, she had laid her cards on the table. At the next meeting of the executive, C. R. Hewitt ('C. H. Rolph' of the *New Statesman*) promised to go with her all the way.

That summer her idea went underground. She was busy with Bowlby's book, then with her Canadian holiday. Perhaps she was airing her idea in the provinces, among those quiet, practical, middle-aged women who had lived in University House. When discussion of her scheme warmed up in London in the following year she drew examples from a local paper on her old territory—the *Hanley Sentinel* of 8 October 1953.

She surfaced again in Broadcasting House, where she had trusted contacts. She was not, she made clear, asking to use broadcasting as direct propaganda, but she wanted listeners to be reminded that care for the victims was an old idea which their more recent ancestors had neglected. She was introduced to Mr T. S. Gregory, who believed the theme could be worked into a Third Programme series on the history of law. Soon she was urging him ahead, because she had found 'some interest from High-ups at the H.O.'. She was deliberately avoiding 'known reformers', but she had hopes of Lord Hailsham and Lord Shawcross (whose current eminence cancelled out the objection that she had once chosen him as temporary assistant secretary to the Howard League).

In her eighty-first summer, when she was preparing her address as a gerontological specimen, she had to bring her compensation scheme down to brass tacks. She was told that her ideas could not be discussed until people knew what they were letting themselves in for. Government actuaries, who she had hoped would do the sums, handed them back to her. She found there were no statistics at the Home Office to help her to estimate the cost. She had to set to work as if she had all the time in the world. She paid shorthand reporters to attend courts in London and the provinces. In May 1955 she told her friends at the B.B.C. she was still not quite ready.

Another year went by. Her amateur researches had produced their effect: the Home Office itself was inquiring into the injuries from violent crime over a three-month period. 'It will be very much more exact than the estimate I had been able to frame,' she wrote to Agnes. On 20 November 1956 she launched her scheme on the air in an unscripted discussion with Mr Richard O'Sullivan, Q.C. From that time onwards she was confident that she had an unanswerable case. Six months later she told Agnes, 'The Home Office has got out "my figure" about the cost of insurance for victims of violent crimes —very satisfactory because it would be so cheap.'

Now her proposals had to be shaped for Westminster. She was no longer alone. She knew her friends—Lord Shawcross, Lord Chorley, and C. R. Hewitt and the young barristers who would put in hard, unpublicized work. Professor Otto Kahn-Freund, then Professor of Law at the London School of Economics, was amazed by her grasp of detail when he lunched with her at Clarendon Road. He took her for a woman in her sixties until she said, 'This won't come in my time, but it will in yours.'

'And of course', she told her old students, 'all the old penal problems are still with us.' They were with her at every level, the deputation about prison sanitation, the party for international criminologists, the finding of a social worker for Holloway Prison, for whom she had obtained a grant from the City Parochial Foundation. When she had found her she fitted out her cell with a table, two chairs, and her own ample medicine chest to hold papers. Then she became chairman of the Holloway Discharged Prisoners' Aid Association. She had to help the trained probation officer who held the post through that period when she was still directed by a committee of amateurs, some rather unwilling to surrender their prerogatives and their intuitions. Margery Fry knew that the time was coming when the position would be reversed: as in the prison education service, the voluntary worker would find scope under trained direction.

The Royal Commission's Report had been followed by no propagandist drive, but the execution of Ruth Ellis in 1955 for shooting her ex-lover in the street, before witnesses, brought an uprush of popular emotion. Victor Gollancz chose his time in the late summer to launch his Campaign for the Abolition of the Death Penalty. The splendidly organized meetings, the mustered eloquence, the showers of pamphlets covered in the fierce yellow which recalled so many earlier pleas for humanity—all these disturbed rather than encouraged some of the less-seasoned members of the Howard League. It seemed a backwater. Margery Fry played her own part. She would use the Third International Congress on Criminology to get hold of people of high standing in abolitionist countries. She arranged for experts from Belgium, Norway, and Sweden to lunch with the Parliamentary Penal Reform Group. As Sidney Silverman's Bill won

MF—Q*

its way through to the Lords, it did not worry her at all that the Howard League was no longer in acknowledged leadership of the supporting campaign. 'You march round the walls of Jericho for a number of years, and they do in the end fall down, but how much this is due to your processions and trumpetings, to your meetings and pamphlets and deputations, and how much to their crumbling from internal rottenness, you will never know, nor should you too urgently ask.'[2] When the Bill was through its third reading, Lord Templewood wrote to Margery that it was now time to attend to her second wish: she must forthwith go down with him to Norfolk to see the bearded tits. But the Bill was again rejected by the Lords. The Homicide Act of 1957 indeed went far towards abolition: far enough to set back total abolition for another span of years.

When the death-penalty campaign was closed there was still popular pressure for reform of the prisons. Conscientious objectors —including women this time—had again proved articulate prisoners. There was a spate of popular writings about prisons and the people in them. Margery Fry was prompt to encourage any serious young writer on these themes, provided he took her advice to avoid sensationalism.

Then the Prison Commission came under violent attack: the whole prison system was rotten and must be swept away. The Howard League began to fear worse things than loss of prestige. It had built its work on good relations with the Home Office and as far as possible with prison officers. According to some angry young men, the League was in the pocket of the Home Office. Again Margery Fry was unshaken. She had known over years the quality of her friends in the Prison Commission: Maurice Waller, Alexander Paterson, Lionel Fox. Though when she looked around everything remained to do, when she looked back thirty years the changes were enormous. Campaigns were useful and necessary, but of their nature evanescent. The League need fear only for its finances: the membership must be kept together for the long pull between campaigns.

One of the advantages of growing old, she reminded her contemporaries in one of her last broadcasts, was that so much of life had drifted into history: 'We have lived through moments when it seemed that everything we valued would be submerged—the rising generation hardly knows the dangers passed. . . . It is for us to try

[2] 'The Most Important Things', broadcast in the B.B.C. Home Service, 12 May 1957.

—how hardly—to take hope from earlier experience without mini-
mizing present danger.'[3]

The American hydrogen bomb had been exploded in her eighty-
first year. A middle-aged friend wondered what this would mean
emotionally to adolescents. The bewildered look of the very old
passed over Margery's face: then she said she would talk to a boy
she knew well who was to visit her that afternoon. But it is doubtful
whether she came near the subject. She found the child who had once
confided in her grown 'alarmingly silent and absent but I think
fundamentally friendly though critical. I don't believe one can *know*
a boy of that age . . . they have to find out quite afresh what relationship to have. And I don't much think they can ever want one again
as they did in childhood as a purveyor of interesting things.' She had
to accept this remoteness not only as part of the process of growing
up, but as a consequence of the independent life which she and her
sisters had longed for in their own youth. Her acceptance brought
privileges: in her eighties she was even taken by two boys for a sail
in their cockle-shell boat off the coast of Essex.

Through tolerance she remained in touch with the generations.
She was still involved in children's matters, though she had been out
of the courts for ten years. There was concern on Children's Committees in London and the provinces about the increasing numbers
of children coming into care, especially those with parents still living.
Stories were also accumulating about families with multiple problems
being further bewildered by the attentions of several entirely un-
co-ordinated social services. Under the chairmanship of Mrs Geoffrey
Fisher a brilliant group of women was brought together to prepare
the way for some national service to prevent where possible the
breaking-up of families. (It was not until 1963, for example, that a
local authority was empowered to pay a housekeeper to hold a family
together in their own home while the mother was in hospital.) More
than one pressure group was at work in the same broad field, and in
October 1956 the Ingleby Committee was appointed by the Home
Office to examine the Children's Courts and to consider whether
local authorities 'should be given new powers or duties to prevent or
forestall the suffering of children through neglect in their own
homes'.

Margery Fry undertook the drafting of the Fisher Group's
evidence to the Ingleby Committee. She now had to straighten out

[3] 'An Indian Summer', broadcast 3 April, 1957.

the questions which had been debated for more than ten years in the Howard League. The Fisher Group proposed that the sole complaint against children of statutory school age should be that they were 'in need of care or protection, guidance or discipline': but if the complaint arose because of some action which would be an 'offence' for an older person, the case was to be proved in strict legal terms. The most original proposal of the Group was its plan for a Parents' Consultative Committee which might wherever possible settle cases on a voluntary basis, acting as a 'sieve' for the children's courts. Here again the most careful safeguards were proposed for preserving the impartiality of the court if a case had in the end to go before it.

'The most important function of the juvenile court', said the preamble of the draft, 'is to prevent the evolution of the naughty child into the adult criminal . . . a much more difficult matter than doling out punishment for childish offences.' For Margery Fry 'juvenile delinquents' had remained 'naughty children'. She drew her terms from the wide, concrete, temperate vocabulary she had heard around her when she learnt to speak. 'To have a dozen or more people waiting impatiently for the court to rise, to have to bring out the secret shames of a family within earshot of even a few people, such conditions inhibit the confidential talk which may help to build up the weak responsibility of the parents, and even for the understanding by the child of his own relation to the world around him, time and trust are essential.' If she used a word which lent itself in its context to cant, she gave it one of her sharp sidelong glances, as when she hoped that the family might be 'brought into co-operation, or at least into non-opposition, with the treatment required by the child'.

She was eighty-two when she drafted the Fisher Group evidence. A few months earlier the death of Joan Mary Fry, at the age of ninety-three, had made the first gap in the sisterhood of five. In 1947 Joan had dismayed her younger sisters by flying to a meeting of German Friends: there in Bad Pyrmont she had spent her eighty-fifth birthday. Five years later she was the only one missing, through illness, when the sisterhood gathered at an exhibition of Roger Fry's pictures. The *Manchester Guardian* reporter who had referred to 'four wonderful sisters' had a reprimand from Golders Green Quakers for omitting 'the most wonderful of all'. She recovered, and Agnes found her at ninety decorating a box for a friend 'with all a child's enjoyment. . . . Age has enriched, not robbed her.' When

Margery was in London she went up every Sunday afternoon to visit Joan at Temple Fortune Hill. It was this physical proximity, Margery assured Isabel, which had brought her so near in affection to the sister whose activities had been directly inspired by religion—always, as Isabel said, 'discovering gaiety in the spiritual life'. 'Our constant seeings meant that affection wasn't always being worried by differences of thinking. She was so tolerant of these that I never felt she was troubled by my agnosticism, tho' of course she'd have liked me to come round to her point of view.'

Constant, not continuous, seeings kept the sisters together. At the first chance each had used her inheritance to form a separate household. Each had her own friendships, her own causes to which the others might give time or money or affection without sense of obligation or guilt. Physically their independence became difficult, as the Frys outlived not only their close friends but also the housekeepers and companions ten, twenty years younger than themselves. When middle-aged people agreed that old people were better left in their own homes, Margery Fry spoke up for those who survived to eighty, ninety, or beyond. There must be special housing for these people, with privacy and dignity: she wanted a 'college for the aged' in every neighbourhood.

Even the sisterhood was forced to compromise when Ruth was left in anxious isolation in Norfolk. At Margery's suggestion she set up house in the top floor at Clarendon Road. It was not easy for either sister. It was thirty years since Ruth had laid down her vast work for the Friends' Service Council. Since then the mysterious discomforts, the 'rheumatic screws' which Margery had often complained of, had seized Ruth with disabling force. She had never been idle. She had been in demand as a public speaker, she wrote and compiled, she maintained an enormous, global correspondence. She was widely and deeply loved. Yet beside Margery she felt again the handicaps of the nursery: in old age her four years' minority should have given Ruth the advantage, but in fact she was the legend, Margery the active presence in the world. She feared sisterly disapproval: not wholly without cause, for there was a lack of sophistication in some of her activities which even the secluded Agnes could not take. Yet it was unthinkable to the sisters that their tender care for one another should fail because, in the phrase then current, they operated on different wavelengths. 'Oh, the family's on a perfect pedestal now,' said Margery in a broadcast discussion in 1957. 'It's the one answer to all questions . . . it may be truly, I think.'

Among themselves the sisters played with differences: this trait was Fry, that Hodgkin or Howard. But looking back from old age Margery saw that her background was extraordinarily homogeneous. She thought this was perhaps one reason why she felt real and continuous, to herself. She could see this person, Margery Fry, walking her own small path through history. She saw, pinned to her best frock, the camellia which Dr Moffat, David Livingstone's father-in-law, had taken from the buttonhole of his frock-coat when he heard at the missionary bazaar that it was little Miss Fry's third birthday. She saw the same child dancing round with the twins chanting a ditty learnt from a nursemaid (for Quakers had to import servants from other Protestant denominations):

> Round and round Sebastopol,
> Up and down the ocean,
> Every time the cannon goes,
> Down goes a Russian.

She saw her cycling in Brittany with Dorothy Scott, when the Boer War was going badly, pedalling away from the workmen who shouted in rude glee, 'As-tu vu de Wet?' She looked down again at the fine damask tablecloth in The Hague in 1907, and heard her father's voice appealing to Marshal von Bieberstein to come to some agreement about floating mines: she saw the old soldier take his watch from his pocket, look at it, put it back without a word. She saw the August sunlight on the railway platform at Bettws-y-Coed, she heard the porter say as he lifted her box, 'Well, I suppose it's war. The Kaiser's stamping all over Belgium.' She felt again her pride when a man in a train in 1918 asked what political party she belonged to.

Now, in the nineteen-fifties, she was seen by television in the sitting-rooms of strangers, perfectly relaxed, almost elegant, with a handsome shawl about her shoulders or lace at her neck, the badger-quiff of her middle years lost now in the whiteness of her hair. 'There's Margery Fry,' said a child who had met her, running up to kiss the screen. 'There's comforting that Margery Fry is,' said a woman in South Wales, scrubbing a floor next morning.

When the Library of Somerville College was half a century old, *Demeter* was produced again: for Margery the poetry of her youth had lost none of its beauty. The Standard Minimum Rules for

Prisoners were adopted by the United Nations just thirty years after Gertrude Eaton had initiated Margery Fry into the office at Geneva. The jubilee of the probation service was celebrated. As the jubilees came round the losses increased. Early in 1957 she lost again by premature death a friend on whom she had built her hopes— Madeleine Robinson.

There were still two letters to write on the twins' eighty-eighth birthday. She could still laugh with Isabel over reminiscences eighty years old, sometimes the rough scourings of memory which Agnes preferred to let lie. Agnes would send her the gist of scientific papers which were now the incidents of her life. 'I want to share my bowl of porridge with you,' she would say, telling also how the beech hedges at Brent Knoll walled her like Jerusalem with pure gold. In return Margery would 'empty the little rubbish-basket of her mind', throwing out the small worries before they became obsessive—'Here I am at the old sort of doings—gate won't open—visitors' room fire won't work.' A taxi to Broadcasting House or Television Centre was now a welcome exchange for a train journey to speak in Scotland or Wales, but the ease of air travel kept her world from serious shrinkage. In September 1956 she was in Provence, staying with her old friend, Jacqueline Merle. Several times since the war Margery had slept in the little wooden *pavillon* in the garden, shaded by a palm tree and a mimosa, sometimes going out alone to sketch a ruined farm-house or a group of olive trees, in the places where she had once painted with Roger. This time she asked Jacqueline to drive her to St Remy, where she wanted to spend a few days near the Maurons.

I thought I already had a deep love and understanding for Provence [says Jacqueline Merle], but on this short trip I understood and loved it more than ever before. . . . On the last day Margery said, 'I have never seen the spring of Vaucluse: let's go back that way.' . . . So we did, and I told her afresh the story of Petrarch and Laura. We went through Noves where Laura was born and near the Château de Sade where she lived. Then we crossed the Luberon hills and the day was so lovely we could not bear to go home and never, no never, have I had so insatiable a fellow-traveller as Margery. We had to see everything, go round this way and that way, and a little further still to see an old abbey. It seemed a day that should never end. . . . I have never had a companion so untirable, so responsive, so child-like as Margery Fry who at this time was over eighty. She left the next day and we never saw her again.

In 1957, when the spring again turned her mind towards travel, she thought of Sweden, the country she had discovered in her old age. In Saltsjöbaden there was another small wooden guest-room, within sound of the sea, where she could rest, 'lapped in comfort, kindness and quiet' by the good Kinbergs. To Olaf Kinberg she could open her whole mind. Here was a penal reformer dedicated to scientific method but grounded in the humanities. He had a feeling like Roger's for the infinite variety of human beings. Though he was an international authority, older than herself, he was still as ready to ask the fundamental questions about responsibility and freewill as a young man with life before him. She did not go to Sweden, but later in the spring she visited Jeanne, already hopelessly ill, and on the same journey discussed with M. Marc Ancel and her other friends at the Centre Français de Droit Comparé the possibility of a con-sultative and non-compulsive committee as ante-chamber to the children's courts. She made two broadcasts, to which Jeanne tuned her radio at Rennes, one on 'An Indian Summer', the other on 'The Most Important Things', in which she spoke of penal reform as the thing on which she had spent most time and effort, though it was not for her the most important thing, filling her whole life. She wrote an article on 'Victims of Violence' for the central page of the *Observer*.

In July she entered Guy's Hospital for investigation of the illness which she had persistently ascribed to 'germs'—carefully traced back to one or another of her acquaintances and attacked with a black herbal panacea which she carried everywhere, as a gesture to science, in one of the newly invented polythene bottles. 'The treatments were horrid, but nice nurses.' It was 'not a handsome illness. . . . I sometimes feel it must seem just hysterical but I'm not really that sort of person.' In August she appeared again in the television Brains Trust. In September she managed to talk to the Magistrates' Association about Victims of Violence.

Parliament was sitting, but a scheme calling for expenditure from the Treasury could not be put through by a Private Member's Bill. She had to give up hope of the Commons for the time being. Soon, however, she told her niece she had a new friend, adding wickedly, 'He's a *real* lord.' He was, in fact, a tenth earl, Lord Drogheda, Chairman of Committees in the House of Lords, whom Margery knew as Chairman of the Home Office Advisory Committee on Offenders. Margery Fry was again in hospital, this time at the West-minster Hospital, when he tabled a motion in the House of Lords.

He wrote to her that it would probably come up for debate in January. By the end of the week he was dead, and the motion died with him. When Viscount Alexander paid a tribute in the House of Lords he spoke of the tabling of the motion as Lord Drogheda's last parliamentary action, linking his name with that of 'the great Margery Fry, still with us'.

She proved to be a co-operative patient, not tiresomely critical, though she had a lively scientific interest in all that went on. She was too exhausted to sew or play with sums. She had little taste for light reading: but though she had always believed herself to be 'very poor on poetry' she found she could recite to herself many of Shakespeare's sonnets and the whole of *The Ancient Mariner*. She liked best, whenever she was well enough, to listen to talk. A page of statistics from the Home Office could still fascinate her. Someone from the Colonial Office, bringing in a paper on juvenile delinquency, met Sir Lionel Fox coming out. She would prolong a twenty-minute appointment to an hour, never satisfied until she had mastered a document. In January 1958 the article 'Wild Justice', which C. R. Hewitt had promised, came out in the *New Statesman*. Kingsley Martin found her delighted with it: she arranged for copies to be sent to every Member of both Houses. She heard how the faithful were preaching compensation for victims of violence in small meetings everywhere. She was sure that her ship would soon reach port.

Men and women of all ages came to her bedside. Then, when the hospital was closed to visitors, she would listen to the gossip of the young nurses. She discovered in each one an interest outside the hospital routine and the play of her immediate emotions. When she left the hospital in February everyone who had nursed her received a specially chosen book. Patients are conventionally expected to feel glad to leave hospital. Margery Fry believed herself to be cured, but she honestly confessed the fear of returning to the normal world where decisions have to be made, or are made by others within earshot. In her absence she found her niece had been busy at Clarendon Road, arranging the house more conveniently for the patient and her attendants.

Isabel, who had come up to London in the winter to visit the sister who had so often cared for her in illness, died on the eve of her eighty-ninth birthday in St Thomas's Hospital. 'Let us try to match our longevities,' Margery had said to her twenty years before, remembering, as she remembered again on the day of Isabel's death, how they had sat on the wall together in their pinafores, gazing at the sunset over Ken Wood.

The first camellias, late and wind-seared, had been brought to Margery's room. She knew that the daffodils were out in the squares, in her own little front garden. She knew she would not see lilac again. Death would be harder even than she had always feared. She would live, perhaps for weeks, under sentence. She spoke of this to some of her friends—'matter-of-factly', as she had always hoped to do.

She had no anxiety about her causes: they were all in good hands. At last she had nothing to do but live. In the extremity of weakness and physical humiliation she could still live in the infinite variety of her friends, exchanging her interest for whatever they had to offer. But she could not take the spiritual comfort which some of those near her most wanted to give. Once she had hoped to learn from the saints, but the people who had taught her most had shown her how to carry with gallantry the burden of unbelief. In the end she could not look to outward authority, either for faith or its opposite. Three centuries of Quaker ancestry had taught her to look within. There she recognized the spring of human love, the longing to know and to be known, answered without intermission for more than eighty-four years, though never in its maturity fulfilled. She found no intimation of a supernatural, personal being, which in her generation was required as the starting-point of a religious faith.

Sunday, 20 April 1958, was a day so beautiful that even the most rooted Londoner longed for the country. Such a day, said Margery, could be measured in minutes. She wondered whether it was perhaps some ignorance of proportion, some primitive misconception of time and space, which made human beings beat against their physical limitations. All individual experience, all significant communication between people was on an infinitesimal scale. With the greatest effort and concentration she wrote to Agnes on this theme.

One of her family, taking a turn round the communal grass plot, looked back at the row of houses and thought that in all those windows Margery seemed the only living creature. She lifted her hand to show she saw him. She was watching through field-glasses the town garden where in thirty years she had seen over thirty different birds. She still knew nothing at all about eternity, but for an instant that afternoon she caught the joy of the speckled woodpecker in flight.

She died the next morning, six weeks after her eighty-fourth
birthday. She had wanted this to be the last of Margery Fry, but in
the end consideration for others' wishes prevailed: there were
flowers—splendid magnolias—'Sheep may safely graze', a reading
from the Book of Wisdom, silence. At Somerville College no service
was held for her in the chapel; they gathered to listen to Bach in the
hall where Roger's portrait of her hung. At University House in
Birmingham, where she had forgotten to send instructions, the
students born in the Second World War sang 'All creatures of our
God and King', while a blackbird fed its fledgling in the Rose Sidgwick Memorial Garden, outside the room where women of seventy
remembered Miss Fry reading prayers.

A fortnight later a letter appeared in *The Times*, signed by
members of 'Justice', the British section of the International Commission of Jurists, under the title 'Victims of Violence: how compensation could be paid'. 'The all-party council of this society was
greatly impressed by the arguments put forward by Miss Fry and
her associates in this cause and whole-heartedly supports her proposals.' Their adoption, it was suggested, would be a fitting memorial.
Lord Shawcross headed the signatories.

Agnes straightened her letters, and the letters sent on by Ruth,
and laid them in a folder. Some of the writers were household names,
others like Lilian and Flossie had once been the mainstay of
Margery's household. Some spoke of Margery's care for people she
had never seen, some of her loving-kindness to her relatives and old
friends. Agnes thought of the honours Margery had received, and
refused. Then, weighing all, judging all, she found a piece of paper
and began a letter to her 'Dearest only sister Ruth'. Agnes had
always been careful with paper. Now the lines of the cheap note-pad
were a support, for she was eighty-nine, in grief, and she could not
bear crooked writing.

Looking at her life from outside, we know she had gt. gifts, 10 talents at
least, and gt. opportunities to use them, wh. does not always come with
the gifts. If she had been born earlier her chance to do the work she did
wld. have been less—I like to note how broadcasting just at the end
offered her a new undreamt of scope.

And I want all these admirers to know she was wonderful as a sister
as well as a penal reformer.

SELECT BIBLIOGRAPHY

A. *Manuscripts*

Family papers in the possession of Mrs Pamela Diamand and Mrs Annabel Cole.

Other letters kindly lent by Lord Bridges, Mrs Maja Kinberg, Miss Marjorie Rackstraw, Miss Pamela Russell, Dr Phoebe Sheavyn, Dame Janet Vaughan.

Note

Up to 1930 unattributed quotations are from letters to Lady Fry, after 1930 from letters to the Fry sisters.

B. *Publications by Margery Fry*

1919 'Co-education in University Life', in *Advances in Co-education*, ed. L. S. Woods. Sidgwick and Jackson.

1923 *Some Facts regarding Capital Punishment*. Howard League and Committee for the Abolition of the Death Penalty.

1933 *Debtor Prisons*. Howard League, from *The Magistrate*.

1936 *The Prison Population of the World*. Howard League.
The Accused. Pamphlets published by the Howard League.

1940 *The Ancestral Child*. Clarke Hall Fellowship.

1942 *A Notebook for the Children's Court* (with Champion B. Russell). Oxford University Press. Revised (3rd edition) 1950 (Howard League).

1944 *The Future Treatment of the Adult Offender*. Victor Gollancz.

1947 Introduction to *Lawless Youth—A Challenge to the New Europe*. George Allen and Unwin.

1948 A chapter in *What Life Has Taught Me*, ed. Sir J. Marchant. Odhams Press.

1950 *Children as Citizens*. National Children's Home Convocation Lecture.

1951 *Arms of the Law*. Victor Gollancz.

1953 A chapter in *What I Believe*, ed. Sir J. Marchant. Odhams Press.
The Single Woman. Delisle.
Child Care and the Growth of Love (by E. J. M. Bowlby, abridged and edited by Margery Fry). Pelican.

1955 *Old Age Looks at Itself*. National Old People's Welfare Council.
Articles in the *Howard Journal*.
Somerville College Reports.
University House Letters.

C. *Family Biographies*

Curtis Brown, Beatrice. *Isabel Fry*. Arthur Barker, 1960.
Fawell, Ruth. *Joan Mary Fry*. Friends' Home Service Committee, 1959.
Fry, Agnes. *Memoir of Sir Edward Fry*. Oxford University Press, 1921.
Woolf, Virginia. *Roger Fry*. Hogarth Press, 1940.

D. *General*

Brittain, Vera. *The Women at Oxford*. Harrap, 1960.
Byrne, St Clare, and Mansfield, C. Hope. *Somerville College 1879–1921*. Privately printed.
Calvert, E. Roy. *Capital Punishment in the Twentieth Century*. Putnam, 1927. 5th edition, 1936.
Farnell, V. *A Somervillian Looks Back*. Privately printed, 1948.
Fox, Lionel W. *The English Prison and Borstal Systems*. Routledge and Kegan Paul, 1952.
Fry, A. Ruth. *A Quaker Adventure*. Nisbet, 1936.
'Justice' report. *Compensation for Victims of Violence*. Stevens, 1962.
Rose, Gordon. *The Struggle for Penal Reform*. Stevens, 1961.
Vincent, E. W., and Hinton, P. *The University of Birmingham*. Cornish, Birmingham, 1947.

Index